CRACKING THE SOLID SOUTH

MERCER UNIVERSITY PRESS

Endowed by

TOM WATSON BROWN
and
THE WATSON-BROWN FOUNDATION, INC.

CRACKING THE SOLID SOUTH

The Life of John Fletcher Hanson,
Father of Georgia Tech

LEE C. DUNN

Mercer University Press • Macon, Georgia • 2016

MUP/ H912

© 2016 by Mercer University Press
Published by Mercer University Press
1501 Mercer University Drive
Macon, Georgia 31207
All rights reserved

9 8 7 6 5 4 3 2

Books published by Mercer University Press are printed on acid-free paper that meets the requirements of the American National Standard for Information Sciences—Permanence of Paper for Printed Library Materials.

ISBN   978-0-88146-526-4
Cataloging-in-Publication Data is available from the Library of Congress

To Davis and Denver

CONTENTS

ILLUSTRATIONS

Old Hanson Home, Monroe County
John Fletcher Hanson
Cora Hanson
Walter Taylor Hanson
Hanson residence, Macon
Bibb Mill No. 1, Macon
Hugh Moss Comer
Harry Stillwell Edwards
Albert R. Lamar
Academy of Music, Macon
Bibb Mill and Power Company, Columbus
Hanson private railroad car
Central of Georgia Railway Shops, Macon
J. F. Hanson headstone

ACKNOWLEDGMENTS

ON A BEAUTIFUL SUMMER evening in Highlands, North Carolina, in 1994, dear friends Betti and Corb Hankey were our engaging hosts for what would turn out to be a night of revelations concerning an ancestor of my husband's we knew nothing about. My father-in-law, Walter Dunn, was also present that evening, and Corb, in his inimitable style, drew Walter into a conversation about his roots. Walter began to describe his great-grandfather, an accomplished Georgian, whom he knew only as "Major Hanson." Having lived in Georgia for eleven years, we were amazed to learn that my husband had roots there—and astonished by the bits and pieces that Walter conveyed about the man he and the family called "the Major." Another four years passed before I embarked upon a genealogical adventure to learn more about the man I quickly discovered was John Fletcher Hanson. The more I uncovered, the more surprised I was that nothing had been written about him. My surprise turned to determination, and I became committed to telling Hanson's story and claiming a place for him in Georgia history.

This book, however, would never have come to fruition without the encouragement, support, and contributions of many wonderful people. I am indebted to Jim Barfield for encouraging me to write the book and his faith in my ability to do so. Staci Catron and Mary Ann Eaddy were instrumental in connecting me with my developmental editor and were also my mentors and early supporters of this effort.

My appreciation extends to Dr. Matthew Hild and Dr. Robert McMath, who were the catalysts for this entire project. Dr. Hild's research of Hanson's involvement with the Knights of Labor shed invaluable light on that facet of his life, and I am grateful to him for sharing his work with me and for writing the foreword. I am also grateful to Dr. Lee Ann Caldwell for a thorough and scholarly analysis of the manuscript. Her suggestions have made this a better book, and any errors or misinterpretations are mine. Dr. James McWilliams also read the manuscript, and his early encouragement and faith in the project assisted in making this book a reality.

The research staff at the Washington Memorial Library in Macon guided me in finding many of the articles and images that helped bring John Fletcher Hanson to life. I am most grateful to Muriel Jackson, and to Dr.

Christopher Stokes, Willard Rocker, and Aubrey Parker for their patience and skill.

Thanks extend to Shanna English, director of one of the most interesting little museums in the South: the Old Jail Museum and Archives in Barnesville, Georgia. I found her repository invaluable to the early Hanson family research. She also generously donated to my personal collection of Hanson archives and shared her time and interest in Middle Georgia history with my mother and me over several lunches in that charming town.

In researching John Hanson's descendants I was fortunate to find the family of Robert Young Garrett III, John Hanson's great-grandson through his daughter Anne Hanson Garrett. Robert and his wife, Mary, have been enthusiastic supporters of this project. They graciously agreed to share their Charles Naegele portrait of John Fletcher Hanson, which graces the cover of this book, and traveled to New York from their home in New Jersey at my request to procure the Central of Georgia Railway records at the Morgan Library and Museum. Special thanks to Robert's daughter-in-law Diana Garrett for her kind assistance in making copies of the family's historic documents for my use. Thank you to Robert's son-in-law Stephen Rubin, former president of the Board of Trustees of Worcester Polytechnic Institute, and Christine Drew, associate director of research at the Gordon Library of WPI, for their initiative in finding relevant historical articles. What a coincidence to find that Hanson's great-great-grandson-in-law was serving on the board of the institution that was the early model for Georgia Tech.

Locating Edward Mayner and his hospitable wife, Betty, was a true delight. Eddie is the great-grandson of John Hanson through Hanson's daughter Frances Hanson White. The couple graciously invited this stranger into their California home, where Eddie gave me one of the most colorful insights into John Hanson and his wife Cora. Eddie's kind and generous gift to me that day will be cherished for generations. The Mayners' son and daughter-in-law Jeff and Kim Mayner also shared their fine hospitality and home with me on another visit to California and encouraged me in my quest to bring their ancestor to life. I am indebted to the Mayner family and regret the passing of Betty Mayner.

I am grateful to Mike Ashcraft, a professor at Truman State University who provided me with my first glimpse of the Hansons at Point Loma and was instrumental in pointing the way to others who could provide background information about Theosophy and the Universal Brotherhood and Theosophical Society at Point Loma, as well as sharing his doctoral dissertation with me. Penny Waterstone, another student of the Theosophical movement, also shared her research, and she deserves my thanks.

The lovely Grace Knoche, leader of the Theosophical Society at its international headquarters in Pasadena, provided me with one of the most interesting days of my explorations. Her generosity in sharing her personal memories of the Hanson family at Point Loma painted an invaluable portrait of their life in the Theosophical colony. The photographs and archival materials housed at the headquarters were also kindly opened to me, and Kirby Van Mater provided copies of pertinent materials. Ms. Knoche's passing is noted with regret.

I am grateful to Bonnie Nickel for being my skilled research assistant in San Diego. She provided me with critical documentation along with the opportunity to see inside the Point Loma home of Ross and Fannie Hanson White—a rare treat.

I would like to thank Ron Williams, a Hanson descendant, for providing me with a copy of his book about the Hanson family of Monroe County. Without it, the life of Enoch Hanson would not have been as vividly portrayed.

A special thank you to David Lambert of the New England Historic Genealogical Society for his expertise and patience in guiding me through the National Archives, the Library of Congress, and the Daughters of the American Revolution genealogical library on the NEHGS's annual trip to Washington, D.C.

Thanks to Charles Pierce, director, and Christine Nelson, archivist, at the Morgan Library and Museum, who helped me locate the Central of Georgia records within the financial empire that was J. P. Morgan.

Cathie Jo Martin, professor of political science at Boston University, eagerly answered my queries about her research that included John Hanson, and she encouraged me in my endeavor to bring him to light, providing me with her articles and the articles of others that might be related to this theme.

David Owings, Columbus State University archivist, is to be thanked for assisting me in my quest to find the best images of Bibb Manufacturing and the Columbus Power Company.

Thanks also to Carole Moore at the Georgia Department of Natural Resources, Historic Preservation Division, for always answering my requests for information quickly and efficiently, and for her support of my work. Andrew Kohr faithfully answered my queries for relevant materials, and I thank him for his kindness.

I owe Jim Cothran for his very special contribution to the book, a debt of gratitude I can no longer repay. His passing has left a void in many lives.

My copy editor, Alison Jacques, deserves recognition for refining the manuscript. Allen Tuten, president of the Central of Georgia Railway Historical Society; and Robert Hanson, a great nephew of John Hanson, also must be thanked for their support of this project.

Thank you to Virginia Remick, who answered the door of the Old Hanson Home when this stranger drove into her driveway. The photographs of the home would not have been included in this book without her welcoming spirit. I particularly enjoyed seeing the graves of the Hanson ancestors in the small family cemetery on the property.

I would also like to thank Craig W. Kessler, director of the Breakbulk and Bulk Operations at the Georgia Ports Authority in Savannah, for his informative tour of the historic former Ocean Steamship Company headquarters building and the entire port facility, and Emily Goldman, also at the Georgia Ports Authority, for her outstanding photographic capabilities in capturing the headquarters building without any twenty-first-century vehicles obstructing the view.

My visit to the California State Railroad Museum was another highlight of my research. Grateful appreciation is extended to Philip Sexton, director of public programs for the California Department of Parks and Recreation, who allowed me to enter and photograph John Hanson's private Central of Georgia Railway car, now in the possession of the museum. Special thanks go to Kyle Wyatt, curator of history and technology at the museum, who allowed me extended time in the archives and provided me with historic documentation on the history of Hanson's private car. Thanks go to Cara Randall, librarian at the museum who provided me with a fine image of the car from their archives, and to photographer Denny S. Anspach, who granted me permission to use it.

Thanks also to Christopher Barr, National Park Service ranger at the Andersonville National Historic Site, for sharing his research and conference paper on the Andersonville Prison Site, which had special application to John Hanson's Memorial Day Address in 1891.

I would be remiss if I didn't mention how grateful I am to my father-in-law, Walter Hanson Dunn, whose ancestor inspired me. His reminiscences added greatly to my understanding of the Hanson family dynamics. I think about him often and wish he could have lived to see this book come to fruition.

Thank you to Mercer University Press, in particular to its director, Dr. Marc A. Jolley, and publishing assistant, Marsha Luttrell, for their support and assistance.

Thanks are due to my daughter-in-law Julie for organizing my files. I realized too late that I should have drawn upon her skills much sooner and more often. Thanks also to my son Michael for enhancing some of the digital images for the book, and to my son Matthew, whose technical support is always appreciated.

To every friend who encouraged me with the words, "How's the book coming?" I want to say a heartfelt thank-you. That simple query always provided me with renewed energy and commitment. Your interest in my journey to complete this work means more to me than you will ever know.

All the information I gathered would never have come together in a cohesive fashion if it hadn't been for the herculean efforts of my developmental editor, Jennifer Yankopolus. I am eternally grateful to her for the remarkable way in which she guided me to a finished product that I never would have achieved without her. She was my compass.

Most importantly, I owe my husband, Mike, a deep debt of gratitude for his unwavering support and encouragement. He understood my passion for the project and urged me to pursue it. I am grateful for his contributions to the book, which came in the form of perceptive insights into the character and motives of John Fletcher Hanson that I wasn't always able to recognize. But I appreciate most of all his complete faith in my abilities, coupled with his capacity to endure time too long spent in the nineteenth century.

FOREWORD

During the late-nineteenth and early-twentieth centuries, John Fletcher Hanson (often referred to as "Major" Hanson, a title that he had earned in the Confederate Army) was one of the best known men in Georgia for his activities in industry, politics, and newspaper publishing, as well as his integral role in the establishment of the institution that is now the Georgia Institute of Technology. Yet after his death in 1910, his name seemed to fade from prominence; the one-time publisher of the *Macon Telegraph* became virtually unknown, in sharp contrast to that of his contemporary Henry W. Grady, whose name is still well known in the twenty-first century.

I first became aware of Hanson during the mid-to-late 1990s. At the time, I was researching and writing a master's thesis on the Knights of Labor in Georgia. While examining the mostly unsuccessful efforts of that organization to persuade the Georgia legislature to pass laws abolishing the convict lease system, child labor in factories, and the 72-hour work week, I kept encountering his name. I was already familiar with him because I had read *Engineering the New South: Georgia Tech, 1885-1985* by Robert C. McMath, Jr., et al., which of course discusses how Hanson became, as Lee Dunn aptly puts it, "the father of Georgia Tech." In my own research, however, I was reading in newspapers and unpublished theses and dissertations about how Hanson, as a founder and head of the textile manufacturing enterprise the Bibb Manufacturing Company, had actually cooperated with the Knights of Labor when the union organized his millhands in 1886, and how he had appeared before the state legislature and urged that body to pass the labor legislation that the Knights sought. This certainly distinguished him from other mill owners in the state, as became very apparent when I discovered that while the Knights of Labor were engaging in strikes and boycotts at mills across Georgia, they never waged such a battle at the Bibb Manufacturing Company.

The more I learned about Major Hanson, the more intrigued I became. In an era when the scourge of Jim Crow was beginning to sweep across the South, Hanson again distinguished himself from his peers by employing black workers in the Bibb mills; in 1888, he delivered an address about the tariff, one of the major political issues of the day, before a black assembly of the Knights of Labor in Macon. Furthermore, his advocacy of the tariff led him to become a Republican at a time when the South was becoming so solidly Democratic that the term "solid South" would be applied to the region for nearly a century.

Clearly, I realized, Hanson was both an interesting and important figure in the history of late-nineteenth and early-twentieth-century Georgia. Yet, he seemed to be a cipher as far as the historical record was concerned. His name appeared in enough books and other scholarly works to suggest that he had been significant, but the frequent mentions of his name were followed by only brief descriptions of his activities, and trying to learn more about him felt like trying to assemble a jigsaw puzzle without having enough pieces. The fact that Hanson, unlike some of his peers, left behind no collection of private papers and correspondence may well have contributed to scholars having shed less light on him than his importance merited. Whatever the reasons may have been, no historian had ever made Hanson the subject of a lengthy, detailed study. While I had done a fair amount of research into his career, I still had a lot of questions about him. Why, for example, did he reverse his earlier stand in favor of legislation against child labor in 1903? What were the reasons for his liberal position (for that time and place) regarding African Americans? Lee Dunn has done a remarkable job of answering these and other questions after combing every source imaginable. In *Cracking the Solid South: The Life of Major John Fletcher Hanson, Father of Georgia Tech*, she presents a clear and compelling portrait of Hanson's life and career. In doing so, she has rescued from undeserved obscurity a man who made a significant impact upon the history of Georgia and whose story challenges many of the notions that historians have long held about the early New South. At long overdue last, his story is now told.

Matthew Hild
The University of West Georgia

CRACKING THE
SOLID SOUTH

The Old Hanson Home in Monroe County, Georgia, built ca. 1825. *Author photo.*

John Fletcher Hanson, 1840–1910, commonly known as the Major. *Courtesy of Mr. and Mrs. Michael Hanson Dunn.*

Cora Alice Lee Hanson, 1847–1923. *Courtesy of Mr. and Mrs. Michael Hanson Dunn.*

Walter Taylor Hanson, 1865–1909. *Courtesy of Mr. and Mrs. Michael Hanson Dunn.*

The Hanson residence on Georgia Avenue in Macon, Georgia, completed in 1883.
Courtesy of Middle Georgia Archives, Washington Memorial Library, Macon, Georgia.

Bibb Manufacturing Company Mill No. 1 in Macon, Georgia (detail below), as it looked in the 1950s. *Courtesy of Middle Georgia Archives, Washington Memorial Library, Macon, Georgia.*

Hugh Moss Comer, 1842–1900. *Courtesy of Norfolk Southern Railway.*

Harry Stillwell Edwards, 1855–1938. *Courtesy of Middle Georgia Archives, Washington Memorial Library, Macon, Georgia.*

Albert R. Lamar, 1830–1889. *George Arents Collection, The New York Public Library, Astor, Lenox and Tilden Foundations.*

The Academy of Music building in Macon, Georgia, completed in 1884.

The Bibb Mill and Columbus Power Company in Columbus, Georgia, as it looked in 1924.
Above: courtesy of Columbus State University Archives, Columbus State University, Columbus,
Georgia; below: courtesy of Library of Congress.

John Hanson's private Central of Georgia Railway car.
Courtesy of California State Railroad Museum, Denny S. Anspach photograph.

Central of Georgia Railway Shops and Roundhouse, as it looked in 1964.
Courtesy of Middle Georgia Archives, Washington Memorial Library, Macon, Georgia.

John Hanson's headstone at Riverside Cemetery in Macon, Georgia. *Author photo.*

INTRODUCTION

It has fallen to my lot to advocate policies that were not in favor with
the people of this state.

—J. F. Hanson

WHEN JOHN FLETCHER HANSON died in 1910 at the age of seventy, he
was one of the most well-known Southern industrialists in the nation.
During his lifetime, he helped Georgia transform from an agrarian economy
into the South's leading textile manufacturing center. He was also
responsible for the establishment of one of the nation's finest engineering
schools, and he helped write the strongest tariff legislation in the country's
history at the time. He lived during the post-Civil War era defined by its
generation as the New South. But unlike other apostles of the New South—
such as Daniel Tompkins, a South Carolina industrialist and publisher;
Henry Watterson, owner of the *Louisville Courier-Journal*; or Henry Grady,
managing editor of the *Atlanta Constitution*—John Hanson is not found in
the prevailing literature that examines the period. In fact, he is virtually
unknown to Georgia historians today though his name appears in various
biographical encyclopedias and is occasionally mentioned in books about
Southern history.

Cracking the Solid South paints a picture of an ordinary man who
believed not only in himself but also in the ability of his state and its people
to overcome the daunting post-Civil War economic conditions and compete
with the rest of the nation, and the world, in manufacturing. In the last
quarter of the nineteenth century, it was commonly held that industry-
alization would be the savior of the South, the diversifier of an economy that
had been held slave to the cotton fields for two centuries. No one in Georgia
held more steadfastly to that mantra than Hanson.

In researching John Hanson, I was forced to rely on the newspapers of
his era. He left no papers, no diaries, and only a few personal letters to influential men of the Gilded Age whose correspondence has been preserved in
archival collections. Hanson's business accomplishments were documented
in the sterile facts and figures of the board minutes and annual reports of the
corporations he led, but those reveal nothing of the man or his motives and
ambitions. Instead, the words of newspaper reporters, the many editorials he

wrote and rousing speeches he gave, and occasional mentions of him in historical works were all I had to work with in putting flesh on the bones of John Fletcher Hanson. But soon a portrait emerged of a man who used his boyish charm, large intellect, sharp wit, and entrepreneurial energy to become not only a successful industrialist but also a champion of the economic potential of the South from the Georgia statehouse to the White House.

As an industrialist and visionary, Hanson personified the phoenix who rose from the ashes, becoming a leading Georgia advocate of the New South in the aftermath of the Civil War. Many have assigned that role to Henry Grady. However, while Grady was a figurehead of the New South movement, he was in fact the Old South with a party mask. In contrast, Hanson was both an advocate of the New South and a disciple of his own version of the New South; he challenged traditional Southern attitudes and policies while creating jobs, expanding the industrial economy, advancing educational opportunities, and promoting a new attitude toward some of the most pressing social issues facing Southerners at the time.

While the region was christened the New South, it also acquired a designation that reflected its political leanings. In the closing decades of the nineteenth century, the South became a solidly Democratic stronghold, giving rise to its political moniker, the "solid South." Hanson worked to crack the political solidity of the region and, at the same time, pursued strategies to crack other solidly held ideologies he believed were preventing the South from advancing its economy and improving the lives of its citizens. Therefore, I use the term "solid South" as an all-encompassing metaphor to describe the solidly held political, economic, and social underpinnings of the South.

After spending his formative years in Pike County and Barnesville, Georgia, Hanson exploded on the Macon scene in 1871. This young, aggressive entrepreneur quickly became involved in the city's civic and social life and founded Bibb Manufacturing, a textile firm, by soliciting the investment capital of Hugh Moss Comer, one of Georgia's wealthiest men. Immediately after starting his own business, Hanson rescued the failing Macon Manufacturing Company, another cotton mill, and over the next thirty years he expanded the Bibb by purchasing and reviving more failing mills and building new mills throughout the state. At the height of his career he controlled nine mills that among them manufactured hosiery, twine, cording, yarn, coarse fabrics, and eventually the fine Egyptian cotton fabrics produced at the mill in Columbus—the fulfillment of a vision for a consolidated textile empire with a broad market share of cotton products.[1]

In the post-Civil War South, two industries dominated in Georgia: textiles and railroads. As a mill owner who shipped cotton products to markets in thirty states, Hanson had a strong interest in the railroads, which led him to become involved in the railroad industry, first as a voice against the unchecked powers of the state railroad commission and then as a board member of several Georgia railroads, where his business acumen and access to investment capital were strong assets. By the turn of the twentieth century, while still leading the growing Bibb Manufacturing empire, he also stood at the helms of the Central of Georgia Railway and the Ocean Steamship Company (a subsidiary of the railway) as they emerged from one of the most widely known financial restructurings in U.S. history. He had inherited enterprises that were suffering from years of mismanagement, including a railroad buckling under the strict governmental oversight of the state railroad commission. In spite of these regulatory and financial difficulties, Hanson modernized the operations and gave them a competitive footing. Amid all this he formed the Columbus Power Company—in an era when electrical energy was in its infancy—to generate hydroelectric power for the newly erected Bibb Manufacturing mill in Columbus and to provide increased electrical capacity for the area, which stimulated manufacturing growth in the region for the next fifty years. He later became the first Ocean Steamship Company president to fuel the fleet with Alabama coal, rather than Pennsylvania coal, and he purchased a large Alabama coal mine, implementing a vertical integration strategy that gave the Central of Georgia Railway and the Ocean Steamship Company a steady, dependable source of fuel.

In his quest for new markets for a cotton industry suffering from over-supply, Hanson became the voice of an emerging Southern drive for the expansion of American trade. Hand in hand with foreign trade, he advocated for the establishment of a merchant marine and for shipping subsidies to encourage the American shipping industry, which was practically nonexistent

---

[1] *History of Bibb Manufacturing Company, 1876–1929* ([Macon]: n.p., 1937) 6. There is a copy at Middle Georgia Archives, Washington Memorial Library, Macon, GA.

in the closing decades of the nineteenth century. He coupled his push for expanding foreign commerce with his support of a protective tariff—a duty levied on foreign goods—which was the primary revenue source for the federal government at the time and an issue that dominated the national political landscape during the last quarter of the nineteenth century. Hanson saw the protective tariff as critical for protecting American industry from low-wage foreign competition and as beneficial for farmers and the working class. On this issue, though, along with many others, Hanson stood apart from his Southern peers. The South was solidly against the protective tariff, thinking that it protected industry at the *expense* of farmers and the working class.

Of all the viewpoints that separated Hanson from his peers, none was more radical than his views on race. On numerous occasions he found himself the lone Southerner expressing ideas that few dared think, and even fewer dared speak. In a period when the South was marching toward Jim Crow and disfranchisement, he advocated for black participation in the election process, even encouraging federal supervision of elections—a bold invitation for a region that was still stinging from Reconstruction.

To promote and defend his viewpoints, Hanson used the power of the press. Politicians and newspaper editors were the most influential people in Hanson's time. Having a strong aversion to political office, which he articulated each of the many times he was encouraged to run, Hanson took up the pen as his first weapon in his efforts to crack the solid South. He purchased the *Macon Telegraph* in 1881, a calculated acquisition that provided him a bully pulpit from which to influence the course of politics and public policy in the state and nation.[2]

---

[2]From its founding as a weekly paper in 1826 to its presence on the newsstands and the Internet of today, the *Macon Telegraph* has gone by various names. Even after it became a daily in 1831, weekly and semi-weekly editions were at times issued alongside the daily. During Hanson's ownership, the paper was known first as the *Macon Telegraph and Messenger* until he simplified it to the *Macon Telegraph* in 1885. Several weekly editions were published during Hanson's ownership: the *Georgia Weekly Telegraph, Journal and Messenger*; the *Macon Weekly Telegraph and Messenger*; and the *Macon Weekly Telegraph*. Regardless of the name changes or issue frequency, all of these publications emanated from the same editorial source: an entity that I refer to as the *Macon Telegraph*—although in the footnotes I retain the distinction between the daily (*Macon Telegraph*) and the weekly (*Macon Weekly Telegraph* and *Georgia Weekly Telegraph*) editions as an aid to future historians in their research.

During his seven-year ownership of the *Telegraph*, he used the paper to educate his readers on a wide range of topics that, when taken together, demonstrate the depth and strength of his vision for a New South. Hanson promoted the need for university-level technical education in order to bring industrialization in Georgia in line with Northern, as well as European, industry; it was a fight he sustained against much criticism and apathy, but that eventually led to the creation of the Georgia Institute of Technology. If Southern industry was ever going to be competitive, Hanson knew that it needed trained engineers to run the mills and bring modern manufacturing technology to the operations—not to mention to prepare Georgians for broader, more viable careers instead of the limited, low-wage jobs available to them. He also challenged the unchecked power of the state railroad commission in an attempt to secure a more equitable regulatory system that wouldn't stifle investment in the industry, a charge he repeatedly levied against the commission.

While in the editor's seat at the *Macon Telegraph*, Hanson came up against a formidable foe: Henry Grady, managing editor of the *Atlanta Constitution*. Both were prolific writers and speakers, and both sought to influence politics and public policy through the power of the press. The two men went head-to-head on many of the most pressing issues of their day, but none was more heated than Democratic Party politics in Georgia. Hanson believed that voters had the right to choose party nominees through a transparent political process. The *Telegraph*'s policy under his leadership was to remain neutral regarding political candidates during the nominating process so as not to unfairly influence voters' choices. Grady, by contrast, through his political machinations, placed his handpicked candidates in office: three in the governor's chair and two in the United States Senate.[3] Hanson also used the *Telegraph* to advocate for a strong two-party system, believing that the Democratic solidity of the state inhibited the free exchange of ideas, and he also urged the Republican Party to form a pro-business platform that Southern manufacturers and entrepreneurs could embrace. Having gotten rid of the Republican influence in Southern affairs less than a decade prior, most Southerners had no interest in encouraging

---

[3]Harold E. Davis, *Henry Grady's New South: Atlanta, a Brave and Beautiful City* (Tuscaloosa: University of Alabama Press, 1990). This book is a comprehensive look at Grady's career with emphasis on his political campaign strategies.

the party's participation in the region's politics. And, of course, the pages of the *Telegraph* were well washed with Hanson's views on the protective tariff.

Hanson's continual push for a pro-business climate eventually led him to join the party of protectionism. He became a Republican in the belief that the party's economic principles would strengthen American manufacturing interests—a move that left him politically isolated from his peers. While most Southerners were still fighting the North on political, economic, and social battlefields long after the Civil War had ended, Hanson rejected sectional thinking and encouraged the South to become more nationalistic in its policies and attitudes. Long familiar with how far outside the mainstream of Southern thought he stood, he reflected on his position late in his career to an audience of Atlanta businessmen, saying, "It has fallen to my lot to advocate policies that were not in favor with the people of this state."[4]

Hanson's controversial opinions and editorials in the *Macon Telegraph* often pinched the nerves of other Southern editors, who chastised him for weakening the Democratic Party through his assaults on its positions. Such responses didn't deter him from speaking his mind, nor did they seriously affect his standing in the community as a man of integrity and business acuity. To the contrary, *Telegraph* subscriptions soared during his ownership, and his pen brought him recognition both north and south of the Mason-Dixon Line. He also planted the seeds of political and social change in interviews with the *New York Times*, *Boston Advertiser*, and other important U.S. publications as well as at speaking engagements before the most influential policymakers of his day. Hanson's message resonated with Northern audiences because he spoke frankly about the challenges facing the South and the solutions that were needed, in contrast to the regressive and narrow-minded rhetoric expressed by many Southern politicians and editors at the time. His message also captured the attention of the national Republican Party. Hanson was invited to join the most influential Republicans of his day in a consortium of like-minded businessmen and politicians called the American Protective Tariff League. As a result, he became friends with William McKinley and worked with such influential industrialists as Andrew Carnegie, Cornelius Bliss, and J. P. Morgan. Hanson assisted McKinley in drafting the McKinley Tariff Act and campaigned vigorously for him in his runs both for governor of Ohio and for president of the

---

[4]"Eloquent Talks at Big Banquet," *Atlanta Constitution*, 18 February 1903, p. 1.

United States. Hanson's opinions as a Southern industrialist were sought by several White House administrations, and he became the national Republican Party's go-to man in behind-the-scenes Georgia politics during the last two decades of his life. Political influence, however, was for Hanson strictly a means to an end, a piece of the foundation he was building for the continued development of the region.

Few books have been written about the nineteenth century's captains of industry in Georgia. *Cracking the Solid South* is one of only a handful of biographies about an economic entrepreneur whose vision, intellect, and willingness to take risks created jobs and financial prosperity for the state and its citizens. Many people build careers or excel at professions, but few create a broad platform on which others can thrive. Hanson laid just that foundation in Georgia on which his impact on technological training, international trade, transportation, energy, and state and federal legislation fostered economic expansion for industry throughout the region. His ownership of the *Macon Telegraph* was of much less value as a commercial venture than as a vehicle that allowed him to reach and influence the constituencies that made up this foundational fabric.

In describing John Fletcher Hanson, it is easy to color him with the phrase "New South industrialist," but he was much more. He was a risk taker, a policy influencer, a strategist, and a leader across a broad spectrum. Hanson's friend and former associate editor at the *Macon Telegraph*, Harry Stillwell Edwards, described him as "the mastermind, [who] carried for generations a purpose weighted with the destiny of thousands."[5] Considering his remarkable achievements, Hanson has rested more quietly in his grave than history should allow.

---

[5]Harry Stillwell Edwards, "John F. Hanson—The Man," *Macon (GA) Telegraph*, 18 December 1910, p. 6.

I

THE HANSONS

I was satisfied that he [Jefferson Davis] was determined never to stop until every man that is able to drag one foot after the other is placed under his control.

—J. F. Hanson

JOHN FLETCHER HANSON—born in Pike County, Georgia, in 1840—was of the second generation of his family to be born on Georgia soil. His paternal great-grandparents, William and Ann Bird Hanson, had begun their lives in Virginia. William was born c. 1770 and Ann in 1771.[1] As one of five sons growing up in Fauquier County, William knew that his father's parcel of land, if divided five ways upon inheritance, would not be sufficient to sustain himself and his own family. Even though Thomas Jefferson had successfully campaigned to end the practice of primogeniture, the law of inheritance by the firstborn son, it was still difficult to acquire an adequate amount of land by inheritance.[2] Early American families were usually large, with many sons who often left the family homestead to seek affordable land in other states on which to farm and raise a family. Against his father's wishes, William and his family migrated to Georgia to improve their chances for a better life.

They traveled along the Great Wagon Road to Georgia, mirroring the trip made by thousands of other Americans in the fledgling nation who ventured west and south in search of their own pieces of land. The Great Wagon Road ran from Pennsylvania through Maryland and Virginia into

---

[1] Monroe County Historical Society (MCHS), *Family Histories of Monroe County, Georgia* (Fernandina Beach, FL: Wolfe Publishing, 2000) 7.

[2] "Life before the Presidency," *American President: Thomas Jefferson*, Miller Center website, accessed 13 August 2014, http://millercenter.org/president/jefferson/essays/biography/2.

North and South Carolina and terminated in Augusta, Georgia.[3] By 1799 William and Ann were living in Jackson County, Georgia, created in 1796 from Franklin County on land originally held by Creeks and Cherokees.[4] In 1804 William purchased eighty-four acres on Wildcat Creek in Clarke County, which had been created from Jackson County land in 1801.[5] It is here that William and Ann raised their eight children, seven to adulthood.[6] William's son Enoch, John Hanson's grandfather, was born in Fauquier County, Virginia, on September 25, 1792, but grew up on Wildcat Creek. Clarke County is also where Enoch met Cindarilla Ruby Barber, whom he married on February 13, 1813.[7] Eleven months later, James Bird Hanson, John Hanson's father, was born. Enoch and Cindarilla spent the next eight years in the Clarke and Morgan county areas before trying their luck in the fourth Georgia Land Lottery of 1821.

In 1803 a special act of the legislature during the term of Governor John Milledge created a lottery system to disperse lands acquired through cessions by the Creek and Cherokee Indians. Eight land lotteries were held in Georgia between 1805 and 1833, the largest land lottery system ever conducted in the United States.[8] The lottery of 1821 opened for settlement the area between the Ocmulgee and Flint rivers extending from the towns of

---

[3]Parke Rouse, Jr., *The Great Wagon Road: From Philadelphia to the South* (Richmond, VA: The Dietz Press, 1995) 93.

[4]R. J. Taylor, Jr., *An Index to Georgia Tax Digests: 1789–1817*, 5 vols. (Atlanta: R. J. Taylor Foundation, n.d.); *New Georgia Encyclopedia*, s.v. "Jackson County," by Elizabeth B. Cooksey, last modified 8 September 2014, http://www.georgiaencyclopedia. org/articles/counties-cities-neighborhoods/jackson-county.

[5]*New Georgia Encyclopedia*, s.v. "Clarke County," by Elizabeth B. Cooksey, last modified 9 September 2014, http://www.georgiaencyclopedia.org/articles/counties-cities-neighborhoods/clarke-county.

[6]William C. Stewart, *Gone to Georgia: Jackson and Gwinnett Counties and Their Neighbors in the Western Migration* (Washington, DC: National Genealogical Society, 1965).

[7]MCHS, *Family Histories*, 29; Mary Bondurant Warren, ed., *Georgia Marriages 1811 through 1820* (Danielsville, GA: Heritage Papers, 1988) 140.

[8]Kenneth Coleman, *A History of Georgia* (Athens: University of Georgia Press, 1977) 107; *New Georgia Encyclopedia*, s.v. "Land Lottery System," by Jim Gigantino, last modified 5 June 2014, http://www.georgiaencyclopedia.org/articles/history-archaeology/land-lottery-system.

Roswell in the north to Ashburn in the south. Each parcel of land was 202.5 acres in size.[9]

Not all those eligible to participate in the Georgia land lotteries of the early nineteenth century were lucky enough to draw a parcel; some draws were blank. As a married man with a child, Enoch qualified for two draws, and he got lucky with both. On May 15, 1821, he traveled to the state capital in Milledgeville to take part in the lottery, drawing two lots, one in Monroe County and one in Henry County. He paid grant fees for both parcels but sold his parcel in Henry County.[10]

In the mid-1820s Enoch moved onto his 202.5 acres in Monroe County, bringing his parents, Ann and William, with him. An industrious man, Enoch built his own house, which still stands today and is commonly referred to as the Old Hanson Home. With the surrounding property still almost free of development, it is easy to envision the rural farm life enjoyed by the family. The bucolic setting looks much like it did in Enoch and Cindarilla's day, with the exception of the large belching stacks of Plant Sherer, the coal-fired power plant, in the distance. Although the livestock outbuildings are clearly of more recent vintage, the two-story Federal-style farmhouse retains many of its original details, including two flanking chimneys. The four narrow windows upstairs over the covered porch appear to be original as well.

Enoch was a successful planter who developed his land with the help of slaves. According to slave schedules, Enoch owned thirty-three slaves in 1860, twelve more than he had in 1850, establishing him as a member of the large planter class.[11] He and Cindarilla also received help on the homestead from their ten children.

Enoch was also a religious man and a member of the Methodist Church. In 1823, two years after Monroe County was opened for settle-

---

[9]David B. Poythress, *Georgia Surveyor General Department* (Atlanta: Georgia Surveyor General Department, n.d.), Georgia Archives and Records Building, Morrow, GA.

[10]Georgia Genealogical Society, *The Third and Fourth or 1820 and 1821 Land Lotteries of Georgia* (Easley, SC: Georgia Genealogical Reprints/Southern Historical Press, 1973) 117.

[11]U.S. Census Office, *1850 Federal Population Census*, Slave Schedule, National Archives microfilm M432, roll 93, Monroe County, GA; U.S. Census Office, *1860 Federal Population Census*, Slave Schedule, National Archives microfilm M653, roll 149, Monroe County, GA.

ment, the Methodist Conference in Savannah designated the county as the Monroe Mission, later changed to the Monroe Circuit. When George Hill, a traveling preacher who was assigned to the territory, crossed the Ocmulgee River on his initial visit to the area, he encountered Enoch Hanson. After meeting with Hill, Enoch began to organize religious meetings in his home for his friends and neighbors, where he or a traveling preacher would preside. Services were held either in his living room or in the open air under the oak trees that abounded on the property. These gatherings became known as the Ebenezer Methodist Church. The informal surroundings served as the area church until May 1, 1829, when Thomas Walker donated one and a half acres on Colvin Road for a permanent building. Three different churches have stood on this property. Today the third Ebenezer Methodist Church still stands on Colvin Road as a reminder of the long heritage of Methodism in the area and the meetings that began at the home of Enoch Hanson.[12]

Stories of Enoch and his farmstead have come down through the recollections of his granddaughter, Carrie Hanson Breedlove, daughter of Enoch's son Francis Marion (and therefore John Hanson's cousin). Carrie remembered her grandfather's beautiful flower garden—and how she was never allowed to play in it. She also recalled fondly one of his slaves, affectionately called Aunt Mary. Whenever Carrie got into trouble or was scolded, she would run to Aunt Mary's cabin for comfort. But her most interesting recollections speak to the wealth that Enoch accumulated later in his life. He was especially fond of celebrating his birthday by inviting interesting people to dine in his home, often including a speaker. Carrie remembered that the dining table was always set with many places. One particular birthday celebration stood out in her mind. At the conclusion of the after-dinner speech, Enoch instructed his guests to look under their dinner plates. There they each found a hundred-dollar gold piece.[13]

On January 27, 1857, after forty-four years of marriage to Enoch, Cindarilla died. Three months later Enoch married Catherine McCollum Brewer, a widow of twenty-two years with four grown children from her marriage to Reverend Brewer, a local minister from the Methodist Episcopal

---

[12]Bill Britt, *History and Directory of Ebenezer United Methodist Church* (Forsyth, GA: self-published, n.d.) 10–11.

[13]Ron Williams, *On Railroad Street: The Story of Carrie Hanson Breedlove and Her Family* (Valley, AL: printed by author, 1998) 4.

Church.[14]After fifteen years of marriage, Enoch Hanson died on May 29, 1872, one month after Catherine. The small family cemetery is the final resting place of several generations of Hansons, including William, Ann, Enoch, Cindarilla, and Catherine. Typical of many rural family cemeteries, the Hanson cemetery sits at the back of a small, enclosed field behind the house. Large trees shade the headstones, many of which are askew, their lettering faded by the ravages of the elements. Enoch's father, William, passed away on March 7, 1842, and his mother, Ann, died on February 5, 1858. Some of the headstones contain only names with birth and death dates. Others contain passages of Scripture or sentiments popular at the time. Reflecting her piety, Cindarilla's headstone reads, "Having been an acceptable member of the M. E. Church for more than 30 years—Jesus smiles and says well done, thy good and faithful servant." Enoch lies beneath the words "Tis sweet to believe of the absent we love, If we miss them below we shall meet them above."

Enoch's oldest son, James Bird Hanson, was named executor of his father's considerable estate, which was valued at $18,417.64 (the equivalent of approximately $354,000 in 2015 dollars), a handsome sum in the antebellum South.[15] Enoch was not just a model of religious piety; he was industrious as well, and his son James followed faithfully in his footsteps. The early years of Methodist preaching in the home made a lasting impression on James, who became a well-known Methodist preacher with a long career at the pulpit. He married Permelia Caroline Freeman of North Carolina on September 25, 1836, and settled in Barnesville, Georgia. Together they raised a family of four boys, James Asbury, John Fletcher, Henry Clay, and Isaac Newton and two girls, Susannah and Mary.[16] John was born on November 25, 1840. John remained close to his younger brother Newt his entire life, and his youngest sister, Mary, would become the grandmother of golf legend Bobby Jones.[17]

---

[14]"Mrs. Catherine Hanson," *Southern Christian Advocate*, 5 June 1872.

[15]Enoch Hanson, will, dated 6 April 1868, Book C, Monroe County (GA) Wills Book, pp. 124–30, Monroe County Library, Forsyth.

[16]Monroe County (GA) Marriage Book, Book A (1824–1845), Monroe County Ordinary Court, Georgia Archives, Forsyth.

[17]Augusta Lambdin and Tallu Brinson Jones Fish, eds., *The History of Lamar County, 1825–1932* (Alpharetta, GA: W. H. Wolfe Associates, 1932) 343, 344; U.S. Census Office, *1860 Federal Population Census*.

With a large family to support, Reverend Hanson needed to be as industrious as his father, Enoch. He rose to the occasion and engaged in many business ventures. He sold insurance and real estate, and he started his own planing mill and walnut furniture factory, a business his son Henry continued later in life. The local farmers organized the Grange Cooperative Store and chose Reverend Hanson to manage it. This experience provided a strong foundation on which he later established a wholesale dry goods business. All the while, Reverend Hanson was preaching at the Methodist churches in the area and upholding his responsibilities as a Master Mason in the Pinta Lodge in Barnesville.[18]

Although not a circuit-riding preacher, Reverend Hanson was known to deliver sermons in the surrounding villages when his services were needed. In his religious discourse he expressed the belief that the human voice was "God's appointed instrument" and, therefore, an organ would have little use in his ideal "house of worship."[19] Many years later John, in memory of his parents, gave the First Methodist Church of Barnesville a magnificent round stained-glass window that radiated beautiful colored shafts of light onto the organ below.[20] The church was destroyed by fire in 1939, and another Methodist church stands in its place today. Reverend Hanson's daughters also felt the effects of their father's strict religious views; he thought that ruffles, frills, and crisping pins (used for curling the hair) were not reflective of "pious womanhood."[21]

Reverend Hanson educated his children in the "old-field schools" along with a healthy dose of Bible study and the reading of local newspapers. Old-field schools, usually one-room schoolhouses built by communities before public schools were established, were typically located in rural or agrarian regions in old fields that may have been over-farmed and abandoned.[22] Tuition varied from fifteen to fifty dollars, and the school year varied from eight to ten months. A student would attend the school from two to nine

---

[18]Lambdin and Fish, *Lamar County*, 343, 344.

[19]Ibid.

[20]"Barnesville, the Old Home of Maj. Hanson, Stricken with Sorrow," *Macon (GA) Telegraph*, 16 December 1910, p. 1.

[21]Lambdin and Fish, *Lamar County*, 343, 344.

[22]James Davidson Hall, "On an Old-Field School," 23 April 1828, available at *Documenting the American South*, University of North Carolina Library, last modified 16 November 2006, http://docsouth.unc.edu/true/mss02-14/mss02-14.html.

years, depending on the wealth of the family and the desired degree of instruction. Reverend Hanson was fond of saying, "Give me Old-Field Schools and plenty of newspapers and I will show you educated men."[23]

The people of Barnesville recognized that Revered Hanson was a man of fine character and leadership skills, and they elected him several times to the Barnesville Board of Commissioners. He was knowledgeable in matters of the law and was often called upon to write wills and deeds and arbitrate disputes between neighbors. He served a long tenure as a justice of the peace, during which "the decisions of 'Squire Hanson' were never questioned."[24]

During the Civil War years, Reverend Hanson served as chairman of the Board of Commissioners, a position equivalent to mayor, when the arrival of wounded soldiers in staggering numbers tested his resilience and that of the people of Barnesville. The train depot and the stores of the town were converted to serve as hospitals for wounded soldiers, and tents were set up along the outskirts of town to house the hundreds of sick and wounded. By July 1864, five field hospitals in Barnesville were taking care of the injured from the battles of Kennesaw and Atlanta and surrounding areas.[25] The women of the town worked tirelessly to help the wounded. By day they worked on their farms but also worked at the hospital cooking meals, writing letters for the soldiers, helping with surgeries, and consoling the dying. By night they washed and boiled bandages in pots in their backyards in order to return them to the hospital the next day. In the morning their toil would begin again, often including the digging of graves and the burying of the dead.[26] Most households were without men because a large proportion of Barnesville's able-bodied males had joined the Barnesville Blues and other regiments in the area. The older men and slaves left behind helped the women manage their farms and property as best they could. Reverend

---

[23]Lambdin and Fish, *Lamar County*, 343, 344.

[24]Ibid.

[25]Confederate Hospital historical markers, GHM 085-4/-6/-9, Barnesville, GA, erected by Georgia Historical Commission, 1955/1955/1957.

[26]Leonora Ginn, *Days to Remember: Commemorating the 150th Anniversary of the Founding of the Town of Barnesville, Georgia* (Barnesville: Lamar County Historical Society, 1983) 13.

Hanson was a "tower of strength" to the women of the town at this time, often being called upon for his advice and protection.[27]

Reverend Hanson was still serving as chairman of the Board of Commissioners of Barnesville in 1865 when the lost cause of the Confederacy was coming to an end. On April 19, 1865, a skirmish occurred on the outskirts of Barnesville, where a detachment of approximately two thousand Union troops of the Fourth Regiment, Indiana Cavalry—called Wilson's Rangers, under the command of General James H. Wilson of General Alexander McCook's division—met with the Dixie Rangers, a local militia unit. According to local accounts, the Dixie Rangers fought gallantly but gradually withdrew from the field, and the flag of the Rangers was captured. A historical marker near Barnesville commemorates the skirmish.[28] General McCook's division then entered the town of Barnesville firing their weapons, but the townspeople made no resistance in the hopes that their property would be spared. The responsibility fell to Reverend Hanson to make the town's formal surrender. Despite this gesture, soldiers still looted and ravaged many of the homes. Gardens and fields were destroyed, and the food and valuables in many of the houses were stolen. Dresser drawers were even taken out of the houses to be used as troughs to feed the soldiers' horses.[29] Less than one month later, on May 15, 1865, ten thousand Union troops, one of Sherman's flanks, camped on the edge of town in their pursuit of Confederate president Jefferson Davis.[30] This was the last of the Union troops that Barnesville encountered. The hardships of war, however, continued long after the last shots were fired, as the days of Reconstruction brought financial stagnation and depression to the South. It was during Reconstruction that Reverend Hanson's example of hard work, courage, and patience gave the greatest comfort to the citizens of Barnesville.[31]

Despite his defense of the old-field schools as being capable of providing the best education, later in his life Reverend Hanson was able to see what an institution of higher learning could mean to the town of Barnesville when its leading citizens advocated for the establishment of a

---

[27]Lambdin and Fish, *Lamar County*, 344.

[28]Federals at Barnesville historical marker, GHM 085-3. Barnesville, GA. Erected by Georgia Historical Commission, 1957.

[29]Ginn, *Days to Remember*, 12.

[30]Federals at Barnesville historical marker.

[31]Lambdin and Fish, *Lamar County*, 344.

college. His leadership ability and business acumen made him a logical choice to be the first president of the board of trustees of Gordon Institute, established in 1872 and named after John B. Gordon, a revered Confederate general who later became a United States senator and governor of Georgia. This was no small feat for the town of Barnesville to accomplish during Reconstruction, when money and resources were scarce and other colleges were struggling. Reverend Hanson served as president for three years and resigned in 1875 at the age of sixty-one. Gordon Institute is now Gordon College, a four-year college in the University System of Georgia.[32]

During the years following the war, Reverend Hanson worked tirelessly in many occupations, some in conjunction with his enterprising son John. Even as late as 1879, when Reverend Hanson was seventy-one, he continued to inspire the citizens with his entrepreneurial skills by purchasing the Variety and Iron Works Company built in 1870 by Stafford, Blalock and Company.[33]

Not much is known about the formative years of John Hanson's life. It may be assumed that his religious upbringing was strict, and it is certain that his education consisted of reading newspapers and the Bible and attending the old-field schools. The influence of Reverend Hanson's strong leadership and advocacy of the old-field schools was tested when John joined the Confederate cause in 1861, at the age of twenty. On April 12, 1861, South Carolina fired on Fort Sumter in Charleston Harbor. The echo of the guns had barely faded when, eight days later, John was in Virginia at the front.[34] He enlisted as a private in the volunteer Spalding Grays military unit, which was organized in Griffin, Georgia, a town seventeen miles north of Barnesville in Spalding County. The Spalding Grays became part of the 2nd Georgia Battalion, along with the Macon Volunteers and the Floyd Rifles, both of Macon. Together these were the first units ordered to Virginia by

---

[32]Ibid., 125, 155; Faith Walton Porch, comp., *Heritage of Gordon Military College in the Heart of the Deep South* (Barnesville, GA: n.p. [1965?]).

[33]Brown, *A History of Barnesville*, n.d., Old Jail Museum and Archives, Barnesville, GA.

[34]Compiled Service Records of Confederate Generals and Staff Officers, and Nonregimental Enlisted Men, microfilm 331, Records from the Military and Military Agencies: Civil War, National Archives at Atlanta.

Governor Joseph E. Brown on April 18, 1861.[35] Reverend Hanson, however, remained a staunch Unionist.[36]

John saw his first action in the war less than a month after his arrival in Virginia, when the 2nd Georgia Battalion was involved in the Battle of Sewell's Point in Norfolk County. Although it was an inconsequential battle for both sides, John forged relationships with men who would remain his friends throughout his life.[37] In his own unit, the Spalding Grays, John served with James W. English from Griffin, who, after the war, settled in Atlanta. English wielded considerable influence in establishing Atlanta as the capital of Georgia and served as the city's mayor, among many other accomplishments.[38] The two men became friends, a friendship that ended only when Captain English, one of the dignitaries representing Atlanta at Hanson's funeral, accompanied John's body to its grave.

The education John received in the old-field schools, along with the example of an industrious father, provided him with the skills he needed to succeed in the military. After completing a year of service in the 2nd Georgia Battalion, John was commissioned adjutant of the 53rd Georgia Regiment on June 5, 1862. An adjutant, a commissioned staff officer who assisted the commanding officer of a regiment, usually carried the rank of major, which was often conferred upon those with money and influence as opposed to merit. Without the advantage of a privileged background, John received his appointment based on his intellect and leadership skills, as well as the bravery he had displayed on the battlefield.[39]

The 53rd Georgia Regiment was formed in May 1862 and sent to Virginia to take part in the Peninsula Campaign, a Union operation

---

[35]National Park Service, Civil War Soldiers and Sailors System (CWSS), database, accessed 23 January 2014, http://www.nps.gov/civilwar/soldiers-and-sailors-database.htm; Richard W. Iobst, *Civil War Macon: The History of a Confederate City* (Macon: Mercer University Press, 1999) 68.

[36]*Cincinnati Enquirer*, 21 December 1890, quoted in "Gath and Hanson," *Augusta (GA) Chronicle*, 30 December 1890, p. 2.

[37]National Park Service, CWSS database.

[38]["Capt. James Warren English"], in *Encyclopedia of Georgia Biography*, vol. 1, ed. Lucian Lamar Knight (Atlanta: A. H. Cawston, 1931) 109–11, available online at http://freepages.genealogy.rootsweb.ancestry.com/~englishsurname/misc/menofmark/jamesWarrenEnglish_2.htm.

[39]"Major John F. Hanson Is Taken by Death," *Savannah (GA) Morning News*, 16 December 1910, p. 1.

launched in Southeastern Virginia by General George B. McClellan. The campaign was an attempt to capture the Confederate capital of Richmond by traveling up the peninsula between the James and York rivers. The 53rd joined forces with units serving under Major General Lafayette McLaws's division of Brigadier General Paul J. Semmes's brigade. It was with the men of the 53rd that John saw some of the bloodiest action of the Civil War.

The 53rd was formed in Henry County with Pastor Leonard T. Doyal of the McDonough Baptist Church as colonel and commander and Lieutenant Colonel Thomas Sloan as second-in-command. The regiment traveled by train from Griffin on June 20, 1862, and arrived in Richmond five days later. Unlike John, who had now seen a year's worth of fighting, his new regiment consisted of raw recruits. The next day, after being issued their equipment, the men marched eight miles in two days to earthworks six miles east of Richmond and only three-quarters of a mile from the Union troops.[40]

On June 29, the exhausted soldiers of the 53rd found themselves on the battlefield at Savage's Station.[41] As the adjutant and veteran of the regiment, John had to provide seasoned leadership. The men were being thrown into a battle that was integral to a larger campaign to save the Confederate capital. The Battle at Savage's Station occurred on the fourth day of what would become known as the Seven Days Battles of the Peninsula Campaign, because it took the Southern army seven days to drive McClellan's army off the Peninsula and save Richmond. Unfortunately, the first battle for the 53rd Regiment was a costly one for the troops. Only four days after stepping off the train in Richmond, ten men from the 53rd were dead and forty-seven were wounded.

Three days later John and the 53rd Regiment were positioned one fourth of a mile from the enemy and poised to take part in the Battle of Malvern Hill, the final engagement of the Seven Days Battles.[42] Late in the afternoon the 53rd, including John, charged the enemy guns after marching through woods and swamps knee-deep in water and mud. The Confederates pushed back the Union soldiers in a total rout of the enemy. John and his regiment slept that night behind Yankee breastworks in the pouring rain

---

[40]John W. Lynch, *The Dorman-Mashbourne Letters, with Brief Accounts of the Tenth and Fifty-Third Georgia Regiments, C. S. A.* (Senoia, GA: Down South Publishing, 1995) 18–19.

[41]Ibid., 20.

[42]Ibid., 21.

with no tents, listening to the moaning of the wounded. The final engagement of the Seven Days Battles was over, after which the men, exhausted but glad to be alive, returned to their camp around Richmond.[43]

John saw more heavy fighting in September 1862 when the men of the 53rd were ordered to march toward Sharpsburg, Maryland, as part of the Maryland Campaign in which Robert E. Lee drove the Army of Northern Virginia onto enemy soil.[44] The regiment crossed the Potomac, wading waist-deep through a portion of the river one-half mile wide. The following day the 53rd became engaged in a battle at Crampton's Gap, which resulted in a loss for the Confederates and a significant loss of momentum for Lee's advance northward. Upon arrival in Sharpsburg, the 53rd was immediately pressed into battle. John, along with 255 men, marched through an apple orchard and then a cornfield under heavy shelling from the enemy. John and his fellow soldiers continued to engage the enemy in their forward march as men on both sides fell dead and wounded in the field. The Union began to retreat, and John and the other men of the 53rd continued rapidly onward over nearly a mile, driving back the enemy as they retreated. Finding themselves out of ammunition, the 53rd Regiment ended the engagement by turning back toward its original lines for a new supply. Union soldiers took cover in a nearby farmhouse and barn at the edge of the woods, while John and the 53rd withdrew toward the Potomac, sleeping under a grove of large trees. John and his exhausted regiment had just waged a twelve-hour battle that stands today as the bloodiest one-day confrontation in American history, in which over twenty-three thousand men died out of a fighting force of one hundred thousand men. It is commonly known as the Battle of Antietam.[45] The official report of the battle praised the many acts of gallantry of the 53rd Regiment and stated that the officers and men "acted in a manner worthy of our cause, and fully sustained the reputation which Georgia troops have ever won upon the field of battle."[46]

---

[43]Ibid., 22.

[44]National Park Service, "The Battle of Antietam," *Antietam: History and Culture*, accessed 16 May 2012, http://www.nps.gov/anti/historyculture/upload/Battle%20history. pdf.

[45]Ibid.

[46]Captain Sam Mashbourne's Official Report and Brigadier General Paul Semmes' Official Report, both in *The War of the Rebellion: A Compilation of the Official Records of Union and Confederate Armies*, series 1, vol. 19 (Part 1), prepared by U.S. War

When the Fredericksburg Campaign was launched in early December, John was not with the 53rd. On November 10, 1862, he had been granted a forty-day furlough by the medical director's office at Richmond. In late December he returned to his unit and helped them set up winter camp near Fredericksburg, Virginia.

John saw his last battle of the Civil War in early May 1863 in the Chancellorsville Campaign. Confederate Brigadier General Paul Semmes had moved his brigade toward Chancellorsville on May 1 and taken a position to the right of General William Mahone's brigade of Virginians. The two brigades faced U.S. General George Sykes and his army in heavy force, with the main assault falling on Semmes's brigade. The Union army was driven back a mile to another line of breastworks, leaving behind all types of equipment that could be used by the Confederate troops. In their advance, the 53rd encountered Union soldiers at Salem Church, a two-story red brick chapel three miles west of Fredericksburg. It is here that they made their stand under a hail of bullets with the battle lasting two hours. The 53rd and the 50th regiments received the brunt of the attack, with the 53rd capturing the colors of the 2nd Rhode Island Regiment, 460 of the best rifles, and several tents. John, as the adjutant of the regiment, had reason to be proud of his leadership on the field.[47] An article reviewing the Chancellorsville Campaign, published in the *Atlanta Journal* on September 14, 1901, stated that "Major John F. Hanson...along with many others...all greatly distinguished themselves not only in this but in every battle Longstreet's corps was in."[48] In a tribute paid to John after his death, Captain James W. English stated that John "was considered by both his superior officers and the men under him as a gallant soldier and a capable officer."[49]

On May 5, 1863, just days after the Chancellorsville campaign, John tendered his resignation from the Confederate Army for medical reasons. A surgeon's letter accompanying his resignation stated that he was suffering

---

Department (Washington, DC: Government Printing Office, 1887) 879; Lynch, *Dorman-Mashbourne Letters*, 33.

[47]Lynch, *Dorman-Mashbourne Letters*, 47.

[48]"10th Georgia Captures 27th Connecticut," *Atlanta Journal*, 14 September 1901, p. 2.

[49]"Funeral Services in Macon This Afternoon," *Atlanta Constitution* (hereafter cited as *Constitution*), 16 December 1910, p. 1.

from nephritis and calculus; however, in a letter John later wrote to Georgia governor Joseph E. Brown, he cited chronic bronchitis as the reason.[50]

Although John resigned his military service, the threat of conscription loomed over him during the waning years of the war. The Conscript Act, passed by the Confederate Congress and signed into law by Confederate president Jefferson Davis on April 16, 1862, required men between the ages of eighteen and thirty-five to serve in the Confederate Army for three years or pay a substitute to serve for them. Medical issues and being the only son in a family were the two allowable exemptions. Governor Brown, one of the most outspoken opponents of the Conscription Law, undermined conscription efforts in Georgia, resulting in much correspondence between himself and Davis. In one letter to Davis, dated April 22, 1862, Brown proclaimed, "I do not feel that it is the duty of the Executive of a State to employ actively the officers of the State in the execution of a law which virtually strips the State of her constitutional military powers."[51] John, unfortunately, became a political football in a conflict of opinions between Governor Brown and Jefferson Davis over the conscription law and what Brown considered state's rights. Some time after he had resigned, John reported for duty with the state-owned Western and Atlantic Railroad in Atlanta, an occupation that Governor Brown felt should be exempt from conscription because of the importance of the railroads to the defense of both the state and the Confederacy. However, the provost marshal would not accept John's official travel documents, which were needed during the war to travel within the state. John returned to Macon and received an appointment as a purchasing agent for the state, another occupation that the governor felt should be exempt from conscription. Again, the military guard in Macon refused to accept his papers. John, concerned that he would be conscripted back into the army and seeking clarity on his civilian position, wrote Brown to ask if an employee of the state would be protected from conscription. He expressed his opinion that Jefferson Davis "was determined never to stop until every man that is able to drag one foot after the other is placed under his control" and further stated that "I am willing to consider

---

[50]Compiled Service Records, National Archives at Atlanta, microfilm 331; John F. Hanson to Governor Joseph E. Brown, 29 March 1865, Governor's Subject Files, Georgia Governor's Office, RG 1-1-5, Georgia Archives, Morrow.

[51]Joe Brown to Jefferson Davis, 22 April 1862, accessed 27 May 2014, http://www.anselm.edu/academic/history/hdubrulle/civwar/text/documents/doc36.htm.

military service while I can live at it but having been forced to resign a grand position which I had survived by hard service, because of chronic bronchitis, I was unwilling to go back as a private to undertake that which I could not stand as a staff officer."[52] Brown responded to John that his state service would protect him from conscription. However, Davis may have felt differently. It is not known how John spent the final months of the war, but he was not conscripted.

It was a great relief when the war ended and John could begin his life without the threat of being pressed into military service. While fighting for the Confederacy in the hills of Virginia, John had met his future bride, Cora Alice Lee.[53] Following his resignation and some time after his return to Barnesville, John brought Cora to his hometown where, on February 15, 1865, Reverend Morgan Bellah, a Methodist preacher, married the couple in the Barnesville Methodist Episcopal Church.[54]

During the years of Reconstruction, the South suffered from the economic woes of a severe depression. Cities and towns were in ruins, no capital investments were being made, and few jobs were available. Farms lay wasted, the agrarian economy built on the backs of slaves was in turmoil, and a new system of sharecropping was emerging to take its place. During this difficult recovery time for the South, John's entrepreneurial spirit was challenged. Following the example of his father, who had his own furniture business, John was inspired to launch a furniture enterprise of his own. However, during Reconstruction little investment capital was available, and what could be obtained would not be offered to a young man in his twenties with little manufacturing experience. For help John looked northward.

One of the most successful furniture companies in the latter half of the nineteenth century was the Wakefield Rattan Company, located in Wakefield, Massachusetts. The popularity of rattan furniture in the Victorian era can be attributed to the genius of Cyrus Wakefield, who transformed rattan from a packing material into a fashion statement. With neither capital nor credit, John visited Wakefield and, with all the boldness

---

[52]John F. Hanson and Governor Joseph E. Brown, correspondence, 22 March 1865, Governor's Subject Files, Georgia Governor's Office, RG 1-1-5, Georgia Archives, Morrow.

[53]*Atlanta Georgian & News*, 18 August 1909, p. 1.

[54]*Barnesville (GA) Gazette*, 16 February 1865, n.p.; Lambdin and Fish, *Lamar County*, 350.

of youth, said, "I have no money and no credit but I wish to start a chair factory. I have confidence in my ability to succeed. I have come to ask you to supply me with the materials I need, though I cannot promise to pay you until I have made and marketed my product." Wakefield then turned to one of his employees and instructed, "Take this young man and let him have what he wants and let him have all the time he needs in which to pay for it."[55] For what appeared to be an act of bravado, John had actually arrived with the expectation of meeting a cold, hard businessman who would refuse his request. Instead, he found a friend who was willing to support an honest and forthright young man with ambition. John would tell this story to his friends many times in his life. He would also remark that this episode helped diminish the bitterness he harbored against the North that remained after the war.[56]

Nine months later, on November 9, 1865, Cora gave birth to the couple's first child, a son whom they named Walter Taylor, after Walter H. Taylor, the assistant adjutant general to Robert E. Lee.[57] John's father, the Reverend Hanson, was particularly fond of his grandson, and on the reverend's many jaunts into the wilderness to fill a vacant pulpit, young Walter was his favorite companion. Reverend Hanson, as a strong student of the Bible, was long-winded in his zeal for the Scripture in his sermons. A story is told that one hot summer day the two traveled by horseback to a country church where little Walter sat in the front pew to listen to his grandfather. The minutes dragged into an hour or more, and finally Walter chimed, "Grandpa, stop preaching and let's go home!" Thus ended the sermon, much to the boy's relief.[58] These experiences with his grandfather left a strong impression upon John's son, who would remain a Methodist all of his life in spite of his later foray into another spiritual philosophy.[59]

John's extended family remained close to him in the Barnesville area. His older brother, James Asbury, lived nearby with his wife, Mary, and their

---

[55]"Major John F. Hanson Is Taken by Death," *Savannah (GA) Morning News.*
[56]Ibid.
[57]Family Bible, in private collection of Mr. and Mrs. Robert Young Garrett III, Princeton, NJ.
[58]Lambdin and Fish, *Lamar County,* 343, 344.
[59]"The Theosophists of Point Loma," *San Diego Union,* 12 August 1901, p. 3.

son, James W., along with Mary's six children from a previous marriage.[60] John witnessed his sister Susannah's marriage to Alexander Morrill Lambdin, from the prominent Lambdin family of Barnesville, a union to which two children were born.[61] With his parents, brothers, sisters, nieces, and nephews all living in Barnesville, the town was his home and the center of his life.

Two years after Walter was born, the Hanson family was expanded with the birth of a daughter, Anne Carolyn, on July 31, 1867.[62] John and Cora had quite a full household at that time. In addition to their two young children, Cora's eighteen-year-old sister, Dorah, was residing with them, along with John's youngest brother, Henry, and his wife, Anne.[63] Henry was a timber contractor, procuring lumber for the milling and furniture business owned by his father and brother John. To help Cora with the household, John employed black domestic servants, who had three children, ages ten, five, and three; this family also lived with the Hansons.[64] Anne and Dorah were probably a great help to Cora with the children, especially when her third child was born, daughter Frances May, on September 15, 1871.[65] Maintaining a household of eleven people was straining John's finances. Adding fuel to the fire was the burden of a sluggish economy. Making ends meet in the post-Civil War economy meant working in more than one enterprise at a time, a challenge at which John excelled.

In addition to his furniture business, John also became involved in a brick business in Barnesville and supplemented his income working as a general agent for the North American Life Insurance Company.[66] The rattan chair business may not have been able to sustain his family, as few Southerners were able to afford the luxury of rattan chairs after the war, and even life insurance may have been a luxury few could afford. To continue to increase his income, John formed a business alliance with his father and

---

[60]U.S. Census Office, *1870 Federal Population Census*, National Archives microfilm M593.

[61]Lambdin and Fish, *Lamar County*.

[62]Family Bible.

[63]U.S. Census Office, *1870 Federal Population Census*.

[64]Ibid.

[65]Family Bible.

[66]"Major John F. Hanson Is Taken by Death," *Savannah (GA) Morning News*; "Funeral Services," *Constitution*; original North American Life Insurance Company letterhead with John F. Hanson listed as agent in possession of the author.

E.H. Bloodworth in 1868, advertising as "carrying on the Mercantile, Warehouse, Commission, Manufacturing and Milling Business." By 1869 John had formed his own partnership with Bloodworth in an enterprise that didn't include his father, advertised as Hanson, Bloodworth & Co. Touting themselves as warehousemen who were able to handle cotton as advantageously "as it can be done in any interior town,"[67] John and his partner were clearly trying to capture some of the cotton warehouse trade that was being conducted in Macon. Partnerships were constantly being formed and reformed during these tumultuous times. John and his father formed another company together—J. B. Hanson, Son & Co., a warehouse business and general commission merchants—in partnership with William Reid Murphey, an influential citizen whose family contributed significantly to the growth of Barnesville after the Civil War. John worked at least seven different jobs in Barnesville, holding several simultaneously. John was also active in the civic and social organizations of his community. He honed his debating skills in the local Barnesville Debating Society, which would serve him well the rest of his life. And like his father, John was a member of the Pinta Lodge of Free and Accepted Masons.[68]

In the small Middle Georgia town of Barnesville the foundation was laid for John's lifetime of achievements. The work ethic and leadership skills that would later bring him prominence were instilled in him by his father, a hardworking Methodist preacher and businessman, and his grandfather, an industrious farmer. John's own experiences in forging a successful economic life for himself and his family filled him with compassion for the struggles Southerners faced after the Civil War. His skills and knowledge would shortly blossom into an economic vision for Georgia's future—and eventually the nation's—that John pursued his entire life.

---

[67] *Barnesville (GA) Gazette*, 2 September 1869, Old Jail House Museum Archives, Barnesville, GA.

[68] Lambdin and Fish, *Lamar County*, 91.

2

THE BIBB

New England had the very best training for the operatives from more than fifty years['] worth of experience, the most accurate system of business, and a thorough understanding of the market in which they buy and sell, and the general laws of trade and finance, buildings that stand as the perfection of three generations.

—J. F. Hanson

BARNESVILLE MAY HAVE been John Hanson's birthplace and home, but by 1871 he was ready to move to the thriving metropolis of Macon and build a new life for himself and his family. Macon, located in Bibb County, was the heart of the cotton trade in Middle Georgia, and Hanson, with an interest in cotton, was drawn to the larger opportunities that such a city could provide. He also knew many men in Macon with whom he had served on the battlefield in the Army of Northern Virginia as well as through his business travels to the city during and after the war.[1]

Located along the fall line where the Piedmont plateau meets the Atlantic coastal plain, in the geographical center of Georgia, Macon, often referred to as the Central City, was the fifth-largest city in Georgia when Hanson contemplated his move. It had served as the transportation hub for Middle Georgia as early as 1836, when several railroad lines converged there. Bisecting the city is the Ocmulgee River, which provided water transportation as well. By 1877 sixteen main rail lines and their branches ran through Macon, connecting Columbus with Augusta and Savannah, and eventually with the city of Atlanta to the north. In *History of Macon, Georgia*, historian Ida Young describes Macon at mid-century as a flourishing market

---

[1]"Brown's Hotel," *Macon (GA) Telegraph* (hereafter cited as *Telegraph*), 18 March 1869, p. 3.

for cotton, with eight cotton warehouses located in the city by 1860.[2] Macon historian John C. Butler classifies Macon in 1879 as "one of the largest interior cotton markets in the South."[3] Macon's strength as a cotton and transportation center was most likely a factor in Hanson's decision to move there.

As co-founder of Hanson, Bloodworth & Co., his cotton warehouse business in Barnesville, Hanson had gained experience in the cotton industry before moving to Macon. After settling in the Central City in 1871, he continued his career in cotton, now as a commission merchant; with William A. Cherry, an established businessman with deep Macon roots, he founded the firm of Cherry and Hanson. In the South, most cotton planters relied on commission merchants to sell their crops. These agents, who were sometimes called cotton factors, bought and sold cotton on a commission basis. Cherry and Hanson also sold fertilizer to the "planting community" as agents for E. Frank Coe's Superphosphate.[4] While operating Cherry and Hanson, Hanson also functioned as an agent for Macon Manufacturing Company, a textile mill in Macon, and served as its secretary and treasurer.[5] He also joined the Georgia State Agricultural Society, formed by the state's farmers to promote agricultural development within the state and to disseminate information about crops and their markets.[6] As a member, Hanson interacted with others in the agricultural industry, allowing him to gain a statewide perspective on dealing with a large agricultural commodity like cotton and providing him an avenue for input as well. During his tenure with the society, the organization successfully lobbied the state legislature to form a Department of Agriculture, in 1874, the first state in the nation to do so.[7]

---

[2]Ida Young, Julius Gholson, and Clara Nell Hargrove, *The History of Macon, Georgia* (Macon: Lyon, Marshall & Brooks, 1950) 185.

[3]John C. Butler, *Historical Record of Macon and Central Georgia* (Macon: Middle Georgia Historical Society, 1969) 288–91.

[4]"E. Frank Coe's Phosphate," *Macon (GA) Weekly Telegraph* (hereafter cited as *Weekly Telegraph*), 27 February 1872, p. 3.

[5]"Notice," *Telegraph*, 9 July 1874, p. 4.

[6]*Transactions of the Georgia State Agricultural Society, from August 1876 to February 1878* (Atlanta: James P. Harrison, 1878) 319.

[7]Ibid., 319; History of the Georgia Department of Agriculture (website), accessed 28 December 2014, http://agr.georgia.gov/gdahistory.aspx; "State Agricultural Convention," *Telegraph*, 15 August 1874, p. 1.

Hanson had settled in Macon just ahead of the Panic of 1873, an economic recession that is considered one of the worst economic recessions in American history, according to the National Bureau of Economic Research.[8] It began in Europe and spread to the United States in 1873 to banks already heavily overextended with railroad construction. Real estate values plummeted, while wages declined and construction came to a standstill. The nation did not begin to recover until 1879.[9] Young also described Macon during this period as "engulfed in hard times and depression," despite it being a flourishing cotton market.[10] American humorist Bret Harte was in Macon on a lecture tour in November 1874 and, in a letter to his wife, expressed his impression of the South as "one of sadness, the wasted ill-kept fields, the scattered negro cabins, the decaying and fallen plantations, the badly dressed people, the helpless and hopeless negro, and the dumb, ill-regulated but earnest striving of the best people for a better state of things."[11] Southern historian C. Vann Woodward, in his book *Origins of the New South, 1877–1913*, describes the Southern region after Reconstruction as standing far behind the rest of the country in every measure. In comparing the South to the rest of the country, Woodward calculated wealth based on the value of private property in the United States in 1880. The figure in the South was $376 per capita, compared with $1,086 in the rest of the nation.[12] In an exercise intended to gather firsthand reports of conditions in the South, the editor of the *New York Herald Tribune*, Whitelaw Reid, sent a team of reporters into the region in 1879. Their assessments revealed a South that economically "still sits crushed, wretched, busy displaying and bemoaning her wounds."[13]

---

[8]R. Glenn Hubbard, ed., *Financial Markets and Financial Crises* (Chicago: University of Chicago Press, 1991) 82.

[9]Samuel Rezneck, "Distress, Relief, and Discontent in the United States during the Depression of 1873–78," *Journal of Political Economy* 58/6 (December 1950): 494–95.

[10]Young, Gholson, and Hargrove, *History of Macon*, 318; Richard W. Iobst, *Civil War Macon: The History of a Confederate City* (Macon: Mercer University Press, 1999) 440.

[11]*The Letters of Bret Harte*, ed. Geoffrey Bret Harte (New York: Houghton Mifflin: Riverside, 1926) 42–43.

[12]C. Vann Woodward, *Origins of the New South, 1877–1913* (Baton Rouge: Louisiana State University Press, 1951) 111.

[13]*New York Tribune*, 3 October 1879, quoted in Woodward, *Origins of the New South*, 107.

However, while the entire Southern region was still suffering from the effects of the Civil War and the nation as a whole was weakened by the global recession, Hanson looked forward. He had been eyeing an abandoned warehouse owned by the Central Rail Road and Banking Company of Georgia (later renamed the Central of Georgia Railway). When the warehouse was built near the east bank of the Ocmulgee River in 1843, the railroad was not permitted to come directly into Macon, necessitating that the building be constructed across the river where passengers and freight were off-loaded and then carried to downtown Macon by wagon. By 1851 the Central was granted permission to cross the river, and a downtown terminal was built and the old one abandoned. During the twenty-five years of its disuse by the railroad, the building had served as a gristmill and later a schoolhouse.[14] Although it stood empty by the early 1870s, the warehouse was fertile ground for the imaginations of Hanson and his brother Newt, who envisioned a new cotton mill and gristmill inside the empty shell.

At such a financially tumultuous period, it was a risky venture to open a new mill. Across town the Macon Manufacturing Company was running at half time and would lose $21,000 that year. I. E. Jones, the superintendent of the mill, recommended closing its doors because its outdated equipment made success futile.[15] But Hanson may have seen this as the perfect time to start a mill with new equipment and take advantage of the market opportunities that the loss of Macon Manufacturing would provide. Hanson was one of the "best people" that Harte described. He was striving to build an enterprise that would bring employment to the citizens of Macon, income to the coffers of the mercantile class, and a secure future for his family.

Hanson gave considerable thought to the financial structure of his new business. Even after the Civil War, the South still preferred individual ownership over the corporate model, which was gaining popularity elsewhere, according to Broadus Mitchell, historian and author of an economic history of Southern cotton mills.[16] William Gregg, one of the

---

[14]*Bibb Manufacturing Company*, April 1975, Middle Georgia Archives, Washington Memorial Library, Macon.

[15]*History of Bibb Manufacturing Company, 1876–1929* ([Macon]: n.p., 1937) 7. There is a copy at Middle Georgia Archives.

[16]Broadus Mitchell, *The Rise of Cotton Mills in the South* (Columbia: University of South Carolina Press, 2001) 38, originally published 1921 by Johns Hopkins Press.

South's early pioneers in cotton milling, advocated differently. Gregg had established a blueprint for success with his own textile operation that he founded in 1847, the Graniteville Company near Charleston, South Carolina, and before the war championed Southern industrialization as a means to increase the region's economic vitality and independence. His seminal work, *Essays on Domestic Industry*, which was first published in the *Charleston Courier* in 1844, drew on his analysis of the textile industries in New England and Philadelphia and outlined, in part, the components of a successful mill operation.[17] Gregg recommended that mills use a corporate form of ownership because it allowed for greater funding for working capital and "the services of skilled directors...which only associated capital could guarantee."[18] It is likely that Hanson would have consulted Gregg's compendium in determining how to establish and operate a mill business, finding much of value in Gregg's abundance of facts and figures, lessons regarding best and worst practices, and detailed recommendations for how to run a mill. Hanson did follow Gregg's advice by choosing the corporate model, which necessitated finding a strong financial partner.

Hanson had been in the business of cotton in one form or another for ten years and had crossed paths many times with Hugh Moss Comer, a cotton merchant in Savannah. An astute businessman, Comer held stock in railroads, fertilizer companies, hotels, a construction company, several banks, a phosphate mining company, a malting company, textile mills, the Savannah Cotton Exchange, real estate, and a cattle enterprise in Texas. By the time he built his Italianate home on Monterey Square at the corner of Bull and Taylor streets, in 1880, he had become Savannah's wealthiest citizen.[19] Hanson, who was fortunate to have come under Comer's eye, approached Comer about partnering in his new cotton milling enterprise in Macon. In Comer's various business dealings with Hanson, he had been able to assess Hanson's leadership skills and business acumen and was impressed with both.[20] Comer agreed to invest, and through this initial partnership the

---

[17]Broadus Mitchell, *William Gregg, Factory Master of the Old South* (Chapel Hill: University of North Carolina Press, 1928) 16–17.

[18]Ibid., 105.

[19]Pamela F. Crews, *A Biography on Hugh M. Comer* (Savannah: Georgia Historical Society Archives, 1991).

[20]"J. F. Hanson, One of the Greatest Builders of the South, Crosses Over," *Telegraph*, 16 December 1910, p. 1.

two men developed a friendship and business association that would be the most important and influential affiliation of Hanson's life.[21]

On February 25, 1876, Hanson, his younger brother Newt, and Comer were granted a charter for Bibb Manufacturing Company, a textile mill and gristmill. The first entry in the company journal confirms that Comer purchased stock in the amount of $17,500, with Hanson purchasing $13,100, and Newt $4,400, making a total initial investment in Bibb Manufacturing Company of $35,000. This placed Comer and the Hanson brothers in a fifty-fifty partnership in their new corporation, but with two of the partners being brothers, Comer was in a potentially weaker position in terms of control.[22] Newt assumed the role of office manager, and Hanson, the oldest at thirty-six and the only one of the three with any experience working inside a cotton mill, functioned as the agent and superintendent of the enterprise in charge of the day-to-day operations of the mill. On the board, Comer served as president and Hanson as the secretary/treasurer.[23]

To further enhance their opportunity for success, Hanson went before the mayor and city council of Macon to lobby for an exemption from city taxes. Although it was Hanson's desire to establish the company in Macon, all three agreed that they would set up operations elsewhere if they did not receive the tax exemption. On April 18, 1876, the city council passed an ordinance exempting the Bibb from taxation for ninety-nine years.[24]

On May 5, 1876, two months after it was chartered, the Bibb Manufacturing Company acquired the old Central of Georgia Railway freight depot in east Macon.[25] This structure was known as Bibb Mill No. 1 for the entire life of the company. With the building secured, Hanson and Comer made every effort to equip the facility with the most advanced technology available in order to put the Bibb on a competitive footing. Repairs to the old depot were begun in July, and the newest carding equipment in the industry was purchased from the Lowell Machine Shop in Lowell, Massachusetts, the premier manufacturer of textile milling

---

[21]*History of Bibb Manufacturing Company*, 2.

[22]Ibid., 2, 5, 6.

[23]Ibid., 4.

[24]"Maj. J. F. Hanson Tells of City's Contract with Bibb Manufacturing Co.," *Telegraph*, 12 November 1905, p. 11.

[25]"The Bibb County Manufacturing Company," *Telegraph*, 22 October 1876, p. 2.

equipment.[26] The mill was powered by a Wright's Patent steam engine, with its innovative "cut-offs" to control the expenditure of steam, designed by William Wright, the period's leading inventor of steam engine technology. The boiler and steam pump also came from Wright's factory in Newburg, New York. In addition to these modern textile marvels, the newest picker, invented by Richard Kitson of Lowell, Massachusetts, was also purchased to clean the cotton and discharge the debris outside the factory through large tubes to keep the interior of the factory free of lint and dirt.[27] Sleeping quarters were also provided in the building so that one of the Hanson brothers would always be accessible if needed.[28]

On September 15, 1876, Bibb Manufacturing opened its doors, marking the beginning of Hanson's career as one of the post-Civil War industrial leaders of Georgia and the Southeast. The factory was not originally designed to manufacture cloth but rather confined its operation to spinning, twisting, spooling, and reeling to make yarn, thread, carpet warp, twine, and rope. Hoping to diversify the company's profits, the factory also had a state-of-the-art corn milling operation, which produced "bolted meal unsurpassed by any in the market."[29] The company's charter granted it the right to manufacture flour from wheat or grain of any kind. However, the cotton milling business outpaced corn milling, and the latter was eventually eliminated to make more space for cotton production.[30]

It wasn't long before Hanson made another bold move. Less than two years after Bibb Manufacturing was founded, he set his sights on his former employer, the Macon Manufacturing Company. Hanson and Comer bought the property out of foreclosure and sold it to Bibb Manufacturing.[31] The Bibb immediately invested more than $100,000 in new equipment, remodeling, and repairs to make the plant operational in ninety days.[32] The Macon Manufacturing Company became known as Bibb Mill No. 2 and began manufacturing a product advertised as "Macon Sheeting," or cloth,

---

[26] See "Lowell Machine Shop," *Lowell National Historical Park Handbook 140*, National Park Service website, accessed 28 January 2014, http://www.nps.gov/lowe/photosmultimedia/machine_shop.htm.

[27] "Bibb County Manufacturing Company," *Telegraph*.

[28] *History of Bibb Manufacturing Company*, 3.

[29] Ibid.

[30] Ibid.

[31] Ibid., 6.

[32] "Sale of Property," *Telegraph*, 6 February 1878, p. 4.

increasing the market share of the type of cotton products the Bibb produced.[33] By fall 1878, two years after Bibb Manufacturing had opened its doors, Hanson was providing jobs for 220 employees in his new Macon enterprise.[34]

Not all of Hanson's life was consumed with his textile business, though. In one of his efforts to assimilate into Macon society, he joined the Floyd Rifles, a militia company formed in Macon and one with which Hanson had served in the 2nd Georgia Battalion during the Civil War. Macon had five militia companies before the war, all of which folded at the end of the conflict. In 1872, arms, which had been scarce after the war, became available once again, and military units reestablished themselves with the state's permission.[35]

Militia companies were as much social clubs as they were actual military units, and membership was a good way for Hanson to meet or become reacquainted with men in the community. The companies drilled and held regular parades four times a year. Hanson began his service in the Floyd Rifles as a private in 1873, and by the following year he was elected second lieutenant of the company.[36] However, his time with the Floyd Rifles was short-lived; he resigned after two years.[37] With his business affairs, Hanson may have decided that he didn't have time to devote to a military organization, or perhaps it served as a reminder of a period in his life he would just as soon forget.

Though no longer a member of the Floyd Rifles, Hanson still loved shooting sports. He helped organize the Ocmulgee Shooting Club in 1879, a pigeon-shooting club that met on the parade ground of the Central City Park.[38] The club, a forerunner of the trapshooting clubs of today, used live pigeons launched from a box as targets. In establishing the club, the members also ordered the latest trap machine, the Bogardus trap, which is similar to modern-day trap machines, and a full supply of glass balls, a forerunner of today's clay targets. After pigeon shooting, the men would

---

[33] Advertisement for Macon Mills, *Telegraph*, 16 September 1879, p. 7.

[34] "Georgia News," *Columbus (GA) Daily Enquirer-Sun*, 12 October 1878, p. 3.

[35] "Reorganization," *Telegraph*, 1 May 1873, p. 4; Iobst, *Civil War Macon*, 23.

[36] "Election of Officers," *Telegraph*, 19 July 1874, p. 4.

[37] "Officers Elected," *Telegraph*, 18 February 1875, p. 4.

[38] "Ocmulgee Shooting Club," *Telegraph*, 26 March 1879, p. 4.

often move to the shooting range for glass ball practice.[39] The members' scores were published in the *Macon Telegraph*, and Hanson and Newt were often listed as having enjoyed an afternoon of pigeon shooting together. Hanson also enjoyed the camaraderie of his friends, and according to the *Macon Telegraph*, on New Year's Eve 1881 he royally entertained a group of men at a private party in his home.[40]

Hanson and Cora enjoyed a full and varied social life. They joined many of the clubs and societies open to them, and the opportunities were many. Attendance at the Social Thalian Dancing Club of Macon, described as "the most popular society organization of the Central City," was one of the couple's favorite social activities. The grand Valentine's ball in Eastman, Georgia, in February 1882, is an example of the soirees hosted by the club. Sixty-five Maconites, including Hanson and Cora, traveled to the ball in two coaches aboard the Macon and Brunswick Railroad. The revelers arrived at eight o'clock in the evening and disembarked into the elegantly appointed Uplands Hotel. Cora was described as "adding to the brightness and elegance of the evening in her beautiful plush green velvet gown, and her emerald ornaments." The group danced until after eleven, when men in suits, white gloves, and boutonnieres served a full supper to the gathering. After a sumptuous meal, the dancing began anew and didn't stop until four o'clock in the morning. The train of weary Thalians arrived back in Macon at six, having feted the goddess Thalia at the St. Valentine's Day Ball.[41]

One of the most important aspects of socializing in Macon was the ability to entertain lavishly in one's own home. In summer 1880, the Hansons were building a large three-story residence on the eastern half of the Nesbit property, at the top of Johnston's Hill on Georgia Avenue. Hanson had commissioned the well-known Macon architect Alexander Blair to design the home, which included a basement and all the "modern improvements."[42] His penchant for the latest technology was not confined to his business. Hanson had made a successful transition to a new life in Macon, and nothing speaks to that more assuredly than the elegant home he provided for his family. Finished in 1883, this Second Empire-style mansion stood on a street blooming with Victorian architecture. The *Macon Telegraph*

---

[39]Ibid.

[40]"Observing the Custom," *Telegraph*, 4 January 1882, p. 1.

[41]"The Thalian Revelers," *Telegraph*, 16 February 1882, p. 1.

[42]"In Brief," *Telegraph*, 16 July 1880, p. 4.

described the house as being able to "fill an ugly gap in Georgia Avenue and add greatly to the appearance of that thoroughfare."[43] Ironically, less than one hundred years later the house was torn down and replaced with the windowless AT&T building, which broke the residential character of the neighborhood and created an ugly gap in the thoroughfare once again.

While Hanson possessed a strong civic and social commitment, he was also concerned about his own financial stability, which was largely tied to the mill in the form of Bibb stock. To diversify his assets he began investing in local property, such as a house and lot at Pine and First streets that he purchased at an estate auction in spring 1880.[44] Hanson's personal investments in real estate led him to become an investor in a real estate corporation formed in spring 1884. The purpose of the Macon Real Estate and Improvement Company was to buy and improve property in the city of Macon and its vicinity.[45] The corporation issued five thousand shares of stock at fifty dollars per share. Within hours of the announcement, forty-one of Macon's most influential citizens had signed up to purchase stock. While tending to his own investment portfolio, Hanson was also encouraging growth and development within the city of Macon.

Although Macon was making strides in recovering from the war, the city's infrastructure, especially its public water system, had not kept pace with its growth.[46] Macon's water system, owned by the Macon Gas, Light and Water Company, piped a modest amount of water from three springs to cisterns located at Mulberry and Cherry streets, where citizens would use buckets to collect and transport water to their homes.[47] This system was inadequate for the city's needs, especially during emergencies, which was particularly evident in 1879 when central Georgia was suffering from a drought and Macon was running out of water. During one week in June of that year, several businesses and homes went up in flames, and the fire department could do nothing to prevent or mitigate the losses because of the lack of water.[48]

---

[43]Ibid.

[44]"Executor's Sale," *Telegraph*, 7 April 1880, p. 4.

[45]"A New Boom," *Weekly Telegraph*, 11 April 1884, p. 5.

[46]Butler, *Historical Record of Macon and Central Georgia*, 289–91; "Manufactories," *Weekly Telegraph*, 7 October 1881, p. 2.

[47]Young, Gholson, and Hargrove, *History of Macon*, 376.

[48]"Fire," *Telegraph*, 10 June 1879, p. 4; "Fire," *Telegraph*, 13 June 1879, p. 4.

Several days after the June fires, an anonymous citizen wrote a letter to the *Macon Telegraph* urging the formation of new and larger municipal waterworks adequate to the city's needs and suggesting it be financed by subscriptions from businesses and merchants. The writer proposed that a committee of Macon's leading citizens, including Hanson, be chosen to undertake this enterprise.[49] Macon did establish a committee to research the problem, but Hanson was not among its members since he was already serving on the board of the Macon Gas, Light and Water Company, a likely competitor to any new enterprise. After meeting and canvassing the city, the committee discovered that few people were willing to lend their capital to such a project, and the initiative faltered.[50]

Hanson and the board of the Macon Gas, Light and Water Company did, however, begin exploring the issue of bringing running water to the city's homes. Hanson had received extra impetus to find a solution when that same year a fire licked at the periphery of one of the Bibb Manufacturing facilities.[51] By spring 1881, Hanson and the Macon Gas, Light and Water Company had created a plan to capture water from Tufts Springs two miles away by digging a reservoir fifteen feet wide and fifteen feet deep to contain it.[52] The water from this reservoir would then be pumped into the city through underground pipes at the rate of one million gallons per day, which was more than adequate for Macon's needs. The city council approved the plan, which was financed by the sale of $75,000 in bonds.[53]

On a sunny June day in 1881, Hanson was able to witness the results of his efforts with the board of the Macon Gas, Light and Water Company. Gathering at the reservoir, called Waterville, those in attendance were invited into the new engine room with its gleaming pine walls "shining in the sun like a bright new dollar." Hanson, whose interest in technology was not confined to the textile industry, brought his three children to see the mechanical triumph. He especially wanted to share his enthusiasm with his son, Walter, who at age fifteen showed an interest in mechanical engi-

---

[49]"Water Works for Macon," *Weekly Telegraph*, 17 June 1879, p 8.

[50]"Water Works," *Telegraph*, 11 July 1879, p. 4.

[51]"Editors Telegraph and Messenger," *Telegraph*, 14 June 1879, p. 4.

[52]"Preparations for the Flowing Streams Which Are to Cool Us," *Weekly Telegraph*, 6 May 1881, p. 2.

[53]Young, Gholson, and Hargrove, *History of Macon*, 376.

neering. Hanson's role, along with his fellow board members, in facilitating improved water delivery to the citizens of Macon led the *Macon Telegraph* to predict that in the hot days of summer the city would "rise up and call them blessed."[54]

Not long after helping to establish the new waterworks facility for Macon, Hanson played a significant role in another civic project. The city had several smaller concert halls but lacked a space large enough to attract popular performers at a ticket price that was affordable to a larger portion of the citizenry. After much urging from the *Macon Telegraph*, prominent businessmen in the community discussed the feasibility of building a concert hall that would meet the cultural needs of the city.[55] On January 31, 1882, citizens interested in becoming stockholders in a private venture to build an opera house met at the Masonic Hall to discuss the idea. Hanson was among those chosen as directors of the new enterprise, and shortly afterward he organized a meeting with his fellow directors in his office to discuss the project, collect funds, and establish committees for accomplishing their lofty goal of building a state-of-the-art performing arts center in Macon.[56] Sufficient money was raised among the city's residents through the issue of stock, and on April 13, 1882, the enterprising stockholders were granted a charter under the corporate name Academy of Music.[57] Two days later they purchased a site on Mulberry Street, next to the Bibb County Courthouse.[58] The committee chose architect Alexander Blair to design the building. Hanson supported the committee's decision to select Blair and may even have influenced their choice, having been working with the architect on the design of his home as well as cottages for his Bibb Mill workers and an addition to Bibb Mill No. 2.[59]

Two and a half years after its charter was granted, the Academy of Music opened its doors to a sellout crowd on September 22, 1884. The *Macon Telegraph* took credit for being the strongest champion of the venue,

---

[54]"Macon's Healthful Flow Begun," *Weekly Telegraph*, 10 June 1881, p. 8.

[55]"The Opening Night," *Telegraph*, 14 September 1884, p. 8.

[56]"Opera House Chat," *Georgia Weekly Telegraph, Journal & Messenger*, 17 February 1882, p. 2.

[57]"Application for Amendment to Charter," *Telegraph*, 16 June 1882, p. 1.

[58]"The Academy of Music, Purchase of the Ground Yesterday," *Telegraph*, 16 April 1882, p. 1.

[59]"With the Architect," *Telegraph*, 9 July 1882, p. 1; "City Items," *Telegraph*, 25 August 1882, p. 4.

claiming, "Its need to the city was advocated in these columns for a long time and we persisted so long and so earnestly for it, that a number of gentlemen with liberal purses and city pride were induced to make the initiatory step, which culminated in the grand temple of Thespis that will be opened Monday night."[60] While the *Telegraph* claimed credit for promoting it, Hanson expressed his satisfaction with the building and credited others for its success, contending that "it is to the skill, taste and fidelity of Mr. Blair, the architect; the workmanship of Mr. Smith, the superintendent, and to Mr. S. R. Jacques, whose hard work, unceasing watchfulness and judicious management of the finances that the public is indebted for the beautiful building."[61] As for the building itself, the *Macon Telegraph* described it as "a model of elegance and a triumph of taste."[62] But it was for the public to judge its success, and they arrived in their finery on opening night ready to be impressed. As the curtain was rising, Hanson ascended to the stage, and in a fitting tribute he "formally dedicated the academy to the public as a temple of amusement and instruction."[63]

Hanson's involvement with the boards of the Academy of Music and the Macon Gas, Light and Water Company went smoothly, but not all his civic endeavors would end as successfully. In June 1882, amid his efforts with the Academy of Music, Hanson was elected to serve on the Board of Trustees of Wesleyan Female College in Macon.[64] In this role, Hanson was asked to serve on the building committee under the chairmanship of his friend Henry L. Jewett.[65] In 1881, George I. Seney of New York, a railroad and banking magnate and prominent philanthropist, had made several large

---

[60]"The Opening Night," *Telegraph*.

[61]"The Academy of Music," *Telegraph*, 23 September 1884, p. 5.

[62]"Academy of Music," *Telegraph*, 14 September 1884, p. 2.

[63]"The Academy of Music," *Telegraph*, 23 September 1884. In 1886, Leonidas Jordan, a leading citizen of Macon and original investor in the Academy of Music, purchased the theater from the stockholders. Jordan sold the theater in 1893 to Atlanta Opera House owner L. DeGive and Sons, and in 1905 a remodeled version of the Academy of Music opened. The exquisite grande dame that once graced Mulberry Street was replaced by a more practical incarnation. The building continues to perform its original function for the city of Macon to the present day ("Work Has Started on New Play House," *Telegraph*, 5 April 1904, p. 8; "Sky-scraper to be Built," *Telegraph*, 19 April 1904, p. 6.

[64]"City Items," *Telegraph*, 11 June 1882, p. 4; "Wesleyan Female College," *Telegraph*, 8 July 1883, p. 2.

[65]"The Wesleyan College Improvements," *Telegraph*, 29 April 1883, p. 1.

donations to Georgia educational institutions, including $100,000 to Wesleyan Female College, which the school was using to erect a new building.[66]

Hanson took his seat on the building committee when the building was already under construction, and it wasn't long before he began to see problems with the performance of the superintendent of the project, B. F. Hartman; he told Jewett that Hartman "did not show capacity for organizing and wielding a large force, such as under his control and direction."[67] The project was running over budget, and the workmanship, in Hanson's opinion, was inferior. Hanson brought his concerns to both the building and executive committees of the college many times over the course of several months. However, Jewett defended Hartman, stating, "He was the best man for the place in the United States." Jewett continued to pay the bills submitted by Hartman until more than $100,000 had been expended—well over the $40,000 Hartman had initially estimated—yet the project was still not completed.[68]

Fearing that rumors of his performance were circulating in the community, Hartman defended his work by writing a letter to the *Evening Graphic*, a competitor of the *Macon Telegraph*, in which he produced the signatures of his contractors verifying that the money they had been paid was commensurate with the work performed. Hartman also made a preemptive strike by bringing Hanson into the controversy publicly: he criticized Hanson for not being a contractor or builder and, therefore, in no position to judge the costs of the project.[69] Hanson responded in the *Macon Telegraph*, outlining for the public the cost overruns for which Hartman was responsible and telling readers that Hartman had threatened him with slander if he said anything about how the project had been handled. Hanson made it clear that he was not the one who had "invited public discussion of these matters" but declared, "I shall shrink from no responsibility...nor will I spare a man, high or low, who is culpable for the condition in which the college is placed, so far as in my power lies, to bring the facts before the

---

[66]"Trouble in a College," *Augusta (GA) Chronicle*, 24 February 1883; "Wesleyan College Improvements," *Telegraph*.

[67]"The Improvement of the Wesleyan Female College Buildings," *Telegraph*, 18 February 1883, p. 1.

[68]Ibid.

[69]Ibid.

public."[70] Hanson acceded to Hartman's assertions that he, Hanson, was not a contractor, adding, "How much advantage Mr. Hartman has of me in those particulars, as developed by his performance at the college, and especially in his estimates as to what it would cost to do the work, I leave the public to judge."[71]

The building committee hired two independent experts to evaluate the project. Their report vindicated Hanson, as the experts agreed that the project had been mismanaged and that the contractor was incompetent.[72] Hanson presented the findings to the *Macon Telegraph*, which published them in great detail.[73] Hanson also pressed the executive committee to make a claim against Hartman in the courts for the losses incurred by the college while also urging that Jewett and some of the members of the building committee be held accountable, but the committee chose not to take his advice. Hanson resigned from the Board of Trustees and admonished the building committee, stating that exonerating itself from any fiduciary responsibility for mismanagement of the money "would doubtless create a profound effect upon the people of Georgia."[74]

Hanson's financial acumen was of use to the community in many instances. He was appointed as a member of Macon's Bond Funding Commission in 1879. Macon was in danger of defaulting on bonded debt, as were many cities after the Civil War. In the Georgia legislative session of 1879, a bill was passed allowing the city of Macon to sell new bonds to fund again the old bonded debt at a lower interest rate of 6 percent over the 7 percent bonds currently held by the city.[75] The 1 percent annual savings could be used to provide city services. The money raised from the sale of the new bonds would retire the old debt, and a fractional increase in taxes would be used to retire the new bonds in thirty years. The legislation specified that the mayor and city council could not serve on the bond commission; rather, its members must come from the citizenry of Macon. The bill included the approval of the members who had been recommended for the commission,

---

[70]"Improvement of College Buildings," *Telegraph*, 18 February 1883, p. 1.
[71]"Wesleyan Female College," *Telegraph*, 20 February 1883.
[72]"Wesleyan Female College: A Thorough Investigation Promised by the Executive Committee," *Telegraph*, 25 February 1883, p. 1.
[73]"Wesleyan College Improvements," *Telegraph*.
[74]"Financial Wreck of Wesleyan Female College," *Telegraph*, 13 July 1883, p. 1.
[75]"The Refunding Commission," *Weekly Telegraph*, 16 December 1879, p. 2.

with Hanson among them. Hanson's experience in financing a successful business made him a good candidate for service to the city in this capacity, which included determining which debts and bonds were refundable and managing the sale of the new bonds.[76] Hanson would retain his position on the commission until 1908, at which time he was the only remaining member of the original commissioners of 1879.[77]

In addition to the bond commission, Hanson served on the board of directors of the public library beginning in 1876, the year he started Bibb Manufacturing, stepping down as its president in December 1879 and passing the gavel to his neighbor Theodore Oscar Chestney.[78] By 1882 he was serving on the board of directors of the Central Georgia Bank, one of Macon's long-standing banks of the era. He also joined the Macon Board of Trade, the forerunner of the Chamber of Commerce, in 1883, rising to become its president by 1890.

While establishing a civic leadership role for himself, Hanson was also becoming a strong and forward-thinking leader of Bibb Manufacturing. At the company's five-year mark, Hanson wanted to raise more money to invest in the growing textile enterprise. This led Hanson to sell 350 shares of stock for $237.50 per share, the first recorded price of Bibb Manufacturing Company stock. This not only provided the capital he needed for expansion, it also provided a benchmark for the worth of the business. In those first five years, amid the continued economic stagnation of the Panic of 1873, Hanson had doubled the value of the business.[79] His conviction to move to Macon from Barnesville was paying dividends.

By 1882, however, Hanson and his fellow Southern mill owners were experiencing a weakening in prices for their goods; the Bibb realized $22,000 less in revenue between 1881 and 1882 despite an investment increase of $50,000. Hanson observed that many mills were being poorly managed and producing inferior products that were driving down prices. Other mills were losing money through inefficient operations. In an interview with the *Macon Telegraph*, Hanson described the state of the Southern textile industry as having been "built without experience or model, equipped by whatever machinery an agent offers at the lowest prices, run by

---

[76]Ibid.; "Funding the Macon Debt," *Weekly Telegraph*, 29 July 1879, p. 4.
[77]"Heard on a Street Car," *Telegraph*, 21 November 1907, p. 6.
[78]"Library Election," *Telegraph*, 9 December 1879, p. 2.
[79]*History of Bibb Manufacturing Company*, 9.

men who have been trained as farmers or lawyers or merchants, buying cotton without judgment and selling goods without knowing anything of the markets, and each mill working in ignorance of what other mills are doing, and setting its own price on yarns or cloth."[80] This was not the vision Hanson held for the Southern textile industry.

According to Hanson, too many people with no experience were enticed to the milling industry by the common perception that Southern mills held a two-cent-per-pound advantage in the price of cotton goods over their New England counterparts. Henry Grady, managing editor of the *Atlanta Constitution*, contributed to the frenzy by urging every town in Georgia to build a mill, without considering the current supply and demand of cotton goods, nor the quality of the goods that would be produced by inexperienced mill management.[81] Hanson believed that any price advantage the South held over New England was lost through its lack of professionalism and experience. Hanson observed that "New England had the very best training for the operatives from more than fifty years['] worth of experience, the most accurate system of business, and a thorough understanding of the market in which they buy and sell, and the general laws of trade and finance, buildings, and machinery that stand as the perfection of three generations."[82]

New England had achieved such success in part through the formation in 1854 of a cotton spinners' association in Massachusetts, which became the New England Cotton Manufacturers' Association in 1865.[83] This organization allowed the New England mills to work collectively on pricing, management techniques, and cooperative production strategies, enabling a manager or owner to benefit from the wisdom and experience of other mills. Hanson attempted to form a similar organization when he called for a meeting of Southern mill owners in Atlanta on January 16, 1883.[84]

---

[80]"Southern Cotton Manufacture," *Telegraph*, 19 January 1883, p. 1.

[81]*New Georgia Encyclopedia*, s.v. "Textile Industry," by Arden Williams, last modified 3 September 2014, http://www.georgiaencyclopedia.org/articles/business-economy/textile-industry.

[82]"Southern Cotton Manufacture," *Telegraph*.

[83]*Wikipedia*, s.v. "National Textile Association," accessed 20 July 2014, http://en.wikipedia.org/wiki/National_Textile_Association.

[84]"Southern Spinners," *Telegraph*, 18 January 1883, p. 1.

Although historian Mildred Gwin Andrews describes the first interest in forming a Southern textile association as having occurred in 1897, Hanson realized the need for a collective association of mill owners as early as 1882.[85] At the first meeting in January 1883, the attendees voted to form the Southern Cotton Manufacturers' Association and elected Hanson its first president. The association determined that its goals would be to "mutually protect and assist each other…and secure fair prices for our products."[86]

As president, Hanson chose to address two issues at the first meeting: "defective management of the mills" and poorly informed selling agents "who are either ignorant as to value, or indifferent as to prices at which products are sold."[87] Hanson wanted to help his fellow competitors manage their enterprises more effectively so that they could compete more successfully in the marketplace, which in turn would strengthen the industrial economy of the entire region.

In organizing this first meeting Hanson had asked the attendees to bring their sales records so he could more accurately assess industry pricing. He had calculated that because of the efficiency with which he managed his operation the Bibb sold its yarns for one cent a pound more than three-fourths of the mill owners present. Hanson used this information to advise the owners on improved selling strategies and professional management practices. Many attendees commented to the *Macon Telegraph* that the practical information on mill management they received at the meeting would allow them to receive one-half to one cent more per pound on their product.[88] Operating approximately fifteen thousand spindles and eighty-eight looms, Bibb Manufacturing was a respectable operation.[89] Hanson's experience enabled him to grasp the shortcomings of the Southern textile industry, and he was more than willing to share his knowledge with other mills in order to improve the quality and efficiency of cotton manufacturing. Although he had formed the Bibb only six years earlier, Hanson was already speaking with one of the largest voices in the industry in the South. Despite

---

[85]Mildred Gwin Andrews, *The Men and the Mills: A History of the Southern Textile Industry* (Macon: Mercer University Press, 1987) 151.
[86]"Southern Spinners," *Telegraph*.
[87]Ibid.
[88]"Southern Cotton Manufacture," *Telegraph*, p. 3; "Southern Spinners," *Telegraph*.
[89]"Manufactories," *Weekly Telegraph*.

the success of the initial meeting, in its first year the Southern Cotton Manufacturers' Association had "failed utterly, miserably" to come to a consensus on the issues facing the industry, according to Hanson.[90]

A year of declining prices in cotton goods precipitated another meeting of mill owners organized in Augusta, called this time by H. H. Hickman of the Graniteville Manufacturing Company, formerly owned by William Gregg. Hickman was interested in forming another association in conjunction with western manufacturers, called the Southern and Western Manufacturers Association. Hanson attended the meeting, served as its chair, and was elected president of this group as well. A lively discussion ensued as to the causes and remedies of the present state of the cotton market. It was Hanson's opinion that overproduction was now driving down the cost of goods, and he strongly urged the mill owners to run their mills at three-fourths of full time to reduce the glut of products currently in the marketplace. While some owners agreed with his position, such as Hickman and former Georgia governor Rufus Bullock, president of the Atlanta Cotton Mills, others disagreed, and a consensus could not be reached. Among those in disagreement with Hanson was William H. Young of the Eagle and Phenix Mill in Columbus, who believed that the "surplus was more apparent than real." His statement gave weight to those who did not want to reduce their production times. After extended debate, Bullock presented a resolution that would reduce the production of yarns and cloth pending the recommendations of a committee of fifteen. The membership agreed, and an executive committee was established and tasked with formulating a plan.[91] Hanson reacted with irritation to the formation of another committee, stating, "If the representatives of the various companies present could not agree among themselves, I could not anticipate any better results from the efforts of the executive committee's recommendations touching this point." In his frustration with the group's inaction, he resigned his role as chair in favor of Hickman.[92]

Despite Hanson's exasperation with his fellow mill owners' seeming unwillingness to be proactive, the Southern Cotton Manufacturers' Association, sometimes referred to as the Southern Manufacturers'

---

[90]"King Cotton," *Atlanta Constitution* (hereafter cited as *Constitution*), 4 April 1884, p. 1.

[91]Ibid.

[92]"Mr. Hanson Explains," *Constitution*, 5 April 1884, p. 4.

Association or the Southern Textile Manufacturing Association, continued as an organized body of mill representatives into the late 1890s with Hanson in a lead role.[93]

Hanson was clearly dissatisfied with the lack of professional standards and the manufacturing inefficiencies in the Georgia textile industry. He had wanted to form an association to strengthen the industry in the South, but his determination was part of a larger economic vision that he held for the region. Hanson was a strategist and adept at calculating the most effective path to accomplishment, whether it was traveling to New England to persuade a successful Massachusetts manufacturer to finance his fledgling furniture enterprise or co-opting one of the wealthiest men in Georgia as an investor in Bibb Manufacturing. Even before he invited the Southern textile mill owners to meet in Atlanta, Hanson had made a strategic investment in an instrument that he calculated would help him influence public opinion and, therefore, economic growth in the South.

In Hanson's world, no single agency had more impact upon public discourse than the press, and if he wanted to expand his sphere of influence, owning a newspaper would be the perfect vehicle with which to do so. Woodward asserts that during this period "newspapers were regarded as the voice of their editors...who were public figures of supreme importance."[94] In December 1881, Hanson purchased controlling interest in the *Macon Telegraph* and became its managing editor.[95]

Most people would have considered this an unwise investment. The paper was without cash or credit, had few patrons, had a mountain of debt, and was facing bankruptcy. Its only asset was its Associated Press franchise.[96] Hanson knew that he could do with the *Macon Telegraph* what he had done with the Macon Manufacturing Company, another enterprise that was failing at the time Hanson purchased it. However, Hanson wasn't acquiring the paper for its economic value, but rather as an avenue for promoting his reform ideas.

---

[93]"To Meet Tomorrow," *Telegraph*, 12 May 1896, p. 1.

[94]Woodward, *Origins of the New South*, 145.

[95]Harry Stillwell Edwards, "John F. Hanson—The Man," *Telegraph*, 18 December 1910, p. 6.

[96]"The Macon Telegraph," *Constitution*, 13 December 1881, p. 3; "Dr. R. L. Brantley Gives History of the Macon Telegraph," *Macon Telegraph Centennial Edition*, 25 November 1926, p. 24.

Being in control of Bibb Manufacturing, Hanson would have little time to manage the *Macon Telegraph* on a daily basis, so his choice of editor-in-chief was an important one. The paper had been owned by a consortium of men that included Harry Stillwell Edwards, a minor shareholder and the paper's associate editor.[97] Hanson began by asking Edwards to fill the role. Edwards was aware that Hanson had held strong opinions about the economic and political issues facing Georgia, and even though Edwards had a law degree, he described himself as "not having a collegiate education, without knowledge of state and national politics, and a limited acquaintance with public men." Edwards thus declined the offer, urging Hanson to choose Albert R. Lamar, one of the leading journalists in Georgia during the days of Reconstruction.[98] Lamar was known for his witty and often acerbic writing style. He also had insight into the politics and politicians of the day, having served as tally clerk in the forty-sixth Congress of the United States and as clerk in the Confederate House of Representatives from 1863 to 1865.[99]

Hanson struck a deal with Lamar on the streets of Atlanta, and with Lamar as editor-in-chief and Edwards as associate editor, Hanson had two capable writers at the helm of his paper who could articulate his views when he wasn't writing editorials himself—which, according to Edwards, he often did.[100] Hanson now had the vehicle he needed to influence the public and effect change on a large scale. The list of issues he wished to address was lengthy; it included the unchecked powers of the state railroad commission, the lack of a strong two-party system in the state, the need for higher education, the necessity of a protective tariff for the South's fledgling industrial economy, and corruption in state politics, among others. Because of the views he championed in the *Macon Telegraph*, Hanson would find himself at the forefront of the South's most pressing political, economic, and social issues of his time.

---

[97]"Macon Telegraph," *Constitution*.

[98]Edwards, "John. F. Hanson," 6.

[99]*Journal of the Congress of the Confederate States of America, 1861–1865*, vol. 6 (Washington, DC: Government Printing Office, 1905) 420; William Harden, *A History of Savannah and South Georgia*, vol. 2 (Chicago: Lewis, 1913) 559.

[100]Edwards, "John. F. Hanson," 6.

3

BATTLE LINES

We deem it our highest duty to help to elect a candidate and not to make one.

—J. F. Hanson

WITHIN MONTHS OF announcing his purchase of the *Macon Telegraph*, John Hanson began to take aim at a group of politicians—known throughout the state as the Atlanta Ring—who were in control of the course of Georgia politics. A history of the *Macon Telegraph* published in 1926 described Hanson's motives for his purchase of the paper, asserting that "its leading efforts were to face political rings and combinations…and…reform the abuses which had crept into the political system."[1] Hanson clearly had ambitious goals for the *Telegraph*, and his support for political reform would put him at odds with one of the most influential writers and orators of his day: Henry Grady.

Although Grady had worked as a reporter at several different newspapers, his journalistic star began to rise when he was hired at the *Atlanta Constitution* in 1876. That same year, Evan P. Howell, an attorney and former captain in the Confederate Army, became a major stockholder in the *Constitution* and its editor-in-chief. During the next four years Grady demonstrated leadership and writing skills for which he was rewarded with the position of managing editor in 1880.[2] One year later, Hanson became the managing editor and principal owner of the *Macon Telegraph*.

In spring 1880 the five men composing the Atlanta Ring took control of state politics. Two members wielded the power of the pen, Grady and Evan P. Howell of the *Constitution*. The other three, Joseph E. Brown, Alfred H. Colquitt, and John B. Gordon, were politicians who already held

---

[1]"Dr. R. L. Brantley," *Macon (GA) Telegraph Centennial Edition*, 24.

[2]Harold E. Davis, *Henry Grady's New South: Atlanta, a Brave and Beautiful City* (Tuscaloosa: University of Alabama Press, 1990) 23 (see Introduction, n. 3).

the reins of Georgia's democracy, serving as governors and United States senators. Historians have labeled the three politicians the Bourbon Triumvirate, and they exercised power and influence in the state through the machinations of Grady and the strong political connections he cultivated statewide, particularly between 1880 and 1886.[3] Grady worked to keep the locus of state power in Atlanta through the governor's chair while also making sure that the prestigious senatorial seats were held by Atlantans or people Grady could manipulate. Together these five men and the newspaper they controlled wielded such political power that it became difficult for candidates outside this circle of influence to mount a campaign for powerful government positions.[4]

Grady's first taste of political influence had come in spring 1880 when two situations arose that foretold a possible loss of influence by the city of Atlanta in the two strongest political offices in the state. U.S. Senator and former Confederate General John B. Gordon decided that he'd had enough of politics and wanted to resign his Senate seat for a job that would pay more money. Alfred H. Colquitt, also an ex-Confederate general, was serving as governor and was in danger of not being reelected because of scandals in his administration. The Ring was at risk of losing influence in Washington and the highest office in the state if candidates from other regions of the state replaced them. (Both Gordon and Colquitt were Atlantans.) Working behind the scenes, Grady took it upon himself to see that the outcome would benefit the Ring and, thereby, the city of Atlanta, which was Grady's primary concern.[5]

He began by sending a message to Governor Colquitt asking him to accept Gordon's resignation and appoint Joseph E. Brown, the president of the Western and Atlantic Railroad and former Civil War governor of Georgia, to fill Gordon's unexpired Senate term, which Colquitt did. Grady then maneuvered a job for Gordon with the Louisville and Nashville Railroad, with the Western and Atlantic Railroad paying a portion of Gordon's L and N salary. Many across the state cried foul, and Brown was

---

[3]Ibid., 62.

[4]C. Vann Woodward, *Origins of the New South, 1877–1913* (Baton Rouge: Louisiana State University Press, 1951) 14–15; Davis, *Henry Grady's New South*, 61–65.

[5]Davis, *Henry Grady's New South*, 66–67.

accused of buying his Senate seat, though none of the accusations had any sticking power.[6]

Next, with the backing of the *Constitution*, Grady went to work on the Colquitt campaign of 1880, his first foray into political campaign management.[7] The *Constitution* endorsed Colquitt's candidacy, and because it was Georgia's leading newspaper, the statewide press followed suit. However, Colquitt's scandal-plagued administration, including the Senate seat swap, made him a weak candidate who faced opposition within his own party. Thomas Norwood of Savannah, a former U.S. senator, ran against Colquitt for the Democratic nomination. Grady began a mail campaign by sending personal letters from Colquitt to voters in every county, which impressed many.[8]

According to Isaac Avery, Colquitt's executive secretary and a former editor of the *Atlanta Constitution*, Grady "kept the whole State in his observation, devised means, wrote letters, sent myriad dispatches, strengthened doubtful localities, and placed help wherever it was needed."[9] Working tirelessly and enthusiastically, Grady proved to be a masterful campaign manager and succeeded in keeping Colquitt in the governor's chair. He also kept the Atlanta Ring in control of the state for the next two years, at which time Colquitt would be unable to run again under the state's constitutional term limit.

Hanson perceived that these men were being elected through manipulation rather than by the will of the people. He owned the *Telegraph* during the reign of the Atlanta Ring and fought against it with all the editorial strength that he and Albert Lamar, his new editor-in-chief, could muster. His efforts were not well received by his competitor, Grady's *Atlanta Constitution*. Harold E. Davis, professor emeritus at Georgia State University who wrote a seminal work about Grady's life, titled *Henry Grady's New South: Atlanta, a Brave and Beautiful City*, describes the *Constitution*'s loathing for Hanson's newspaper, declaring that "language approaching the

---

[6]Ibid.
[7]Ibid., 69.
[8]Ibid., 70.
[9]Isaac W. Avery, *History of the State of Georgia from 1850–1881* (New York: Brown & Derby, 1881) 569; Davis, *Henry Grady's New South*, 239.

violent poured upon the Macon competitor even as the *Constitution* blandly and unconvincingly insisted that it loved the people of Macon."[10]

Hanson attempted to expose political corruption primarily through Lamar's quill-driving efforts.[11] Lamar had been working in the office of the solicitor general in South Georgia, and within days of his hiring by Hanson, newspapers throughout the state expressed their support and congratulations for Lamar's return to the "list of most esteemed contemporaries" within Georgia's circle of journalists. He received praise for his "scholarly mind, and judicial temperament and his thorough familiarity with all phases of politics."[12] Foreshadowing what was to come from Lamar's pen, the *Augusta Chronicle* said of him, "There are few men anywhere who have such skill in composition, and fewer still whose experience has been wider and deeper, politically and socially. We and many others will look forward to some of the raciest writing in Georgia, when Lamar gets well warmed in his seat."[13] Harry Stillwell Edwards, the *Telegraph*'s associate editor, confirmed these editorial quips, adding that Lamar's "greatest gift was the invective and in the exercise of this he brought into play the finest irony, ridicule and sarcasm I have ever seen outside the Junius letters." [14]

Hanson also expressed his views on the editorial pages, but in a manner quite different from Lamar's, which Edwards described as having "a directness almost bald in its style, but always clear and forceful." According to Edwards, Hanson's "work was constructive and he dealt with issues and ideas without respect to individuals."[15] Regardless of who was holding the pen, the themes and positions taken by the *Telegraph* reflected Hanson's opinions as owner and managing editor.

The first opportunity Hanson had to challenge the Atlanta Ring came in the 1882 campaign for governor, which began in earnest less than six months after Hanson acquired the *Macon Telegraph*. Augustus O. Bacon, a state representative from Macon, a former Macon city attorney, and the

---

[10]Davis, *Henry Grady's New South*, 43.

[11]"Georgia Press," *Macon (GA) Telegraph* (hereafter cited as *Telegraph*), 20 December 1881, p. 3.

[12]*Atlanta Constitution* (hereafter cited as *Constitution*), 13 December 1881, 3.

[13]*Augusta (GA) Chronicle* (hereafter cited as *Chronicle*), quoted in "Georgia Press," *Telegraph*, 16 December 1881, p. 2.

[14]Harry Stillwell Edwards, "John F. Hanson—The Man," *Telegraph*, 18 December 1910, p. 6.

[15]Ibid.

then-current speaker of the Georgia House, was ready to take on higher office and had his sights set on the governor's chair. Bacon was a strong candidate and fully qualified to be the governor. He was an "efficient presiding officer in the house" and a "scrupulously fair" man who had built relationships with his contemporaries that yielded him a strong political network of statewide support. According to Davis, Bacon's candidacy was "the catalyst that converted the politics of the decade into pro-Atlanta and anti-Atlanta camps, and the threat that he and his friends posed to Atlanta gave the new Ring a continuing reason to exist. Bacon, in short, became the vehicle by which central Georgia and much of the rest of the state sought to shift political power away from Atlanta."[16] Hanson, through his editorial positions in the *Macon Telegraph,* became the loudest voice driving that vehicle. But for Hanson, it was less about bringing the locus of power to Middle Georgia and more about advocating that qualified statewide candidates have a fair opportunity to be elected. Lamar would try to expose the Ring's political maneuvering through the power of the pen, as did Hanson, but the two men were no match for Henry Grady's political machine.

Early in the gubernatorial campaign of 1882 there seemed to be no other Democratic candidates of substance in the way of Bacon's ascent to the governorship. However, the political contest was about to change. An Independent movement of Democrats had begun in North Georgia in the 1870s, led by Dr. William H. Felton and his wife, Rebecca Latimer Felton—"the most famous husband and wife political team in Georgia history," according to historian and author Matthew Hild.[17] Dr. Felton, from Bartow County, had served three consecutive terms in Congress beginning in 1874. Rebecca managed her husband's campaigns, was an outspoken critic of the convict lease program, was active in the temperance movement, and "brandished one of the sharpest political pens in the state."[18] At its zenith of influence, in 1878, the Independent Party had ninety members holding office in the state legislature. The Independent Democrats were attempting to separate themselves from the Bourbon Democrats, who had come into power after Reconstruction. Often called the Redeemers, the

---

[16]Davis, *Henry Grady's New South,* 71.

[17]Matthew Hild, *Greenbackers, Knights of Labor, and Populists* (Athens: University of Georgia Press, 2007) 35.

[18]Ibid.

Bourbons returned the power of government in the South to the white ruling class and worked to disfranchise blacks. The Independent Democrats, with the Feltons at the helm, were leading the charge against what they perceived as rampant corruption among politicians and government, something Hanson could certainly agree with.[19] Hanson and the *Macon Telegraph*, however, did not support an Independent Party but rather tried to reform the Democratic Party through the power of the press.

As leader of the Independent movement, Dr. Felton wrote Alexander H. Stephens, the former vice-president of the Confederacy and a U.S. congressman, asking him to run for governor as the Independent Party candidate. Stephens had been serving as a Democrat congressman from Crawfordville, Georgia, since 1873, although was not a friend of the Bourbon Democrats.[20] In March 1882 Governor Colquitt made a special trip to Washington to also encourage Stephens to enter the race for governor, but as a Democratic candidate. An outgoing governor courting his replacement seemed like an unusual move and was branded by Rebecca Felton as another Atlanta Ring political maneuver, which she characterized in her memoirs as Colquitt "'laying pipe' for Senator Hill's place," since he was unable to run for another gubernatorial term.[21] Senator Benjamin Harvey Hill was waging a battle with cancer at the time and was not expected to finish out his term.

Stephens was seventy-one years of age, in pain, and in ill health, and many felt that he was prevailed upon to become a candidate knowing that his vanity wouldn't allow him to turn it down. And he didn't. Stephens— who had previously stated that he planned to retire from politics—decided to run for governor, but as a candidate of the Democratic Party. This did not please the Feltons, who were hoping to bring a change in political power to Georgia by placing an Independent in the governor's chair.[22]

Grady was not going to let the power of the state rest in the hands of Bacon and Middle Georgia. As the former vice-president of the Confederacy, Stephens was still highly revered by many throughout the state, which Grady knew he could use to the candidate's advantage. Grady

---

[19]Ibid.

[20]Davis, *Henry Grady's New South*, 72.

[21]Rebecca Latimer Felton, *My Memoirs of Georgia Politics* (Atlanta: Index, 1911) 36.

[22]Ibid., 367–71; Davis, *Henry Grady's New South*, 72.

became the vocal leader of the Stephens campaign, which received the wholehearted support of the *Constitution* as well.

Immediately the *Macon Telegraph* came out against the idea of a Stephens candidacy because of his age and poor health and most especially because the newspaper felt his candidacy was gained through manipulation and party politics. Branding this as another move on the part of the Atlanta Ring to control the nomination process, Hanson believed that Stephens would never have mounted a campaign for governor at his age and in such frail health without outside influence and suggested that the campaign came about "suddenly and unexpectedly, and by devious methods and marshalling antagonistic elements."[23] Hanson's comments refer to the Independents and the Democrats, who were both using Stephens's candidacy as a weapon against the other. Because of these manipulations, Hanson described the nomination process as "so closed that the general public cannot be permitted to take part in anything but the voting."[24] He expressed the position of his own newspaper in this regard when he stated that "we deem it our highest duty to help to elect a candidate and not to make one."[25] Through these editorial comments Hanson was trying to expose the collusions of Atlanta's power brokers. The *Hawkinsville Dispatch* seemed to understand Hanson's mission, describing him as a "credit to Southern journalism" and comparing the *Telegraph* to the *Daily Sun* in New York, "a paper that is independent of rings and cliques, the organ of the people, a paper that is fearless in the comments upon public men and measures."[26]

However, as the *Telegraph* was a good Democratic organ, Hanson stated that if Stephens became the Democratic Party's nominee "he shall have the support of the *Telegraph and Messenger* in no half-hearted way."[27] The *Constitution*, however, would not make the same claim about Bacon. Howell made it clear that the two contenders for the nomination were Bacon and Stephens, but if Bacon won the nomination the *Constitution*

---

[23]"Sentimentalism in Politics," *Telegraph*, 9 July 1882, p. 2.

[24]"The Anxious Inquirers," *Georgia Weekly Telegraph, Journal & Messenger* (hereafter cited as *Georgia Weekly Telegraph*), 30 June 1882, p. 6.

[25]"A Word with a Disconsolate Contemporary," *Georgia Weekly Telegraph*, 9 June 1882, p. 4.

[26]*Hawkinsville (GA) Dispatch*, quoted in *Macon (GA) Weekly Telegraph* (hereafter cited as *Weekly Telegraph*), 1 September 1882, p. 8.

[27]"Mr. Stephens and the Governorship," *Weekly Telegraph*, 12 May 1882, p. 4.

would not support him, a statement that rejects the will of the people over the will of the Atlanta Ring.[28] Grady's strength as a campaign manager was now evident to his boss, and Howell probably knew he would not have to eat his words.[29]

It was the policy of the *Telegraph*, under Hanson's leadership, not to endorse a candidate in the primary, and it did not endorse Bacon in his primary bid for governor in 1882.[30] However, the *Telegraph* made it quite clear that it didn't think Stephens was a qualified candidate due to his health and his political history of not being in line with Democratic principles, a reference to his Independent leanings. The *Telegraph* explained its opposition to Stephens by stating, "We have opposed him only from a matter of conviction and duty, and not to elevate any man, or to promote the views, wishes or ambitions of any set of men."[31]

The *Constitution* assailed the *Telegraph* for its stand against Stephens, and the two publications were engaged in pen-to-pen combat almost weekly. The *Constitution* prodded the *Telegraph* to endorse a candidate in the primary, chastising the paper by claiming that "every well regulated newspaper must have a candidate." Lamar addressed the issue with his usual satire, claiming that the *Constitution* has "exhorted us that if we do not hearken to the voice of grace and unbind our stiffness of neck that the gates of political paradise will be closed against us and that our chance in the plan of salvation will surely draw a blank."[32]

In early July, Hanson picked up on a movement to change the way a nominee was chosen at the state Democratic convention. Instead of a two-thirds majority vote, as had been the process for years, Grady and some of the Democratic Party leaders wanted a simple majority to decide the nominee. It was not just the *Telegraph* that was opposed to a Stephens candidacy; the Democrats of Georgia were not lining up in great numbers behind the candidate, and the members in control of the party knew that it would be difficult to get two-thirds of the Democratic Party to support Stephens.[33] But if it were to come down to a simple majority vote, many

---

[28]"Will the Constitution Stand?," *Weekly Telegraph*, 30 June 1882, p. 4.
[29]Davis, *Henry Grady's New South*, 71.
[30]"Disconsolate Contemporary," *Georgia Weekly Telegraph*.
[31]"Sentimentalism in Politics," *Telegraph*.
[32]"Disconsolate Contemporary," *Georgia Weekly Telegraph*.
[33]"The Situation," *Georgia Weekly Telegraph*, 7 July 1882, p. 4.

thought Stephens could very well win. The *Telegraph* had other ideas and suggested that if neither Bacon nor Stephens could command a two-thirds vote at the convention, "there are plenty of good, honest, fair-minded, able Democrats in the party who can command this support. Already the names of Judge Crawford, Hon. W. E. Smith of Dougherty, Mr. Northen of Hancock, and others have been mentioned."[34]

The *Telegraph* excoriated the Atlanta Ring's plan, stating, "This is the result of blind partisanship on the part of those who advocate his [Stephens's] nomination. It shows a willingness to sacrifice the party in the interest of a man." The paper went on to state that "if a candidate cannot secure a two-thirds vote in the July convention, there is no need of any further evidence to show that he is not the man to be nominated. If neither of the candidates before the people can secure the indorsement [*sic*] of a two-thirds vote, it will be the duty of the convention to give the people a nominee who can."[35] The workings of a political machine could be seen in the party element that was pushing for the change. The *Columbus Enquirer* also wrote an editorial on the matter concurring with the view of the *Telegraph*, reiterating that "a man who has not sufficient influence and is not sufficiently satisfactory to the people to obtain a two-thirds vote of the delegates elected by a majority of the people is not the proper candidate to be placed before the people as their standard-bearer."[36]

The Democratic convention convened in Atlanta on July 19, and the Atlanta Ring maneuvered the committee to pass the simple majority rule in choosing their nominee. At that point Bacon could see the handwriting on the wall and immediately resigned.[37] The Democratic Party chose Stephens as its nominee, but when the convention called for making the simple majority a permanent rule, it was "promptly tabled by an overwhelming vote."[38] This confirmed for the *Telegraph* that the disregard for the two-thirds rule was done purely for the sake of electing one specific man. The *Telegraph* regretted that Bacon was defeated through manipulation by machine politics, attesting that he had "character admirably equipped with

---

[34]"Sentimentalism in Politics," *Telegraph*.

[35]"Blind Personalism," *Georgia Weekly Telegraph*, 14 July 1882, p. 6.

[36]*Columbus (GA) Daily Enquirer-Sun*, quoted in "Sentimentalism in Politics," *Telegraph*.

[37]Davis, *Henry Grady's New South*, 73.

[38]"The Convention—Our Position," *Georgia Weekly Telegraph*, 28 July 1882, p. 4.

all the qualities to make up a chief executive...had the campaign not been...marred by the small tricks and practices of the politician."[39] Other delegates to the convention were quoted in the *Telegraph* describing the political machinations a little more harshly. One proclaimed that "he wanted the next state convention held in Fort Valley, or somewhere out of the reach of Atlanta. Between the Atlanta pothouse politicians and Atlanta whisky, there is no man on earth who could spend a half hour in the city as a delegate or legislator without becoming corrupt in both body and soul."[40]

The *Macon Telegraph* continued to assail the Stephens nomination, claiming that there were other more worthy candidates in Georgia, that he was an unpopular Democrat in his own state, and that he was physically unfit to hold office. So fervent were the *Telegraph*'s editorials against Stephens that other papers around the state couldn't resist making retorts, to which Hanson and Lamar were happy to respond; therein ensued many exchanges, such as this one with the *Griffin News*: "THE MACON TELEGRAPH is off on a tangent again, and is opposing Stephens for governor a great deal more vehemently than is necessary. The TELEGRAPH is a good paper, but lacks ballast; it should buy a few rocks to put in the hold. A little rock and rye would not be bad in lieu of something else." To which Lamar replied, "If ballast is the thing that induces a paper to support dead men for office, the *Telegraph and Messenger* doesn't want any of it. We don't want any 'rock and rye' either. This is a sober institution. It would have to be fearfully drunk to take stock in the political graveyard business."[41]

Hanson would not allow the *Telegraph* to back down in its attacks on the nomination of Stephens. In a bold (or, some would say, crazy) move, he advocated the withdrawal of Stephens and took the position that another Democratic convention should be convened to nominate a true Democrat.[42] Lamar expressed this viewpoint in his sarcastic style, penning, "To willfully place in the executive chair of Georgia a man who has so far entered on his second childhood as to need a guardian, is not the part of wisdom or of

---

[39] "Mr. Bacon's Canvass," *Weekly Telegraph*, 28 July 1882, p. 2.

[40] "The Bosses," *Weekly Telegraph*, 28 July 1882, p. 1.

[41] *Griffin (GA) News*, quoted in "The Georgia Press," *Weekly Telegraph*, 28 May 1882, p. 8.

[42] "The Herald and the Telegraph," *Georgia Weekly Telegraph*, 1 September 1882, p. 2.

patriotism.... Of the powers that he once possessed, only his vanity and his ambition are left him unimpaired. The State needs some other qualifications than those in her Governor, and it is absurd to hold that it is out of the power of the Democratic party of Georgia to attend to this need, merely because the recent convention failed to do its duty to the party and the State."[43]

This was the *Telegraph's* last attempt to persuade the Democratic Party to change its course and select a new candidate, and both Hanson and Lamar knew it was fruitless. But the *Telegraph* did not shrink from answering the accusations by the *Augusta Chronicle*, who reproached the *Telegraph* for whining about a Stephens candidacy simply because its candidate, Augustus O. Bacon, was the loser. The *Telegraph* answered in strong terms, stating, "Nothing could be more unfounded; nothing could be more ridiculous. The TELEGRAPH AND MESSENGER is not a Bacon paper.... [T]here are scores of men in the State to whom it would have given as earnest and as unhesitating support." The *Telegraph* closed the editorial by saying that the paper "wasn't ready to indorse [*sic*] a candidate with nothing to commend him but the suspicious earnestness with which he was forced on the party by A. H. Colquitt and Joseph E. Brown."[44] Hanson described that process as a ratification rather than a nomination, as the candidate had already been chosen by a handful of men "who assumed to be the Democratic party in Georgia."[45]

Hanson was outspoken in his charges of influence in the nomination process, and he was more than willing to name the men in question as the bosses of the Atlanta Ring. However, despite their reproachful editorials, Hanson and Lamar had the difficult task of bringing the newspaper into line with the Democratic Party and its nominee as they pledged they would in the beginning of the campaign.

The *Telegraph* was now looking for a way to support Stephens without abandoning its reasons for opposing him. Hanson began to apply pressure on the executive committee of the Democratic Party to bring the disaffected back into the fold, including himself, by making Stephens adhere to a party platform that all Democrats could support. A long *Telegraph* editorial in

---

[43]Ibid.

[44]"For Georgia—Not for Bacon," *Telegraph*, 29 August 1882, p. 6.

[45]"An Imperative Duty," *Georgia Weekly Telegraph*, 1 September 1882, p. 6.

September described the lack of harmony within the state Democratic Party and outlined what Stephens could do to unite Democrats and quash "Independentism," a term used frequently at the time to describe the movement led by the Feltons to move away from the policies of the Bourbon Democrats, a position Stephens supported. The *Telegraph*'s editorial asked Stephens to "place himself in a position where he can be fairly and conscientiously supported." To Hanson this meant denouncing Independentism and adhering to strong Democratic Party principles, including a commitment not to elevate blacks above whites but rather to "guarantee to the negro under all circumstances, equal and exact justice; nothing less, nothing more." He also called for the Democratic Party to banish rings, cliques, and bosses from the organization and to work together "in an effort to rehabilitate and harmonize the Democratic Party for the reason that all of the hopes of the people of Georgia are bound up in the destiny of the party."[46] All told, three editorials appeared in the *Telegraph* outlining what the Georgia Democrats needed to do to make the Stephens candidacy palatable to the *Telegraph*, and by association to its constituency.

The executive committee of the Democratic Party heard Hanson's call and created a platform that included everything he had called for in his editorials. Stephens gave an address at the Masonic Hall in Macon on September 9 in which he concurred with the executive committee's platform, saying, "I agree to every word, syllable and sentence in it." Hanson had led the effort to expose the folly of a Stephens candidacy, but when the choice was made he did not abandon the fight. He was determined that the Democratic candidate should represent the party to which he had been nominated to serve. And in an effort to more fully justify his position during the campaign, Hanson wasted no time in pointing out to the statewide press that the candidate was now standing on the platform on which the *Telegraph* had insisted. The *Telegraph* described itself as "exemplifying what fighting inside the party means, and how prompt and efficacious a remedy this is when properly and fearlessly applied." The newspaper was proud to point out that "it had demonstrated that the cunning of bosses, the trickery of politicians and the machinations of a hungry horde of camp followers, all

---

[46]"The Situation," *Georgia Weekly Telegraph*, 8 September 1882, p. 2.

combined are not sufficient to withstand the assaults of a free, courageous and unpurchasable press."[47]

The only negative aspect of Stephens's candidacy remained his age and health, for which nothing could be done. And upon that score Hanson and the *Telegraph* were vindicated. On October 4, 1882, Alexander Stephens was voted governor of Georgia, and 120 days after taking office, Stephens died in the governor's mansion. Grady and the Atlanta Ring had won a short-term victory.

Amid the *Telegraph*'s battle over the Stephens nomination, Lamar, who had been with the *Macon Telegraph* for only seven months, struck a nerve with the editor-in-chief of the *Atlanta Constitution*. In his zeal to challenge the *Constitution*'s support of what the *Telegraph* considered a quasi-Democratic candidate, Lamar stated in an editorial that "two prominent citizens of Atlanta" had told him that "they were daily expecting the *Constitution* to come out as an independent or republican sheet," which he followed with the exclamation: "Georgians, do you hear that of the immaculate and omnipotent organ!"[48] Nothing could be more heinous to an editor in post-Reconstruction Georgia than to be accused of heading a Republican paper. Lamar may in fact have heard this comment from two individuals, or he may have been taking a poke at the *Constitution* to get a rise out of its editor. If the latter was the case, it certainly achieved its objective, for the *Constitution* lashed out, characterizing the story as a "cowardly insinuation" and "a lie hatched in whole by the editor of the *Macon Telegraph and Messenger*." Being called a liar was almost as heinous as being called a Republican newspaper editor. Howell concluded with a veiled threat of violence toward Lamar, initiating the possibility of a duel by declaring that "the tenor of your note can have but one meaning. I shall immediately place myself beyond the possibility of arrest." Leaving Lamar a way out of the impending disaster, he further declared, "Whilst I am ready to respond promptly to any demand for satisfaction that you may have to make, I do not wish to be a party to a ridiculous fiasco, and accord to you the same desire." Being threatened with bodily harm went beyond the pale, and

---

[47]"Mr. Stephens's Speech—Our Proposition," *Telegraph*, 12 September 1882, p. 2.

[48]"The Howell-Lamar Duel," *Atlanta Weekly Constitution* (hereafter cited as *Weekly Constitution*), 18 July 1882, p. 8.

Lamar felt he had no choice but to defend his honor.[49] And thus began one of the most bizarre escapades in the history of Georgia journalism.

Hanson intervened in the editorial quarrel in an effort to make peace, traveling to Atlanta to meet with the *Constitution*'s editor. The men met at Atlanta's premier hotel, the Kimball House, which was the first hotel in Atlanta to have an elevator and central heating and was the center of the social universe for businessmen and legislators traveling to the capital city. After the heated exchange between the two newspapers had appeared in print, the very public meeting of Hanson and Howell caused curious tongues to wag at the possibility of a settlement of the issues. It was assumed that when Lamar arrived the following day, July 3, that he had been summoned by Hanson to help negotiate a settlement between the two editors.[50] Written communications began to fly back and forth between the hotel and Howell's office over a two-day period with neither party willing to apologize for their insulting statements. In the end there was nothing left for the offended editors to do in the chivalrous South of the 1880s but to challenge each other to a duel. Evan P. Howell and Albert R. Lamar were going to settle this dispute with their pistols.

Arrangements were made between the two men and their go-betweens—Captain Harry Jackson for Howell, Ben G. Lockett for Lamar—to meet across the state line from West Point, Georgia, in Alabama. Hanson, Lamar, and Lockett boarded the midnight train to West Point on July 4, and Jackson took Howell by carriage. In making the arrangements, Jackson had spilled the beans about the looming duel, resulting in Hanson, Lamar, and Lockett being arrested for disturbing the peace before the train could leave the station. Howell arrived in West Point to find Lamar and his entourage missing in action. They were, fortuitously for Howell, spending the night in the Atlanta city jail.

The next morning, Hanson, Lamar, and Lockett appeared before Judge Hillyer in the Superior Court of Atlanta represented by former governor James M. Smith. It was an expensive lesson in humility for both Hanson and Lamar, who were each fined two thousand dollars. Lockett was set free

---

without bond. When Howell and Jackson got within seven miles of the city, they too were arrested. The two had their own day in court on July 6.[51]

The "ridiculous fiasco" that had just transpired was settled by a panel of three men, I. N. Whittle, Judge Logan E. Bleckley, and Judge Clifford Anderson. They examined the issues on both sides and created a document for Lamar and Howell to sign stating that each was wrong in his hasty comments made in the heat of political passion and, further, that each withdrew all statements made to the other in this regard. The signatures of acceptance were published in the paper and a truce was finalized.[52]

The unconsummated duel and arrests of two of the South's most highly regarded editors made headlines in the *New York Times*, probably shocking the sensibilities of its readers, and most certainly embarrassing Evan P. Howell. The *Marietta Journal* summed up the Southern opinion of the whole affair when it opined, "This weather is too caloric for chivalry. Use plenty of ice, gentlemen, and keep cool."[53] This incident foreshadowed problems that Hanson would later have with his editor-in-chief when his support of Lamar's editorial excesses would cost him more than money.

Not long after Hanson and Lamar's editorial debacle, in the middle of the gubernatorial campaign, Benjamin Hill passed away on August 16, 1882. Hill was a popular senator who had served in the Confederate Senate before becoming a United States senator in 1877. Macon paid tribute to Hill with a tolling of the bells in the clock tower at noon following the announcement of his death. On the morning of the funeral, leading citizens of Macon called a meeting in the courthouse to solicit recommendations or resolutions to be presented from Bibb County. At the meeting Hanson was chosen as one of thirty-two delegates to represent Macon at the funeral. Before the meeting was adjourned, Hanson, by motion, requested that the mayor ask the merchants of Macon to close their doors from four until six, during the hours of the funeral, and that the church and engine house bells be tolled from four to half past four. The motion was adopted.[54] Hanson was also part of a committee to solicit funds to contribute to the erection of a monument

---

[51]"The Lamar-Howell Duel," *New York Times*, 6 July 1882, n.p.
[52]"The Howell-Lamar Duel," *Weekly Constitution*.
[53]*Marietta (GA) Journal*, 13 July 1882, p. 2.
[54]"The Dead Senator," *Georgia Weekly Telegraph*, 25 August 1882, p. 7.

to Hill to be placed at the state capitol, and he offered the *Telegraph* newspaper office as a collection location for funds.[55]

It wasn't long after Hanson had paid his respects to Senator Hill that he and Lamar began waging another battle with the *Constitution* over Grady's political maneuvering to fill Hill's vacant Senate seat with an Atlanta Ring candidate. Conveniently, Colquitt, the outgoing governor, was available. Grady, having already made his Senate-seat-for-sale deal with Joseph E. Brown and determined that Atlanta men would sit in both Senate seats, became Colquitt's campaign manager.[56]

Speculation about who would become Georgia's next Senator occupied the state press for several months preceding the November vote on the matter by the state legislature, the body that elected U.S. Senators at the time. The *Telegraph* was most preoccupied with Colquitt, however. It revived previous accusations that Colquitt had traveled to Washington, D.C., in March, not to urge Stephens to run for governor but rather to broker mutual support: Colquitt would support Stephens's gubernatorial candidacy in exchange for Stephens supporting Colquitt for U.S. Senator when Hill's seat became available. Colquitt and Stephens denied the quid pro quo accusations, and Hanson, Lamar, and the *Telegraph* took every opportunity to point out to the people of Georgia that a conspiracy was afoot to keep control of the state's affairs in the hands of a few men in Atlanta.[57]

In late October the *Post-Appeal*, an Atlanta paper, printed a story stating that it had in its possession a signed letter from Stephens, written before he had declared his candidacy for governor, stating that he would not be a candidate for the Senate seat when it became available but that Colquitt was the "most fit man for the place of any mentioned."[58] Lamar commented that "the exalted nonsense that Colquitt is the ablest man offering for the Senatorship, gives a sort of unreal, jocular character to the whole effusion."[59]

The existence of such a letter from Stephens signaled to Hanson that he and the *Telegraph* had been right in their assertions that Stephens had

---

[55]"The Hill Monument," *Telegraph*, 22 September 1882, p. 1.

[56]Davis, *Henry Grady's New South*, 73; Raymond B. Nixon, *Henry W. Grady: Spokesman of the New South* (New York: Alfred A. Knopf, 1943) 200.

[57]*Telegraph*, 18 October 1882, p. 2.

[58]"The Mask Dropped," *Telegraph*, 24 October 1882, p. 2.

[59]*Telegraph*, 14 November 1882, p. 2.

indeed entered into an agreement with Colquitt that each would support the other in their respective quests for political office. However, Stephens had claimed in several of his speeches that he was beholden to no man and that he "toted his own skillet."[60] Both Brown and Stephens were now aggressively supporting Colquitt for Senator, and the *Telegraph* was asking the voting public if either of these men actually believed that Colquitt was the strongest, most experienced, and most competent person to represent Georgia in Washington. Lamar inquired, "Is there a Georgian outside of a lunatic asylum, who can read and write, who can now doubt the existence of a ring and its purposes? Will the young and rising men of the State, who have borne the burden and heat of party conflicts, for good government, submit to sit beneath the blighting shade of this little political corporation?"[61]

The *Telegraph* was making headway in its editorial charge of corruption within the ranks of the Democratic Party. Other editors around the state began to comment on the political maneuvering of the Atlanta Ring. Following Lamar's sarcastic style, the *Augusta Evening News* lamented, "What a pity for the big ring that Atlanta cannot have three Senators, so as to give Brown, Colquitt and Gordon all a chance!" Lamar, as the master of the form, followed suit: "Better to send Bob Toombs to the Senate than fill Ben Hill's place with Gov. Colquitt. Better to have a man who once was great than a man who never will be." Finally, the exchange was capped by this question posed by the *Augusta Evening News*: "Why should not south Georgia name the United States Senator? He ought to come from either Augusta, Macon or Savannah." Lamar mockingly responded, "Why, this will be thought to be rank treason against Atlanta. Augusta, Macon or Savannah could furnish a clever Senator, but isn't it Atlanta's turn? Gov. Colquitt has a mortgage on the office; and so he will weep for Georgia on the floor of the Senate."[62] Lamar was referring to the deal Colquitt had brokered that furnished Gordon with a handsome salary from the Western and Atlantic Railroad through the generosity of Joseph E. Brown as president of that railroad in exchange for Brown receiving Gordon's Senate seat. Feeling that they had no input into their own political process, many

---

[60]"The Mask Dropped," *Telegraph*.
[61]Ibid.
[62]"The Georgia Press," *Georgia Weekly Telegraph*, 1 September 1882, p. 8.

editors used sarcasm to convey their contempt for the small group of influential men who were controlling their state's political destiny. Even North Carolina couldn't resist weighing in on the subject with this comment in the *Wilmington Star*: "It is thought that Governor Colquitt will succeed Senator Hill from Georgia. But what a difference in the mental weight and debating powers of the two men."[63]

Grady, as the mastermind of the Ring, was pushing for Colquitt's election in the halls of the Capitol, as well as in the public and private rooms of the Kimball House. On November 15, 1882, after only two ballots, the state legislature voted for Pope Barrow to serve Hill's unexpired term until the spring, at which time Colquitt would begin serving a full six-year term as United States senator from Georgia. Colquitt expressed his gratitude to Grady by presenting him with a beautiful pair of chestnut horses.[64]

Hanson had led a determined campaign to expose the collusion among the powerful members of the Atlanta Ring by allowing Lamar free reign to spotlight their machinations. During the 1880s, business leaders, politicians, and members of the press began to recognize Hanson as a man of influence. This became apparent when the statewide press, and many of his peers, began referring to him by the title of major, his Civil War rank at discharge. In the South a title such as major, often used as a courtesy, reflects a level of respect and authority that an individual commands within his community. Although Hanson never insisted upon such a title, by the end of the decade he was referred to as "Major Hanson" almost exclusively in the press. So strong was the title that his grandchildren referred to him as "the Major" during his lifetime. Even his descendants two generations after his death knew him only as the Major.[65]

---

[63]"Wilmington Star," *Telegraph*, 30 July 1882, p. 2.

[64]Davis, *Henry Grady's New South*, 74.

[65]Walter Hanson Dunn (great-grandson of the Major), interview by author, July 1994.

4

THE BATTLE CONTINUES

Would any merchant, any insurance man, any foundry man, any banker or any man of any profession or trade be willing to turn over his business to General Gordon? Gentlemen, I would just as soon turn loose a crazy monkey in a powder magazine with a red hot poker!

—J. F. Hanson

THE ELECTION OF Alfred H. Colquitt to the Senate did not discourage the Major in his efforts to expose political corruption. He continued his assault on the Atlanta Ring in the editorial columns of the *Macon Telegraph* and was reinvigorated for the fight when the death of Alexander Stephens in early 1883 put the governor's chair up for grabs.

Augustus O. Bacon once again set his sights on the governor's mansion. By law the president of the state Senate, James Boynton, assumed the governorship until a statewide election could be held to fill Stephens's unexpired term. Boynton made it known that he would like to keep the position, and as a Spalding County resident, he was a viable Middle Georgia candidate who could seriously challenge the Atlanta Ring's control of the seat of power in the state.[1] The race appeared to be between Bacon and Boynton until Henry D. McDaniel, a state representative from the town of Monroe, decided to throw his hat into the ring. McDaniel had attended school in Atlanta, and his father owned a business in Atlanta, although McDaniel was now a resident of Walton County. The Major would have been content with any of these candidates, while Henry Grady would have been content to see anyone but Bacon, according to Grady scholar Harold E. Davis, who describes the *Constitution*'s attitude toward Bacon as "frigid."[2]

---

[1]Harold E. Davis, *Henry Grady's New South: Atlanta, a Brave and Beautiful City* (Tuscaloosa: University of Alabama Press, 1990) 74.

[2]Ibid., 74–75.

Boynton called for a nominating convention to meet in Atlanta on April 10, 1883, with an election to follow on April 24 to select the Democratic Party's nominee. On the day of the convention, five preliminary ballots were taken and Bacon held the lead in four, but without a majority. When news of the results hit Grady's ears, he sprang into action. The locus of power was about to shift from Atlanta to a strong Middle Georgia candidate, and Grady was determined to stop it. Leaving houseguests at home, he went to the Kimball House, where the party caucuses were being held. As Grady surveyed the candidates, he realized that McDaniel, although weak, was someone he and the Atlanta Ring could manipulate, and he began the political machinations for which he had become famous.[3] Grady biographer Raymond B. Nixon describes Grady in this situation as a "behind-the-scenes manipulator of anti-Bacon strength."[4] Grady devised a plan to change the nomination process. He worked tirelessly throughout the night meeting with legislators to sell his idea: instead of the entire nominating committee of over 350 casting their votes, a special committee of eighteen would choose the nominee—a number Grady could more easily manipulate.[5]

When the nominating convention convened the following morning, one of the plotters of Grady's plan made a motion to appoint just such a committee. The Bacon forces, sensing Grady's hand in the motion, argued vigorously against it. Nonetheless, it passed by a vote of 203 to 147. In the first nomination ballot, Bacon and Boynton tied with six votes each and McDaniel had four, with a minor candidate, Philip Cook, drawing two. In another balloting, as arranged by Grady, the Boynton forces announced that they were throwing their votes to McDaniel, giving him ten, and with that, McDaniel became the Democrat nominee and then, running unopposed, the governor.[6]

Grady's night of clandestine maneuvering had prevented him from returning home to his houseguests that evening, although he had sent them a letter, explaining, "I was struck squarely between the eyes—the hardest lick I ever had in politics in my life. I was astonished, sore at heart, and almost

---

[3]Ibid., 74–76.

[4]Raymond B. Nixon, *Henry W. Grady: Spokesman of the New South* (New York: Alfred A. Knopf, 1943) 209.

[5]Ibid., 210.

[6]Ibid.

dismayed. It was the first time I ever encountered treachery flagrant and unblushing. To have had Bacon elected by the Tel. and Mess. would have disgraced me and hurt me. But I tell you now that if I had come home that night Bacon would have been governor."[7] In that letter Grady confessed to manipulating a legitimate nominating process in order to place his candidate in the governor's chair. By Grady's own admission, had he stuck to reporting the news rather than trying to make it, Bacon would have been the next governor of Georgia.

After losing another contest to Grady's political machine, Bacon lashed out at the *Constitution*, repeatedly referring to it as a "'tool' of an 'Atlanta Ring.'" The *Constitution* countered that Bacon was part of "a small clique of reformers" led by the *Macon Telegraph*.[8] The *Constitution* assessed the motives of the *Telegraph* accurately. The Major, through the editorial pages of his newspaper, was leading a reform effort in the state Democratic Party against the very kind of machinations that Grady performed in winning the nomination for McDaniel. This latest achievement by Grady provided more fuel to the reform efforts of the *Macon Telegraph*.

During the bid for the governor's seat, Lamar stumbled once again into editorial impropriety. The *Post-Appeal*, a small competitor of the *Atlanta Constitution*, suggested in its columns that the *Telegraph* had tried to form an alliance with the *Post-Appeal* to promote Bacon in the recent nominating process. In his response to the *Post-Appeal* denying the allegations, Lamar made personal references to the editor, Colonel M. E. Thornton, that were in poor taste, writing, "The state has furnished an institution in which unfortunate people are kindly cared for. If the charitable lady who has undertaken to furnish Colonel Thornton with bed and board will permit him to go at large and become a public nuisance, we shall feel it our duty to apply to the Ordinary of Fulton County for a writ of *de lunatico inquirendo*." Mentioning Thornton's wife in his remarks sent Thornton into a rage, which was given voice on the pages of the *Post-Appeal* by Thornton's friend, Judge Emory Speer, who penned a poisonous response to Lamar's words. He called Lamar "a scavenger of partisanism, a vulturous ghost of private, inoffensive, helpless character, using the tactics of the hyena in raking up venom as a weapon of warfare and political diet, a damage to any cause he

---

[7]Ibid., 209–10.
[8]Ibid., 210.

champions by his insolence and malignity." He also took exception to Lamar's reference to Thornton's wife, pointing out that "the domestic relations of the editor of this paper [*Post-Appeal*] are sneeringly dragged into this most ungentlemanly article." The *New York Times* took great pleasure in reporting to its readers the editorial "squabbles" between the Georgia editors, elucidating that Colonel Thornton was actually a young civilian gentleman, not a colonel, who was married to a woman many years older than he.[9]

Immediately after the *Post-Appeal* ran its vitriolic response to Lamar's comments, Lamar was in Atlanta; some thought it was to challenge Thornton to a duel. However, shortly after his return from Atlanta, Lamar penned a most gentlemanly apology to Mrs. Thornton in the *Macon Telegraph*, stating, "It is due to myself as a gentleman as it is to her as a lady that I should do everything in my power to make every amend possible for the language I used in the heat of political excitement." Thornton replied in the *Post-Appeal*, accepting Lamar's apology. The *New York Times* expressed the last word on the situation, commenting, "And peace reigns among the unassigned Colonels of Georgia."[10]

This latest episode of editorial acrimony stood in complete contrast to the Major's editorial and personal style. Indeed, going beyond the bounds of good taste and gentlemanly character may have caused some harm to Lamar's relationship with the Major. The only serious disagreements the two ever had were over Lamar's extremes.[11] Editorial excesses aside, the *Telegraph* continued to be a leading voice of opposition to the Bourbon Triumvirate.

In September 1883, not long after the Major resigned from the Wesleyan College Board of Trustees, the legislature passed a bill to build a new capitol in Atlanta. The Kimball Opera House in Atlanta had served as the capitol since January 1869, but the state had outgrown it.[12] The bill included a one-million-dollar spending cap, stipulated that construction be

---

[9]"Editors Calling Hard Names," *New York Times*, 22 April 1883, n.p.

[10]Ibid.

[11]Harry Stillwell Edwards, "John F. Hanson—The Man," *Macon (GA) Telegraph* (hereafter cited as *Telegraph*), 18 December 1910, p. 6.

[12]Timothy J. Crimmins and Anne H. Farrisee, *Democracy Restored: A History of the Georgia State Capitol* (Athens: University of Georgia Press, 2007) 23–25.

completed by 1889, and gave the governor the authority to appoint a board of commissioners to oversee the project.

Governor McDaniel was considering the Major for an appointment to the Capitol Commission, which the *Columbus Enquirer* endorsed, claiming that the Major "had done more than anyone else to secure the passage of the bill."[13] The *Telegraph* also wrote that "its liberal views...contributed materially to the passage of the bill."[14] Evidence would suggest the contrary, however. At this particular juncture, the legislature was considering a bill to establish a technological school for Georgia, and the *Telegraph* was editorializing that one million dollars would be better spent on a technical institute than a new capitol.[15] But that was in July; by September's passage of the bill for a new capitol, the Major was being given credit and his newspaper was taking it.

Whatever the Major's editorial stand with regard to a new capitol for Georgia, he did not seek an appointment to the commission though others did so in earnest on his behalf. One of his most unlikely supporters was the *Atlanta Constitution*, whose editor, Evan P. Howell, appeared personally before the governor to urge the Major's appointment, as did Representative Nathaniel Harris of Macon.[16] Support for the Major's nomination was not unanimous, however; his own congressman, James H. Blount, and several members of the state legislature voiced opposition.[17]

When objections to his nomination began to surface, the Major met with the governor to withdraw his name from consideration. He told McDaniel that he "understood the appointment was favorable to the Governor" but was being opposed and that "he was a better friend, than to wish to be appointed at the risk of antagonizing anybody, and assured him that if his name was dismissed from consideration with the matter, it would not affect his friendship for him or interest in his administration." Hanson concluded by saying that "he would not accept the appointment unless it came from him in such a manner as to convey the assurance that he regarded

---

[13]"Major J. F. Hanson," *Columbus (GA) Sunday Enquirer*, 16 September 1883, p. 2.

[14]"Atlanta Letter," *Telegraph*, 9 September 1883, p. 1.

[15]"The Capitol Bill," *Telegraph*, 26 July 1883, p. 2.

[16]"Mr. Blount and Mr. Hanson," *Atlanta Weekly Constitution* (hereafter cited as *Weekly Constitution*), 25 September 1883, p. 4.

[17]"Macon Rises to a Question of Privilege," *Telegraph*, 19 September 1883, p.1; "Capitol Commissioners," *Columbus (GA) Sunday Enquirer*, 16 September 1883, p. 2.

the appointment as in the interest of the State." McDaniel told the Major that no one could raise an objection about his qualifications, but simply that his appointment would be "unsatisfactory," a statement Congressman Blount had made to McDaniel. The Governor declined to appoint the Major to the commission.[18]

Despite his gracious offer to withdraw his name from consideration, the Major was disturbed by what he considered behind-the-scenes political maneuvers by politicians who thwarted the will of the people for their own personal interests. He had witnessed this with the Atlanta Ring and could now understand the frustration Bacon had endured in his political contests. The governor's decision to exclude the Major from the commission set off its own small firestorm within the state, and the *Macon Telegraph* fanned the flames.

The people of Macon were perturbed that the city was left with no representation on the commission, given that it was one of the commercial centers of the state whose citizens contributed a substantial amount of tax dollars to the capitol project, and they expressed their displeasure in the pages of the *Telegraph*.[19] Macon was not the only city disappointed by the governor's decision. Many statewide journals ran articles expressing their displeasure at the governor's change of heart over the Major's appointment.[20]

The *Hamilton Journal*, for example, expressed sorrow that the Major wasn't chosen for the commission, describing him as "possessed of great executive skill, a man of undoubted integrity, and great moral courage, with a wonderful insight into the character of men, with him upon the commission the people might have been assured not only that every dollar of their money would be honestly expended, but that it would be expended to the very best possible advantage."[21] The *Rome Courier* expressed dismay that anyone would be antagonized by the appointment of a man "whose character and qualifications are indisputable."[22] The *Griffin News* took a more

---

[18]"Atlanta Letter," *Telegraph*, 9 September 1883; "Atlanta Letter," *Telegraph*, 16 September 1883, p. 1.

[19]"Macon Rises," *Telegraph*.

[20]"Major J. F. Hanson," *Columbus (GA) Sunday Enquirer*; "Our Position," *Telegraph*, 21 September 1883, p. 2.

[21]*Hamilton (GA) Journal*, quoted in "A Regret," *Telegraph*, 19 September 1883, p. 2.

[22]*Rome (GA) Courier*, quoted in "An Offer of Oil," *Telegraph*, 20 September 1883, p. 2.

aggressive stand when it decided that "the malcontents of Georgia must go" for opposing "a man of unblemished character."[23]

The *Macon Telegraph* declared that since Blount had told the governor that the Major's appointment to the Capitol Commission would be "unsatisfactory," Blount should apply that same standard to his own candidacy and "follow the example of Mr. Hanson in getting out of the way for the sake of harmony." If Blount refused to step down as congressman, the newspaper informed its readers that it would vigorously oppose him in the next election. This editorial placed the entire state on notice so that "the public may rest assured—we shall not stab Mr. Blount in the back. We do not propose to oppose him with the *Telegraph and Messenger*, but with the truth and in the light of day."[24]

A reporter for the *Macon Telegraph* thought that there was more to it than Blount's personal animus toward the Major and drew McDaniel into the conspiracy by speculating that McDaniel wanted to be nominated for another term as governor and thus was unwilling to antagonize Blount by appointing the Major to the commission. The report accused the men of prioritizing their personal ambitions, and in the process "the taxpayers of Georgia are forgotten, disregarded and insulted to further their [Blount's and McDaniels's] own personal ends."[25]

The Major pressed the issue further by asking other legislators for letters of testament about Blount's involvement in the nomination process. William E. Collier, a resident of Fort Valley, wrote a letter to the Major stating that Blount had been invited to the governor's office but that he hadn't set out to derail the Major's nomination. When the governor had asked Blount for his opinion of the Major, Blount referred the governor to Senator George Gustin. The governor said that Gustin was prejudiced against the Major, to which Blount replied, "So am I." Blount told the governor that the Major was qualified to serve on the commission "but being a man of strong will, will try to rule the commission, and should he fail in this, he would become dissatisfied and no longer work in harmony with the

---

[23] *Griffin (GA) News*, quoted in "Let the Disciplining Proceed," *Telegraph*, 20 September 1883, p. 2.

[24] "Our Position," *Telegraph*, 21 September 1883.

[25] "Atlanta Letter," *Telegraph*, 9 September 1883; "Atlanta Letter," *Telegraph*, 16 September 1883.

commission but would make war on them in his paper."[26] This characterization of the Major refers to his service on the Wesleyan College Board, during which he exposed "the deplorable waste" by the building committee.[27] Others, however, referenced the Major's work on the Wesleyan board as one of the strongest reasons why he would be a most competent choice to serve on the Capitol Commission. The *Lumpkin Independent*, for instance, wrote, "His unearthing of the jobbery in building the new Wesleyan College showed his eminent fitness in supervising the construction of buildings."[28]

The Major could not let the issue rest. He was irritated with Blount and wanted proof of Blount's statements to the governor. The Major wrote a letter to McDaniel on October 20, 1883, in response to the governor's suggestion that the two meet for a "frank talk."[29] With the issue of the Major's non-appointment still in the press, McDaniel may have wanted to clear the air with the Major. In their meeting, according to the *New York Times*, the Major asked McDaniel for a certified statement as to what Blount had said to him as well as to the fact that the Major was not an applicant for the Capitol Commissionership. The governor refused.

Several days later, according to the *Times*, Colonel Peter W. Alexander, an acquaintance of the Major's, approached the governor on the Major's behalf and asked him to sign a similar letter. Alexander even produced a copy for him to sign, which threw the governor into "righteous indignation," exclaiming that he wouldn't sign statements others had written for him. The governor immediately composed a letter to the Major in which "he gave his mind very plainly about Hanson and his go-between Alexander."[30]

The *New York Times* concluded its article about the entire capitol affair in late December by stating that "the go-between, Alexander, has been rewarded by Hanson with the chief editorship of the *Macon Telegraph and Messenger*" and that a "vigorous war will be opened on Gov. McDaniel and

---

[26]"Mr. Blount and the Capitol Commission," *Telegraph*, 27 November 1883, p. 2.

[27]Ida Young, Julius Gholson, and Clara Nell Hargrove, *The History of Macon, Georgia* (Macon: Lyon, Marshall & Brooks, 1950) 412.

[28]*Lumpkin (GA) Independent*, quoted in "Why He Wasn't Appointed," *Telegraph*, 26 September 1883, p. 3.

[29]Major John Hanson to Henry D. McDaniel, Henry D. McDaniel Papers, Georgia Archives, Morrow.

[30]"A Bitter Political Fight," *New York Times*, 20 December 1883, n.p.

Congressman Blount which will eclipse anything before known in Georgia politics. Mr. Alexander, on the failure of his mission to reconcile the Governor and Hanson, is reputed to have said: 'we're sorry the Governor has precipitated this war. He will live to regret it.'"[31]

The *New York Times* may have reported the change of editors, but nothing official had been published in the *Telegraph*. On January 1, 1884, the *Constitution* commented on the new editor, stating, "rumors of every nature are afloat to-night. The subject is on every tongue." But as the Major was on business in Savannah, he was not available for comment, and when the *Constitution* called on the Major's brother and *Telegraph* business manager, Henry Hanson, he would only state that "there would be changes, but the management was not prepared to disclose them to the public."[32] It wasn't long into the new year when Alexander was found in control of the editorial pages of the *Macon Telegraph*.

Harry Stillwell Edwards, in his tribute to the Major after his death, said the switch in editors had less to do with a reward for services rendered and more to do with Lamar's acid quill. Edwards believed that some of the Major's friends had convinced him that he should replace Lamar as editor because Lamar's bitter editorials were weakening the paper's influence.[33] The switch occurred only two months after Alexander had sought to reconcile the Major and McDaniel and eight months after Lamar's most egregious comments about the editor of the *Post-Appeal*.

Peter Wellington Alexander began his career as a Civil War correspondent for the Confederacy but spent most of his life as a practicing attorney. On the eve of the Civil War he signed Georgia's Ordinance of Succession as an elected representative from Upson County.[34] Rather than enlist as a soldier, he became a war correspondent for the *Savannah Republican* and during the next four years made a name for himself with reports from the battlefield to such papers as the *Atlanta Confederacy*, *Richmond (VA) Dispatch*, *Columbus (GA) Sun*, *Mobile (AL) Advertiser and Register*, and even the *London Times*. Alexander was held in high esteem by other newspapers and was considered one of the top two Southern reporters

---

[31]Ibid.

[32]"News of Georgia," *Weekly Constitution*, 1 January 1884, p. 1.

[33]Edwards, "John F. Hanson," 6.

[34]Carolyn Walker Nottingham and Evelyn Hannah, *History of Upson County, Georgia* (Macon: J. W. Burke, 1930) 633.

of the conflict, along with Felix Gregory de Fontaine. The *Charleston Courier* described Alexander as "The Prince of Correspondents."[35] After the war Alexander practiced law. When the Major chose him as editor-in-chief of the *Macon Telegraph* in 1884, he had been retired from journalism for twenty years.

Alexander's approach was more subdued and lacked the acerbic wit and political savvy that the Major had relished in Lamar—and that the public had looked forward to reading. Although the Major wasn't always in agreement with Lamar's editorial style, the paper's readership suffered because of the change that Alexander brought to the paper, and no one realized it sooner than the Major. After only six months at the editorial helm of the *Telegraph*, Alexander stepped down as editor-in-chief. When asked to explain the change in management, Alexander replied, "I retire on account of differences of judgment as to the course the paper should pursue," but also reported that he and the Major parted as friends.[36] The *Constitution* summed it up best when it said, "Colonel Alexander's idea was to put sugar in the ink. Colonel Lamar's to spike the ink with the vinegar." The *New York Times*, always ready to comment on the editorial changes at the *Macon Telegraph*, had its own take on why the Major returned Lamar to the editor's chair. Governor McDaniel was getting ready to face the voters for election, having nearly completed Stephens's unexpired term. According to the *Times*, the *Macon Telegraph* was about to launch a campaign against the reelection of McDaniel, and Alexander stood in the way: "Hence the management of the *Macon Telegraph* was turned over to Col. Albert R. Lamar, who has a deep-seated hatred of what is termed the Atlanta Ring."[37] This seems to be a stark turnaround from the position the *New York Times* had reported six months previously when it quoted Alexander as saying that McDaniel had "precipitated a war he would live to regret," a position that was far from standing in the way.[38]

With the 1884 gubernatorial race on the horizon, Grady wanted to keep McDaniel in the governor's chair in an unopposed election to avoid the

---

[35]J. Cutler Andrews, *The South Reports the Civil* War (Princeton: Princeton University Press, 1970) 50.

[36]"An Editorial Change," *Atlanta Constitution* (hereafter cited as *Constitution*), 15 June 1884, p. 6.

[37]"Making Slates in Georgia," *New York Times*, 21 June 1884, n.p.

[38]"Bitter Political Fight," *New York Times*.

drain on time and financial resources that political campaigns demand. To accomplish this, he decided to give the public something else to focus on.[39] Drawing attention to the national stage, Grady announced in the *Constitution* that Samuel J. Tilden would be running for president on the Democrat ticket in 1884. Many Democrats in Georgia felt that the presidency had been stolen from Tilden in 1877, who received 184 electoral votes to Hayes's 165, with twenty votes in dispute. The Republicans made a deal with the Democrats to give the twenty disputed electoral votes to Rutherford B. Hayes in exchange for Hayes removing federal troops from the South, thus ending Reconstruction. Grady was certain that the announcement of a Tilden candidacy would be popular in Georgia. Tilden was planning nothing of the sort, however; he was in ill health, living in retirement at Graystone (his home near Yonkers, New York), and making no overtures to run for the presidency. Grady scholar Harold Davis describes this diversionary tactic as "the most calculated uses of a newspaper ever documented in Georgia."[40]

On March 4, 1884, the *Constitution* launched its campaign to name Tilden the Georgia Democrat nominee for president. Grady stated, "The renewal of the Tilden agitation comes in such shape that there is no room for doubt."[41] Georgia Senator and Atlanta Ring member Joseph E. Brown had already been apprised of Grady's plan to stir up a Tilden wave in Georgia.[42] In a letter to Brown, Grady wrote, "The Tilden boom we have started is doing immense good in tying things together. It reawakens hope, turns attention to national politics and discourages the idea of factional differences here at home."[43]

Grady's success was evident in the columns of many Georgia newspapers, which echoed the *Atlanta Constitution*. From the *Eatonton Messenger* came these words: "The political atmosphere is Tildenish." Larry Gantt, editor of the *Athens Banner-Watchman*, fell for the *Constitution*'s ruse of a Tilden campaign by stating, "It is now a settled fact that the democracy will again try the old ticket, and not only elect it, but their candidates will

---

[39]Davis, *Henry Grady's New South*, 75.

[40]Ibid., 77.

[41]Ibid.

[42]Ibid., 78.

[43]Joseph E. Brown Papers, Box 3, folder 69, Hargrett Rare Book and Manuscript Library, University of Georgia, Athens.

this time be seated." The *Darien Timber Gazette* followed suit, writing that "the indications now point unmistakably to the nomination of Hon. Samuel J. Tilden of New York, for president, and Thomas A. Hendricks, of Indiana for Vice President, by the democratic national convention in Chicago on the 8th of July." Each of these comments and more were printed in the columns of the *Atlanta Constitution* on March 11, 1884, to shore up its own reporting of a Tilden candidacy.[44]

One newspaper in Georgia saw through Grady's subterfuge, however: the *Macon Telegraph*. These diversionary tactics did not fool the Major or Lamar, who used his typical sarcasm to make his point by penning the following in response to "The Tilden Brigade":

> Never before has such a triumph over time, space, wind and water been achieved. In one week, by means of its extensive corps of correspondents, mounted couriers and local reporters, the *Constitution* found out and interviewed every Tilden man in Georgia, roughly estimated at five hundred in number. The stupendous character of this work can be well understood when it is remembered that there are about 175,000 voters in the state.... The *Telegraph* tenders its most sacred sympathies to its esteemed contemporary over the accidental discovery that the great Tilden organ of Georgia, whose weekly edition alone "is read by 140,000 people," has been able to affect the views or coincide with the opinions of only 500. It is a bitter realization for the whole journalistic brotherhood, who are accustomed to believe that subscribers swallow the gifted editor's views along with their coffee and hot muffins in the morning.[45]

This challenge to the *Telegraph*'s "esteemed contemporary" could not have made the Major a popular man, as Tilden was well-regarded in Democrat circles. But the *Telegraph* refused to go along with the idea of his candidacy just because the *Constitution* was trying to distract the public from the pressing issue facing the state: the upcoming gubernatorial election. The *Telegraph* called the charade by pronouncing, "We find a 'Tilden boom' was created to over shadow the 'real issue.'"[46]

Despite the *Telegraph*'s bold assault, no other candidates challenged McDaniel for the governor's chair, although Grady still had much behind-

---

[44]"The Tilden Boom in Georgia," *Constitution*, 11 March 1884, p. 4.

[45]"The Tilden Brigade," *Macon (GA) Weekly Telegraph* (hereafter cited as *Weekly Telegraph*), 21 March 1884, p. 4.

[46]"Tilden as a Candidate," *Weekly Telegraph*, 28 March 1884, p. 5.

the-scenes work to do to keep Brown in his Senate seat. Since the senators were chosen by the state legislature, Grady followed the legislative contests throughout Georgia, encouraging the support of pro-Brown candidates. Evan P. Howell, the *Constitution*'s editor-in-chief and a member of the Atlanta Ring, even attempted to bribe the editor of a weekly newspaper who was running for the state senate in order to ensure that the editor, if elected, would vote for Brown.[47] Grady kept Brown informed of the results of the county races, and in the end Grady achieved his goal, returning both Brown and McDaniel to office in unopposed elections. In describing the political genius of Grady in these two campaigns, Davis states, "If ever two noncampaigns had a masterful manager, Henry Grady was that manager in the uncontested elections of 1884."[48]

Although neither the Major nor the *Macon Telegraph*'s battle against Grady's machine politics had derailed the Atlanta Ring, the politicians of Central and South Georgia were now beginning to recognize that they needed to come together to work toward its defeat.[49] Technically McDaniel could run again in 1886 since he had not served two complete terms, but Bacon had made it clear that he would mount another gubernatorial campaign. The Ring advised McDaniel not to run, fearing that their candidate wouldn't emerge victorious in a head-to-head campaign with Bacon.[50] On March 13, 1886, McDaniel announced that he would not be seeking the governor's chair again.[51] It appeared as though 1886 would finally be the year that Augustus O. Bacon would receive the Democratic Party's nomination for governor and the Atlanta Ring would no longer be in control of the governor's mansion.

Bacon had been campaigning for the office of governor since 1882 and over the years had garnered sizable statewide support; he was in a strong position to become the Democrat Party's nominee. Many of the statewide newspapers were endorsing a Bacon candidacy, and the *Macon Telegraph* showcased for its readers the endorsements of Bacon from the *Acworth News and Farmer*, *Athens Banner-Watchman*, *Buena Vista Patriot*, *Camilla Clarion*,

---

[47]Joseph E. Brown Papers, Box 3, folder 69, Hargrett Rare Book and Manuscript Library, University of Georgia, Athens.

[48]Davis, *Henry Grady's New South*, 79.

[49]Ibid.

[50]"The Inside of Atlanta," *Telegraph*, 24 March 1886, p. 4.

[51]Davis, *Henry Grady's New South*, 79.

Conyers Weekly, Covington Star, Coweta Advertiser, Eatonton Messenger, Gainesville Eagle, Irwinton Southerner-Appeal, Jefferson Herald, Milledgeville Chronicle, Oglethorpe Echo, Sparta Ishmaelite, Sylvania Telephone, Thomaston Times, and *Thomasville Enterprise.* All of these papers felt that the most promising and deserving candidate was Bacon.[52] However, the *Waynesboro True Citizen* failed to detect the subtle difference between a newspaper's reporting about a candidate's statewide support and actually coming out in support of a candidate on its editorial pages, a fine line that the Major and the *Telegraph* walked gingerly during the nominating process. One issue of the *Waynesboro True Citizen* referred to the *Macon Telegraph* as "a pronounced Bacon organ." While the Major understood that the remark was not made in an "offensive spirit," he wanted to clarify his position for his readership, writing, "So far as eternal enmity to rings and cliques of tricksters is concerned, the *Telegraph* may be considered an organ of the people." With regard to the *Telegraph* and Bacon himself, the Major declared, "In common with the people of Georgia, it recognizes in Mr. Bacon a man of character and ability, whose services have given him strong claims upon the people of the State. But Bacon has not tried to control the opinions of the paper and the *Telegraph* has at no time sought to control, direct, or affect his views or speech upon any subject."[53]

If Grady and the Atlanta Ring wanted to remain in control of state politics they needed to thwart a Bacon nomination, and Grady had plans to do just that. Eleven days after McDaniel stated he would not run again, the *Macon Telegraph* made a headline announcement that General John B. Gordon was the Atlanta Ring's candidate for governor, following some speculation of his candidacy in the *Atlanta Journal.*[54] Grady knew that it was going to be difficult to derail a Bacon nomination, so he decided to put forth a candidate who would appeal to Confederate hearts and minds: none other than General Gordon, although Grady was not yet ready to make that publicly known.[55] Gordon, who had received a well-paying railroad job in exchange for his Senate seat through Grady's manipulations, was now fifty-four years old, but after a lifetime of business failures, his greatest strength

---

[52]"State Politics," *Weekly Telegraph*, 20 April 1886, p. 11.
[53]"Not an Organ," *Weekly Telegraph*, 13 April 1886, p. 6.
[54]"Inside of Atlanta," *Telegraph*, 24 March 1886.
[55]Davis, *Henry Grady's New South*, 80.

remained his service to the lost cause. This was about to become his most important asset.

Alabama was laying the cornerstone of its Confederate monument at the state capitol, and the ex-president of the Confederacy, Jefferson Davis, was to be the honored guest at the ceremony. Because Davis was too ill to give the dedication, Alabama veterans pushed for Gordon to give the speech on his behalf. Grady, seizing the opportunity to have Gordon appear with the president of the Confederacy, invited Davis to Atlanta following the ceremony in Montgomery to help dedicate the statue of the late senator Benjamin Hill at the Georgia capitol. Grady understood that the sight of Gordon accompanied by Davis would ignite the passions of Georgia's veterans. By raising the Confederate flag, as he had done with the Stephens candidacy, Grady hoped to elevate Gordon to the governor's chair. Although Jefferson Davis had not been popular with Georgians when he was president, Georgia's veterans "were absolutely ready for a hero and a dose of nostalgia, and they were about to get both."[56]

The entire train ride from Alabama to Georgia was one long—though unannounced—campaign opportunity for Gordon with Davis by his side. At a stop just outside the Georgia line, Davis was unable to speak; turning to Gordon, Davis declared to the crowd, "This is my Aaron; let him speak for me." While working their way toward Atlanta, Gordon appeared on the platform along with Davis at every stop.[57]

When Grady organized something like this, no stone was left unturned. Upon the arrival of the ex-Confederate president in Atlanta, the buildings of the city were decorated, schoolchildren lined the streets with flowers, banners of General Robert E. Lee and Davis were hung in the railroad depot, and red, white, and blue bunting decorated the Kimball House. Trains overflowing with people given discount rates brought visitors to the city. Over fifty thousand people thronged to see Davis, many sleeping on the sidewalks. The Georgia Press Convention, which had been meeting in Macon, arrived in a group, some not very happy with the affair. The owner of the *Rome Daily and Weekly Courier*, W. H. Hidell, was furious at

---

[56]Ibid.
[57]Ibid., 81.

the spectacle Grady had created, which was transparent to many others in the press.[58]

Grady served as master of ceremonies at the unveiling of the monument to Hill, and when the drape over the statue was pulled, the crowd began to chant "Gordon! Gordon!" Gordon was not on the platform with Davis, which was deliberately planned by Grady so as not to make it appear too obvious that this was a staged event for Gordon's nomination. However, a reception was held later for Gordon at the Kimball House, which "infuriated" the Bacon supporters. Grady was heard to say, "Confederate money will be good before Midnight!"[59] Grady had orchestrated another triumph for his not-yet-announced candidate for governor. Davis continued on to Savannah the following day with Gordon at his side, and it was there that word leaked out that Gordon intended to run for governor. Gordon made an official announcement from his home in DeKalb County several days later, on May 9, 1886.[60]

Gordon's candidacy did not please everyone. Some were outraged that Jefferson Davis had been used to further Gordon's campaign ambitions. But the *Constitution* claimed it was the people's fault for cheering for Gordon when he appeared with Davis, thereby encouraging his ambitions. The *Americus Recorder* replied, "If that assumption were true then Davis might as well construe the grand ovation tendered him as a desire on the part of the people that he should be a candidate for President of the United States."[61] Despite what appeared to be a shameful use of Davis and the transparent motives of Grady and the Atlanta Ring, Gordon was in the race, and the *Telegraph*'s prediction of a Gordon candidacy was realized.

Gordon, in announcing his run for governor, asked that the state deviate from its usual policy of allowing the counties to choose delegates to the convention and instead use the primary system to choose the party's nominee. The *Macon Telegraph* saw this as another move on the part of the Atlanta Ring to manipulate the process and accused Gordon of trying "to dictate the campaign and the election of delegates, usually left to the Democracy of the counties." The *Telegraph* asked its readers if this was an attempt "to override the will of the party and threaten a break-up of

---

[58]Ibid., 82.
[59]Ibid., 83.
[60]"Gordon in the Field," *Telegraph*, 9 May 1886, p. 4.
[61]"From the Americus Recorder," *Weekly Telegraph*, 11 May 1886, p. 11.

conventions and the disruption of the Democracy, in order that the Atlanta ring may retain control of the State government?" Patrick Walsh, editor of the *Augusta Chronicle*, put it in stronger terms when he suggested that the Democratic Party in Georgia should "in a friendly way, but firmly tell him [Gordon] to stand aside."[62]

It was now a two-man fight for the Democratic nomination, but the *Constitution* was the only daily journal in the state supporting Gordon. According to Grady biographer Harold Davis, "Outside of Atlanta, not a daily newspaper was helping and few weeklies were" supporting a Gordon candidacy because "they saw the operation of the Atlanta Ring in the background, and they were utterly opposed to it."[63] The Major and the *Telegraph* were gaining ground in their pursuit of the Atlanta Ring, and the statewide press seemed to finally be joining them in this campaign. The *Telegraph* was relentless in exposing Gordon's political and business record, forcing Gordon to defend himself. In a speech in Americus, Gordon stated, "I should like to have a little time to discuss the issues of this campaign or of state politics, but all my time is occupied with the issues raised by the *Macon Telegraph*." In that same speech, he referenced the *Macon Telegraph* sixteen times, but stated, "I am at peace and in the best possible humor. Why should I not be, when the *Macon Telegraph* has abused me. I am dead in love with the *Telegraph*.[64] The *Macon Telegraph* replied to Gordon's comments: "We are pleased to note the fact that he recognizes his inability to meet our positions successfully, and hence has undertaken to weaken their force by accusing the *Telegraph* of abusing him."[65]

One of the most glaring issues highlighted by the *Telegraph* was that as a senator, Gordon abdicated his responsibility to the people of Georgia when he sold his Senate seat, to speak nothing of the ethical violation of the behind-the-scenes maneuver. The *Macon Telegraph* challenged Gordon to "put his finger upon any statement it has made, with reference to himself that is not true. If he will do this, the *Telegraph* stands pledged to make the charge good or retract it."[66] The exchange between Gordon and the

---

[62]"The Campaign Opens," *Telegraph*, 10 May 1886, p. 3.

[63]Davis, *Henry Grady's New South*, 87–88.

[64]"General Gordon at Americus," *Augusta (GA) Chronicle* (hereafter cited as *Chronicle*), 14 May 1886, p. 5.

[65]"Don't Dodge," *Weekly Telegraph*, 18 May 1886, p. 6.

[66]"An Open Challenge to General Gordon," *Weekly Telegraph*, 18 May 1886, p. 6.

Telegraph was doing wonders for the newspaper's coffers. The *Telegraph* reported on May 18 that during the final six days of the campaign the soaring subscription rate was "without precedent in the history of the paper."[67]

The *Macon Telegraph* did not endorse a candidate during the nomination process. However, the Major was more than willing to personally take to the campaign trail on behalf of Bacon. One such appearance took place on June 12 before the Democratic Executive Committee of Clay County. The citizens of Clay County organized the event as a joint discussion about the candidates, with the Major representing Bacon and Hon. W. C. Glenn of Dalton speaking on behalf of Gordon. The Major made it clear to those in attendance that he did not feel that Gordon had the qualifications to be the state's chief executive, citing Gordon's poor performance in business and his resignation from the U.S. Senate. He also pointed out that Gordon used convict labor through Georgia's convict lease program, which the Major opposed.[68] In a practice that began after the Civil War, the state leased prisoners to private companies who would pay the state a fee to use the men for manual labor. It was extremely profitable for Georgia, and equally profitable for businesses. However, the system led to abuse and exploitation of the laborers, and dangerous offenders often escaped. There was a growing movement in Georgia to do away with the convict lease program, and the Major advocated for its banishment in the columns of the *Telegraph*. The Major often criticized Gordon for using convict labor on his plantation on the Flint River in Taylor County, both in his speeches and in the columns of the *Telegraph*.[69]

At the conclusion of his speech, the Major responded to questions from the audience. One person in particular inquired about his party loyalty, asking the Major who he would vote for if Gordon was nominated. The Major replied, "Born and reared upon the soil of Georgia, it is natural that her interest should be to me of first importance, and regarding the solidity of the Democratic party as essential to the control of our State government by the white people, I will vote for General Gordon if he is nominated, rather

[67] *Weekly Telegraph*, 18 May 1886, p. 2.
[68] "The Campaign," *Weekly Telegraph*, 15 June 1886, p. 11.
[69] "Absolute Proof," *Telegraph*, 11 June 1886, p. 1.

than see a division of the white people and the balance of political power placed in the hands of the negroes. It will go pretty hard with me, but I will vote for him if nominated, as a choice of evils."[70]

The Major's answer to the question reflects the fear that most white Georgians felt after the Civil War. The Republican Party was the dominating political force during the Civil War and Reconstruction. With the passage of the Fifteenth Amendment in 1870, black males were given the right to vote, and most voted as Republicans. In some states, Radical Republican legislatures during Reconstruction denied the right to vote to white males who had taken up arms against the Union. This was done in order to weaken the Democratic stronghold in the South. In some Southern states, blacks outnumbered whites, giving blacks (and therefore the Republican Party) an advantage at the polls. This black majority resulted in what became known during Reconstruction as "negro domination." After Reconstruction, the fear of a black majority at the ballot box drove a great many white voters to the Democratic Party, thereby creating a Democratic political stronghold in the South.[71] Although on the point of race and politics, the Major would soon try to bring a more enlightened viewpoint to the South.

The next time the Major spoke, the event was a bit more contentious. On June 22 the town of Dublin in Laurens County invited Gordon to speak, followed by the Major, who had been invited by the Bacon Club of Dublin. Gordon spoke for two and a half hours, at which time the audience was invited up to the podium so that Gordon could shake hands and speak with his supporters. Immediately the crowd began to shout "Hanson! Hanson! Hanson!" and the Major was surrounded by men urging him to take the platform, stating they would clear the way for him. The Major, however, declined to step on the platform as long as Gordon was holding his impromptu reception.[72] Instead, the Bacon supporters adjourned to the courthouse, according to the *Telegraph*, to hear the Major "reply to the General's misrepresentations of Major Bacon."[73] The Major delivered his speech in the courthouse, outlining Gordon's shortcomings. The Major's

---

[70]"The Campaign," *Weekly Telegraph*.

[71]Kenneth Coleman, *A History of Georgia* (Athens: University of Georgia Press, 1977) 222–23.

[72]"Hanson and Gordon," *Weekly Telegraph*, 29 June 1886, p. 3.

[73]"General Gordon at Dublin," *Chronicle*, 25 June 1886, p. 2.

speech "bore its full fruit" when, in the largest mass meeting of Democrats in Laurens County history, on July 6, 1886, Bacon received 360 votes against Gordon's 218.[74]

The Major was invited to speak again to the Muscogee County Democratic delegation in Columbus on July 2, which caused much excitement in town. The Bacon forces flooded the city with posters announcing that the Major would be speaking at the Springer Opera House. The *Columbus Enquirer-Sun* described the Major as a "terse and winning talker who had his audience's undivided attention." He spoke of the corruption that had seeped into the state government from its foundation to its dome and placed the blame squarely at the feet of the Atlanta Ring. The Major was sharply critical of Gordon, and his speech was "repeatedly interrupted, and at times his voice was literally drowned by the applause which his snapping points elicited." He concluded by saying, "Would any merchant, any insurance man, any foundry man, any banker or any man of any profession or trade be willing to turn over his business to General Gordon? Gentlemen, I would just as soon turn loose a crazy monkey in a powder magazine with a red hot poker!" This caused the hall to erupt in a roar of laughter and applause.[75]

The Major was doing his best to take his case for Bacon's nomination to the people, but he was no match for Grady's masterful campaign strategy. To play on Confederate sympathies, Grady planned as many rallies as he could with veterans joining Gordon on the platform. In addition, Grady had reporters working for the *Constitution* in every county in Georgia.[76] When a reporter saw that a county was ready to swing its delegate votes to Bacon, a call to Grady was made. The *Augusta Chronicle* accused Grady and the *Constitution* of sending out "whips and organizers, the strikers who hire the wagons and pack the conventions and pay the money and do the yelling at the meetings" and fixing the election on a "grand scale and calling it the people's will."[77] By the end of July, Grady's hard campaigning efforts had paid off. It was clear that most of Georgia's counties were in the Gordon camp.

---

[74]"Dublin," *Weekly Telegraph*, 13 July 1886, p. 10.
[75]"Gordon and Bacon," *Columbus (GA) Enquirer-Sun*, 3 July 1886, p. 8.
[76]Nixon, *Henry W. Grady*, 202.
[77]Davis, *Henry Grady's New South*, 93.

On July 28, 1886, the state Democratic Convention in Atlanta nominated General John B. Gordon for governor. Despite the fact that Bacon was well qualified, having served as Macon city attorney and speaker of the Georgia House of Representatives, he was no match for the Confederate hero, and Grady knew it. The election wasn't won or lost on the issues, but rather on loyalty to a hero of the "lost cause," according to the *Constitution*, which later remarked that Gordon would have been "disgraced" by a loss, and no one in Georgia wanted to see one of its heroes disgraced.[78] True to his word, the Major and his newspaper endorsed Gordon's candidacy. Nonetheless, the *Telegraph* couldn't resist taking one more jab at Grady's outgoing man, Henry McDaniel, as Lamar penned this gem about the retiring governor: "It may be said that he returns to his position in private life with less reputation than he brought out of it."[79] When Gordon arrived in Macon after winning the nomination, the Major greeted him with "open hand and extended the hospitalities of his home." Gordon could not resist him and accepted both.[80]

After reconciling his differences with one Confederate hero, the Major was confronted with another opportunity to do so. He served on the fund-raising committee for the 1887 visit of the president of the Confederacy, Jefferson Davis, to the State Agricultural Fair in Macon, an event that would be, in the Major's words, "the last grand reunion of Confederate veterans." The Major had been critical of Davis's conscription efforts and had voiced his criticism to Governor Brown during the waning days of the Civil War. The Major now took a leading role in the planning stages of the momentous occasion and helped loosen the community's purse strings with his eloquent statements to a crowd assembled at the Academy of Music. The Major declared, "What city could be more appropriate than Macon for that assemblage? If he [Jefferson Davis] were in the presence of the assembled multitudes, he would confirm that Macon is as loyal to the government under which we lived as any; but Macon realizes that there is no government to pension the living or honor the dead heroes of the Confederacy." This statement refers to the fact that the federal government pensioned the Union soldiers but gave no pensions, nor parades of honor, to Southern soldiers.[81]

---

[78]Ibid.

[79]"Governor McDaniel," *Telegraph*, 10 November 1886, p. 2.

[80]Edwards, "John F. Hanson," 6.

[81]"In Honor of Davis," *Telegraph*, 7 September 1887, p. 1.

The event would need funding, and the Major was aware that these sentiments would make a success of the occasion of Davis's visit. Indeed, he encouraged people "to put their hands into their pockets often and freely."[82]

After a frantic six weeks of preparations, the day of Davis's visit arrived, and Macon celebrated as only Macon could. The Major was one of twenty-three members of the reception committee who greeted the Davis family at the train depot along with more than seven thousand citizens who crowded the station.[83] In carriages on a parade route through the streets with pyrotechnic displays that could have resulted in a complete conflagration of the town, the Davis family arrived at the home of Captain Joseph Marshall Johnston and his wife, Martha "Mattie" Fannin Hugenin Johnston, where they would remain during their four-day visit.[84] The Major's wife, Cora, was also part of the excitement. She was chosen to accompany Mrs. Davis on one of her carriage rides to the fair, an honor accorded to only one other lady. And the Major and Cora were invited to the only private dinner held for President Davis during the family's stay at the Johnston home. It was an elaborate affair, with attendees in full dinner dress, hand-embroidered dinner cards at every plate, and an eleven-course meal that lasted two hours. The evening finished with a final parade of veterans and citizens six thousand strong, with a torchlight procession that could be viewed from the Johnston home on Coleman Hill.[85]

The Major had reason to be proud of his city for its sterling tribute to Davis. On a more personal level, the visit of the former president of the Confederacy in fall 1887 provided closure for the Major to a chapter in his life that had been a source of pride, but also of disappointment and frustration. By paying his respects to Jefferson Davis he was able not only to honor his past, but also to close the door on that past and focus his sights more fully on Georgia's future.

The year 1888 dawned with another gubernatorial race on the horizon in which Gordon ran unopposed. However, with the death of Henry W. Grady in 1889, the influence of the Atlanta Ring would be greatly diminished. For seven years, the Major, with the *Macon Telegraph* as his platform, had led the assault on the Bourbon Triumvirate and their Atlanta Ring

---

[82]Ibid.
[83]"Once More in Macon," *Weekly Telegraph*, 1 November 1887, p. 5.
[84]Ibid.
[85]"Fifty Thousand People, an Elegant Dinner," *Telegraph*, 27 October 1887, p. 1.

leaders, Evan P. Howell and Henry W. Grady, awakening the press and the people to the corrupting influence of political cliques within the Democratic Party in Georgia.

5

GEORGIA TECH

I am so firmly convinced of the wisdom of this policy that I would rather my wife and children, when I am gone, should point to one brick that I had placed in a building for such an institution than to have the proudest monument that could be reared to my memory.

—J. F. Hanson

THE MAJOR, THROUGH his editorial columns in the *Macon Telegraph*, tried to reform Democratic Party politics in Georgia during much of the 1880s but met with little success. The *Macon Telegraph* was one of the few papers to seriously challenge Henry Grady and the Atlanta Ring. When the Major purchased the newspaper, however, he had a goal in mind even broader than political reform. He had a vision for education that would have far-reaching consequences for the economic prosperity of the region.

Not long after he purchased the *Macon Telegraph*, the Major began to champion the need for a technological school for Georgia.[1] Because of its agrarian roots, the South lagged far behind the North in industrialization. The Major fervently believed that transitioning from an agrarian society to a more balanced economy with a thriving industrial component would help Georgia recover from the economic malaise of post-Civil War life.

The Major was not alone in his beliefs, nor was he the first to endorse industrialization as a solution to the state's weak economy. Georgia Senator Benjamin Hill delivered a passionate address at a University of Georgia Alumni Society banquet in 1871 in which he advocated industrialization as the means to economic progress in the South and cited slavery as the cause for the lack of it. After the International Cotton Exposition in Atlanta in

---

[1]Harry Stillwell Edwards, "John F. Hanson—The Man," *Macon (GA) Telegraph* (hereafter cited as *Telegraph*), 18 December 1910, p. 6.

1881, Henry Grady became a manufacturing booster for the South.[2] In fact, Georgia had many advocates for an industrialized economy, the Major among them. But the Major was not merely an advocate for a cause. He was a Georgia industrialist who had the ability to contribute significantly to the growth of a manufacturing economy and who saw the lack of advanced technical education as the most serious hindrance to the fulfillment of that objective. Although the University of Georgia began offering civil engineering classes in 1866, the Major envisioned a separate technical institute for the study of all phases of industrial education.[3] No school of this kind existed in the South at the time.

The Major's interest in advanced technical education grew out of Bibb Manufacturing's need for skilled labor, which was in short supply in Georgia. Although a broad term, "skilled labor" as the Major defined it included workers with the knowledge and training, acquired through education at a university or technical institute, to build, operate, and sustain a technical manufacturing operation. The Major knew that if Georgia was to become industrially competitive with the rest of the nation and the world, the state needed a technological institute that could train students in chemical, mechanical, textile, and electrical engineering.

Although some Northern factory operatives were working in Southern mills, the industry couldn't depend on skilled labor migration from New England to fill Southern factories. The Major felt it imperative that Georgia educate its own engineering workforce because "skilled labor was always the last to emigrate and…it was useless to look to England or New England for the people demanded by the improvement in machinery for cotton goods."[4] The Major's own experience with superintendents from New England was less than satisfactory and may have led to his convictions that New England labor was not the answer to Georgia's employment problem. In a conversation with Harry Stillwell Edwards, the Major expressed his exasperation at the resignation of another factory foreman who returned to

---

[2]James Patrick McCarthy, Jr., "Commerce and College: State Higher Education and Economic Development in North Carolina and Georgia, 1850–1890" (Ph.D. diss., University of Georgia, 2002) 94.

[3]Ibid., 85.

[4]Edwards, "John F. Hanson," 6.

New England, stating, "We can't keep those fellows down here: they feel too far away from home."[5]

The Major was in need of good foremen to run his factories, but he also wanted to advance the state of cotton manufacturing in the South in order to compete more effectively with New England mills. At that time, the South was producing only a coarser grade of cotton goods because it lacked workers with both the advanced training and experience in chemical dyes and the production techniques needed to create the finer goods manufactured in New England.

In his desire for a larger skilled workforce, the Major also had to contend with a common public prejudice against manufacturing work.[6] In the South, aspiring men from the middle and upper classes generally pursued studies in law, medicine, and the classics, which led to them being "inoculated with the idea that manual labor is considered vulgar and that the trades are not respectable," as the *Atlanta Constitution* wrote in one of its editorials in support of trade schools.[7] The Major fought these embedded ideologies by advocating not just for training of a skilled labor force but also for "revolutionizing of the social sentiment" against labor to attract Georgia youth to the industrialization movement. In an interview with the *Macon Telegraph* shortly after the formation of the Southern Cotton Manufacturers' Association in 1883, the Major remarked, "We want to make labor honorable in every sense of the word by turning the tastes of our young men to mechanical pursuits and training them for it."[8] As a newspaper editor and factory owner, he was able to illuminate his point with a concrete example: an advertisement in his paper for a clerk with a six-hundred-dollar-per-year salary would receive one hundred applications in a day from men in Georgia, while an advertisement for a cotton factory supervisor at five thousand dollars per year would bring very few responses, and only from New England. The Major contended that "false pride" kept men in the South

---

[5]"Georgia Tech Came Into Being through Telegraph Editorial," *Telegraph*, 24 November 1933, p. 17.

[6]"Southern Cotton Manufacture," *Telegraph*, p. 1.

[7]"Practical Education," *Atlanta Constitution* (hereafter cited as *Constitution*), 23 May 1882, p. 4.

[8]"Southern Cotton Manufacture," *Telegraph*.

behind a retail counter when they could learn a professional trade that would allow them to work in a factory and would pay them much more.[9]

It was clear to the Major that his vision for an industrialized economy for Georgia would hinge on the establishment of a technological university, an effort that he would have to direct. To accomplish his goal he developed a two-pronged approach involving the state legislature and the *Macon Telegraph*. Just as the Major had used the *Macon Telegraph* to challenge the Atlanta Ring, he used it as a bully pulpit from which he could preach his message of advanced technical education for Georgia.[10] The Major began in March 1882 by orchestrating an editorial campaign in the pages of his newspaper that described the merits of a technological school for the state. He shared his vision of technical education with Edwards and asked him to write the first editorial on the subject.[11] Edwards expressed the Major's ideas in what became the first public endorsement in the state for a technical college. Edwards also revealed the Major's strategy for bringing technical education to Georgia by stating that "it is the duty not only of the press, but of the legislature" to create an opportunity for technical education. The Major did not restrict the hope for technical education to the male population. He was sympathetic to his female employees, asking Edwards to advocate for a college "where a boy or girl—rich or poor—may enter" and learn "the intricacies and combinations of machinery, the power of steam and electricity, the rules of architecture and drawing,...technical skill,...[and] how to manufacture," noting that for those women "whom necessity or inclination drives to labor wages, the field of action is even more circumscribed."[12]

In early July of that year, the Major followed Edwards's editorial with a forceful appeal to the state about its obligation to develop its resources, especially "the capital which is known as skill, technical and mechanical

---

[9]Ibid.

[10]Robert B. Wallace, Jr., *Dress Her in White and Gold: A Biography of Georgia Tech* (Atlanta: Georgia Tech Foundation, 1963) 2; "Major J. F. Hanson[,] the South's Empire Builder[,] Is At Rest," *Telegraph*, 17 December 1910, p. 1.

[11]"A Polytechnic College Needed," *Macon (GA) Weekly Telegraph* (hereafter cited as *Weekly Telegraph*), 17 March, 1882, p. 6; "A Talk on Mechanical and Technical Education," *Telegraph*, 8 July 1882, p. 2.

[12]"Polytechnic College Needed," *Weekly Telegraph*; Robert C. McMath, Jr., et al., *Engineering the New South: Georgia Tech, 1885–1985* (Athens: University of Georgia Press, 1985) 124.

skill." He explained that "the labor of a skilled mechanic more than trebles that of a farm laborer," making the case that an agricultural country is never wealthy, whereas a country that manufacturers to the highest extent the resources within its borders gains "nearly all the profit" and keeps its "currency in rapid circulation."[13]

The Major and the *Macon Telegraph* promoted technical education in at least five different articles in the course of a year. The Major's forceful editorial opinions launched a movement among many newspapers statewide for the creation of a technical institution. The *Columbus Daily Enquirer-Sun* grasped the need for university-level technical education and encouraged the young men of Georgia to "quit crowding the law and study chemistry, this newest and most promising science, especially practical chemistry as it applies to the invention in cheapening methods in dyeing, in production of oil combinations."[14] The *Augusta Chronicle* also came forward with editorials in support of technical education, stating, "We want skilled labor. Education and invention go hand in hand. By all means let us have a polytechnic school in Georgia."[15]

The Major's second approach to establishing technical education in Georgia was through the state legislature, which he felt was the logical entity to inaugurate such an institution. The Major found his opportunity to persuade the legislature through Macon attorney Nathaniel Harris, who declared his intentions to run for the Georgia House of Representatives in spring 1882. Harris was a partner with Walter Barnard Hill in the law firm of Hill and Harris and had served as a city attorney for eight years when he decided to run for a seat in the Georgia House.[16] The Major decided to back Harris's campaign through the *Macon Telegraph* if Harris would agree to sponsor a bill that would help establish a technological school for the state. The Major called on Harris at his home in May 1882 to discuss the idea, telling him that "[a] school of technology is the great want of the State at this time. The legislature ought to appropriate a million dollars to found and

---

[13]"A Talk on Mechanical and Technical Education," *Telegraph*.

[14]"A Word to Young Men and Boys," *Columbus (GA) Daily Enquirer-Sun*, 13 January 1883, p. 2.

[15]"Georgia News Furnished by the Press and Correspondents," *Telegraph*, 14 October 1882, p. 3.

[16]Nathaniel E. Harris, *Autobiography: The Story of an Old Man's Life with Reminiscences of Seventy-Five Years* (Macon: J. W. Burke, 1925) 195, 203.

endow such an institution."[17] Harris was unfamiliar with the concept of a technical institute, but after the Major explained his idea and its benefits to the state, Harris replied, "I would rather be the author of a law establishing such a school than to be the Governor of Georgia." The two agreed that Harris would enter the race on that legislative issue and the Major would give his campaign "the strong endorsement and the editorial support of the influential *Macon Telegraph and Messenger.*"[18]

The second part of the Major's two-pronged strategy was realized when Harris won his seat in the Georgia House. True to his promise, in November 1882 Harris introduced a resolution authorizing the appointment of a committee to study the issue of technological education for Georgia. Although the resolution was adopted on December 8, 1882, Harris still faced an uphill battle in convincing the legislature of the need for such a school.

The committee's first task was to visit the leading technological institutions in the country and report their findings to the legislature. The committee met in May 1883 in Atlanta for the funeral of Governor Alexander H. Stephens and agreed to meet again in New York on June 9 to tour Eastern technological schools.[19] The committee visited the Massachusetts Institute of Technology in Cambridge, Massachusetts; the Worcester Free Institute (now Worcester Polytechnic Institute) in Worcester, Massachusetts; Stevens Institute of Technology in Hoboken, New Jersey; the Cooper Union in New York City; and Rensselaer Polytechnic School in Troy, New York. The men were most interested in the fields of mechanics, mining engineering, and textile work. After touring the schools, the committee made its recommendation at the legislature's summer session, stating that the Worcester Free Institute was "the embodiment of the best conception of industrial education," and recommending that Georgia's technical school "be as near as practicable...to the curriculum and course of training as the Free Institute, Worcester, Massachusetts."[20] The Worcester Free Institute employed a model of technical education called shop culture, in which an emphasis on practical

---

[17]N. E. Harris, *Address on Technical Education* (Macon: J. W. Burke, 1884) 5.

[18]Wallace, *Dress Her in White and Gold*, 2–3.

[19]Ibid., 5.

[20]Wallace, *Dress Her in White and Gold*, 5; "The Free Institute," *Worcester (MA) Daily Spy*, 9 August 1883, p. 4.

skills prevailed and the students' products were sold to provide income for the school. Because of the financial constraints of Georgia's budget, this type of school was particularly appealing to the committee. The alternative to the shop culture was the school culture, in which the emphasis was on higher mathematics, theoretical science, and original research, a model that Georgia Tech eventually followed.[21]

The *Atlanta Constitution* did not support the committee's recommendations. In fact, the paper stated that Georgia students needed something "far simpler and cheaper than a richly endowed and highly developed polytechnic institute," and "doubted that many in Georgia were ready to take advantage of the education a polytechnic institute could provide."[22] The *Constitution* advocated instead that Georgia model its technical school after Washington University in St. Louis, which offered a more elementary curriculum than Worcester and accepted students at a younger age.[23] And although Grady had touted the need for technical education in his speeches, he didn't fully understand the concept of a university-level technical institute and was more focused on a statewide system of trade schools. Thus Grady and his *Atlanta Constitution* were the last to support the idea of a technological institute for Georgia. In July 1883, thinking it prudent to stand with the other advocates "in support of this new departure in education" proposed by Harris, the *Atlanta Constitution* finally offered its lukewarm support.[24] Although the paper would have preferred the school to be a simpler version than those found in New England, the *Constitution* emphasized that whatever plan was chosen, "it should not preclude the establishment of industrial schools in every city as a part of the public school system."[25]

On July 24, 1883, Harris and William A. Little of Muscogee County introduced House Bill 732, which called for the creation of a technical institute for Georgia. The Major's editorials in the *Macon Telegraph* had launched a wave of strong public support for the idea, and he turned now to his oratorical strength to convince the state legislature to pass the bill. On

---

[21]James E. Brittain and Robert C. McMath, Jr., "Engineers and the New South Creed: The Formation and Early Development of Georgia Tech," *Technology and Culture* 18/2 (April 1977): 189–91.

[22]"Technical Training in Georgia," *Constitution*, 27 June 1883, p. 4.

[23]McMath, *Engineering the New South*, 20.

[24]"Technical Education Again," *Constitution*, 13 July 1883, p. 4.

[25]Ibid.

August 1, 1883, the Major addressed the joint finance committees of both the house and senate, bringing to the meeting his strongest arguments for a technological university for Georgia, a speech that Harry Stillwell Edwards described after the Major's death as being "unanswerable" due to his logical and forceful presentation of the rationale for such a school.

The Major addressed the legislature in the senate chamber and chronicled the depressed state of Georgia's economy, setting the stage for his argument for the need to increase industrialization. The Southern economy was struggling greatly after the Civil War, but the Major rejected the prevailing theory that Georgia's financial issues resulted from the war. Dismissing the notion that Georgia was rich before the war and poor now, the Major told the assemblage that Georgia was actually poorer before the war. He explained that "the institution of slavery and the property value of slavery were destroyed by the war, but the productive capacity of the negro race remains, and judged by the cotton crops of the last few years, the negro is more productive now than [at] any period prior to the war. For this reason I am compelled to maintain that the destruction of slavery cannot be traced as an effect upon our present financial condition."[26]

Nor did the Major feel that the prevailing political will, which espoused the need for diversified agriculture as opposed to cotton cultivation alone, was a viable solution to Georgia's sluggish economy. He believed agricultural diversification to be impractical, telling the legislature that Georgia farmers "aren't poor because they raise cotton, they raise cotton because they are poor." Georgia, according to the Major, could not compete with the Midwest and West in the production of wheat, nor could it compete with feed corn, which Georgia raised at seven bushels an acre compared to Illinois's forty bushels. The only crop that could provide Georgia farmers an adequate return on investment was cotton. The raising of produce for transportation to market, referred to as truck farming, had proved to be unsuccessful as well. Spoilage occurred because of unavoidable transportation delays as a result of the state's sparse population and the poor condition of its roads. Cotton was the only staple crop that had a strong market and no spoilage issues. The Major suggested that diversified crop production would only become an economic solution for farmers when the population of the state increased, and he felt that the population could grow only through an

---

[26]"Technical Education," *Telegraph*, 15 August 1883, p. 1.

increase in manufacturing. He hinged the growth of a strong manufacturing base on the development of a strong skilled labor force, which the Major felt could only be realized through the establishment of a technical institute.[27]

His strongest arguments for technical education centered around the industry he knew best and the one that predominated in Georgia: textile manufacturing. In an attempt to persuade the legislature to pass the funding bill, the Major was blunt in his assessment of the state of cotton manufacturing in Georgia. Based on his seven years of experience as a mill owner, the Major reported to the legislature that cotton products in the South sold for 3 to 7 percent less than goods of the same weight and value from New England. Because of defects that had occurred in some Southern mills due to insufficient training and limited technical expertise, many buyers were left with the impression that all Southern goods were inferior, requiring Southern mill owners to make concessions in the price of their goods even when the quality was on a par with those from Northern mills. He stated to the committee, "We may dislike to own the fact; it is unpleasant and even mortifying; but in truth, we have not the skill of New England in planning or operating mills."[28]

The Major attributed the poor quality of Southern goods to the lack of skilled labor. He explained to the committee that, in his estimation, 75 to 90 percent of the mills with more than five thousand spindles employed superintendents from New England or Europe, men whom he believed couldn't compete for the better paying jobs except in the South where experienced professional labor was scarce. Therefore, what skilled labor did exist in Georgia, the Major felt, was not as capable as that in New England. This lack of skilled labor contributed to the South's inability to compete with New England in the production of the finer grades of cotton goods. Particularly in bleaching and dyeing operations, the Major contended that the Southern mills had undertaken nothing but the ordinary work because the factories didn't have workers with the necessary knowledge of chemistry. He was not only concerned about the science of chemistry in the textile industry; he predicted that the "golden knowledge" of chemistry would protect the population from "adulterations...of food of all kinds," and he admonished the committee that if Georgia did not support technical

---

[27]Ibid.
[28]Ibid.

education "the people of other states will supply our lack of service and reap the benefits that should accrue to us."[29]

He broadened his argument for technical education to include iron manufacturing. The Major told the assembled body that the machinery needed in Georgia's textile mills and railroads was being made in New England when it should be made and repaired in Georgia, where it would provide jobs for Georgians and grow the state's—rather than New England's—economy. Georgia suffered from high unemployment after the war, and the Major felt this was because his generation had not "enlarged the list of vocations nor opened up multiplied avenues of employment" through technical education. He urged the legislature to make a "noble contribution to posterity by enlarging to our children the list of vocations that to us were so much restricted."[30]

Comparing France, Germany, England, and Russia to the United States, the Major concluded that these other countries were far ahead of New England in providing technical education for their citizens and that New England was far ahead of the South. The Major emphasized that Georgia needed to build a technological school now to train its own citizens in the industrial arts if she wished to be competitive with other states and the world. The Major ardently stated, "I am so firmly convinced of the wisdom of this policy that I would rather my wife and children, when I am gone, should point to one brick that I had placed in a building for such an institution than to have the proudest monument that could be reared to my memory."[31]

In his speech the Major had addressed the most pressing needs of the state—employment and diversification of crop production—describing manufacturing as the answer to both. He also explained why large-scale manufacturing in the state would be impossible until Georgia began to produce a technically educated and skilled workforce. After nearly two hours in the senate chamber the Major had expressed in an "easy, earnest and logical" manner the critical need for university-level technical education.[32]

Despite the Major's editorial and oratorical juggernaut, Harris's bill was defeated in September, with considerable opposition. Many factors worked

---

[29]Ibid.
[30]Ibid.
[31]Ibid.
[32]"School of Technology," *Telegraph*, 2 August 1883, p. 1.

against it: a misunderstanding of the concept of technical education, the prejudice against factory labor, and opposition from agricultural interests, a strong political force within the state at the time.[33] The University of Georgia chancellor, Patrick Hues Mell, was another opponent of a technical institute because it threatened to drain the Morrill Funds from the university. The Morrill Act of 1862 had given federal land to the states to sell in order to fund colleges. Those funds were critical to the success of the University of Georgia after the Civil War.[34] Mell was already doing battle with state agricultural interests who wanted the Morrill Funds for an agricultural college separate from the one that had been established as part of the University of Georgia. He didn't want to see a further erosion of the funds for a separate institute of technology. Mell had been working to strengthen the University of Georgia's technology offerings, having received $32,000 from the trustees to start a technology school within the agricultural college in 1881.[35] However, critics claimed the university was "out of touch with the needs of the New South"[36]—a term coined in the period that, in its broadest expression, reflected people's hope for a new beginning for the region following the Civil War.

Another key stumbling block for the passage of Harris's bill was the state constitution written in 1877, whose laws made it difficult for the state to incur any kind of debt, even for education. Robert Toombs of Wilkes County, the primary author of the document, was quoted after the convention as saying, "We have locked the door of the treasury and have thrown the key away."[37] According to scholar James P. McCarthy, the state constitution ratified following Reconstruction "championed traditional and agrarian interests and, in its attempts to limit the expenditure and scope of the state government, also had a far-reaching effect on education in Georgia."[38]

Despite the bill's defeat, Harris took the Major's message to the Georgia Agricultural Society meeting on February 12, 1884, in Savannah, a

---

[33]Wallace, *Dress Her in White and Gold*, 7.

[34]McCarthy, "Commerce and College," 133.

[35]Ibid., 174.

[36]Ibid., 134.

[37]Franklin M. Garrett, *Atlanta and Environs*, vol. 2, *A Chronicle of Its People and Events, 1880s–1930s* (Athens: University of Georgia Press, 1969) 169.

[38]McCarthy, "Commerce and College," 152.

constituency whose backing would be critical to any future efforts.[39] There he enlisted the help of Representative Joseph M. Terrell of Meriwether County, who would become a governor and U.S. senator from Georgia, and Richard B. Russell of Clarke County, who would become chief justice of the state supreme court. The three men convinced the agricultural society to support the passage of a new bill and managed to garner public support from Chancellor Mell, along with other prominent University of Georgia faculty members.[40]

With the Major's strong testimony before the legislature and the support of important constituencies, Harris was ready to take up the issue of a technical institute once again. Early in the summer session of 1885, House Bill 8, a rewrite of the old House Bill 732, went back to the floor of the house. After several days of heated debate and rewrites, the Major and Harris won their battle for a technological school for Georgia by a vote of sixty-nine to forty-four. Governor McDaniel signed the bill into law on October 13, 1885, with the state appropriating $65,000 for the school, far from the million the Major wanted, but a beginning nonetheless.[41]

Getting the bill passed, however, proved to be only half the battle. In January 1886, Governor McDaniel appointed a commission to organize and run the technical school. McDaniel's first choice for the commission was Nathaniel Harris, in honor of his perseverance in getting the bill passed. Also chosen were Samuel Inman of Atlanta, Oliver S. Porter of Newton County, Judge Columbus Heard of Greensboro, and Edward R. Hodgson of Athens. The commission's first order of business was to select a site for the school, setting a deadline of October 1, 1886, for bids from cities that wanted the institute in their community.[42]

Many Georgia cities formed a bid committee to compete for the school.[43] The Major, not surprisingly, helped Macon's committee formulate its plan, which they presented to the community on September 6, 1886.[44]

---

[39] Harris, *Address on Technical Education*, n.p.

[40] Wallace, *Dress Her in White and Gold*, 7.

[41] Ibid., 7.

[42] Ibid., 8, 9.

[43] "Macon Wants the School," *Weekly Telegraph*, 31 August 1886, p. 5.

[44] Ibid. Others on the committee included W. A. Huff, W. W. Carnes, W. B. Hill, Henry Horne, S. H. Jemison, T. C. Hendrix, Isaac Hardeman, C. B. Willingham, L. A. Jordan, T. D. Tinsley, S. T. Coleman, S. R. Jaques, W. F. Price, R. F. Lawton, G. W. Gustin, J. A. Orme, W. G. Solomon, A. E. Boardman, R. H. Plant, and Ben C. Smith.

Since the city of Macon had no cash to contribute, the committee proposed raising fifty thousand dollars by selling stock to the citizens of Macon in twenty-five-dollar increments, due when Macon won the bid. An old laboratory in Vineville, just outside the city limits, with its surrounding 137 acres was selected as the prospective site of the school. The committee determined that seven thousand dollars would be needed to make the necessary repairs to the building, twenty thousand to supply the school with machinery and equipment, and five thousand to build cottages for the professors. The committee proposed granting the school ten of the 137 acres, holding the rest of the property for future subdivision as a way for investors to recoup their money.[45] At the end of the campaign to raise funds, Maconites had pledged ten thousand dollars, far short of the fifty thousand hoped for by the committee.

In early October, Governor McDaniel revealed the final contenders: Macon, Milledgeville, Athens, Penfield, and Atlanta. Each had a compelling reason for the school to be located in their city. Athens planned to wrap the school into the University of Georgia, which was the goal of Chancellor Mell and may have been the reason he gave his support to Harris.[46] Milledgeville was "still grieving over the loss of the state capital." Penfield had lost Mercer University when the school relocated to Macon and was offering the site of the former Mercer campus.[47] The Atlanta bid, which had an aggressive group of advocates, consisted of seventy thousand dollars in cash, with the majority coming from the city and the rest from private individuals. The city was also providing a two-thousand-dollar annuity for twenty years. With a site valued at ten thousand dollars, the total bid from the city of Atlanta was worth $120,000.[48] The *Atlanta Constitution* became the coordinating force behind Atlanta's bid, with Evan P. Howell, editor-in-chief, the principal spokesman around Atlanta.[49] Henry Grady added personal money to sweeten the city's offering, but admitted to a group of thirty businessmen convened in Atlanta to discuss the new school in 1886

---

[45]"The School of Technology," *Weekly Telegraph*, 7 September 1886, p. 4.

[46]"Technological School, Choosing the Location," *Milledgeville (GA) Union Recorder*, 5 October 1886, p. 6.

[47]Harold E. Davis, *Henry Grady's New South: Atlanta, a Brave and Beautiful City* (Tuscaloosa: University of Alabama Press, 1990) 188–89.

[48]McMath, *Engineering the New South*, 29.

[49]Davis, *Henry Grady's New South*, 188–89.

that he had no idea what a school of technology was, even though the issue had been debated in the halls of the capitol and on the pages of newspapers statewide for over three years.[50] Grady, however, was able to recognize a good economic opportunity for the city of Atlanta. The Macon bid committee, upon learning of the financial strength of the Atlanta bid, turned to its city and requested three thousand dollars per year in perpetuity to financially strengthen Macon's bid. The request was granted.[51]

In early October of 1886 the commission inspected the proposed sites.[52] The Major and the *Macon Telegraph* began an editorial campaign to sway public opinion toward Macon as the most qualified city. Statistical data—a strength of the Major's editorial style—about Macon's population, cost of living, central locale, and heavy tax base were featured on the pages of the *Telegraph*. The paper even went so far as to claim that it was the healthiest city in the United States, with the lowest death rate, the purest water, and a magnificent climate.[53] In the heat of the competition, the *Telegraph* accused Atlanta of being "poorly drained and unhealthy." The *Atlanta Constitution* fired back, claiming the remark was an "amazing pitch of stupid hatred."[54] In addition to publishing editorials in his paper, the Major met with the commissioners behind the scenes, including Judge Heard, working his hardest to convince them of Macon's merits.[55] Finally, on the day the commission came to visit Macon, the Major reiterated the claims in support of his city that he had made on the editorial pages of the *Telegraph*.[56]

On October 19, the commission met in Atlanta in a secret closed-door voting session at the capitol. Representatives from all the bid cities were in the building awaiting the results, including the Major. The Major and the Macon delegation were confident that their city would be chosen; the commission had been impressed with Macon during its site visit, and Macon

---

[50]Garrett, *Atlanta and Environs*, 170.
[51]"Technological School," *Union Recorder*.
[52]"The School of Technology," *Weekly Telegraph*, 12 October 1886, p. 9.
[53]"Macon and the School of Technology," *Weekly Telegraph*, 5 October 1886, p. 2.
[54]Quoted in Davis, *Henry Grady's New South*, 189.
[55]"Judge Heard's Card," *Weekly Telegraph*, 2 November 1886, p. 4.
[56]"Looking at Macon," *Telegraph*, 10 October 1886, p. 7.

had what it considered a competitive bid when the property value of the proposed site and the city's perpetual annuity were considered.[57]

After twenty-one successive ballots with no majority, the commission adjourned for the evening to meet again the next morning. The Major spent the night in Atlanta to await the final verdict. The commission took twenty-four ballots to decide. On October 20, 1886, one year and one week after Governor McDaniel had signed Nathaniel Harris's bill, and much to the Major's disappointment, Atlanta was selected as the location for the Georgia School of Technology (now the Georgia Institute of Technology).[58] In the final tally, Inman, Porter, and Heard had cast their ballots for Atlanta, with Harris holding out for Macon and Hodgson holding firm for Athens.[59]

As the Macon delegation was returning home that afternoon, the Major saw Heard at the train depot and assured him that he held no hard feelings about his decision to vote for Atlanta, and they parted amicably. However, the next day the *Macon Telegraph* ran an editorial accusing Heard of being influenced by the governor to cast his vote for Atlanta. The train ride back to Macon had been enlightening for the Major, with Harris filling him in on what had gone on in the closed-door sessions. According to Harris, Heard's behavior was called into question when he left the room with Palmer, the governor's private secretary. Sometime after his return to the room, Palmer called Heard to the door again, and the two appeared to be having a serious discussion. It was after this second interchange that the final ballot was taken, with Heard casting the deciding vote for Atlanta. This change in allegiance surprised everyone on the committee because after Heard had given up on his initial vote for Penfield, he was insistent that the school be located in either Macon or Athens, not Atlanta. In his discussions on the train with Harris and others, the Major was certain that Heard and Governor McDaniel had acted inappropriately, and he did not hesitate to approve the editorial to run the next day accusing Heard of irregularities in his voting. Heard wrote a reply to the *Telegraph* in which he expressed surprise at the tone of the editorial, considering that the Major "voluntarily said to me that he did not blame me in the matter." In his letter Heard defended his vote for Atlanta and denied having been influenced by the

---

[57]"Macon and the Technological School," *Weekly Telegraph*, 19 October 1886, p. 2.

[58]"The Inside of Atlanta," *Weekly Telegraph*, 26 October 1886, p. 3.

[59]McMath, *Engineering the New South*, 32.

governor any more than he had been influenced by his conversations with the Major, "who earnestly urged upon me the claims of Macon."[60]

The *Macon Telegraph* published Heard's entire letter to the editor and accepted his defense of his actions. It also apologized for accusing Heard of being influenced by the governor to vote for Atlanta and for accusing the governor of influencing the selection committee. The Major, however, stood firm on his accusation that Heard had not been true to his word that he would not vote for Atlanta. Heard did not deny that he had told Harris and Hodgson he would no longer vote for Penfield and would instead throw his support to Macon or Athens if the two men could agree on which city to support. The Major concluded that Heard's vote should be rendered illegal because he had reneged on his word not to vote for Atlanta. The Major was trying desperately to find an excuse to disqualify Heard's vote; one might even go so far as to say he was a sore loser. The *Athens Banner-Watchman* defended Heard, reporting that Heard would have voted for either Macon or Athens if Harris and Hodgson could have come to an agreement, but since neither would abandon his city of choice, Heard threw his support to Atlanta in order to bring closure to the process.[61] The controversy over the decision to locate the technological school in Atlanta continued for several weeks on editorial pages throughout the state.

In reflecting on the effect of this new school, the *Athens Banner-Watchman* anticipated that the university and the technical school "would be at daggers drawn."[62] This was an accurate prediction, according to McCarthy, who states that because Mell was unable "to appropriate the technological education movement," the formation of the Georgia Institute of Technology created a "diffusion of state funds" that caused "a major setback for the nineteenth-century expansion" of the University of Georgia while simultaneously expanding "state funded educational opportunities for Georgians," which had been the Major's objective.[63] However, contrary to the Major's original intentions, females were not granted full admission to Georgia Tech until 1952.[64]

---

[60]"Georgia News," *Weekly Telegraph*, 2 November 1886, p 6.
[61]Ibid.
[62]Davis, *Henry Grady's New South*, 189.
[63]McCarthy, "Commerce and College," 145.
[64]McMath, *Engineering the New South*, 273.

On October 5, 1888, the day of the formal opening of the campus, the *Macon Telegraph* took a nostalgic look back at the struggle that had led to the founding of the school and praised both the Major, for being the first to impress upon the state legislature the importance of the school to the future of Georgia, and Harris, for championing the bill through the legislature. The paper also claimed credit for being the first to advocate for the school.[65] On October 7, a formal opening ceremony was held at DeGive's Opera House in Atlanta.[66] Isaac Stiles Hopkins, the first president of the school, chose Nathaniel Harris, "the man who had labored so diligently...to make Major Hanson's dream a reality," to deliver the first address to the audience.[67] And in response to the committee's decision to locate the school in Atlanta instead of Macon, Harris stated, "My heart was almost broken."[68] He spoke for everyone in Macon that day, including the Major.

The universal mantra of the New South was industrialization. Political statesmen, factory owners, and newspaper editors all cried for industrialization, but the Major was the first to press for the establishment of a school to move the South closer to this objective. Without the vision of John Fletcher Hanson, a technological school of the caliber of the Georgia Institute of Technology would most assuredly not have become a reality for many years to come, if at all. According to Robert McMath, former vice-provost for undergraduate studies and academic affairs at Georgia Tech, historian, and author of *Engineering the New South*, "More than any other individual, John F. Hanson deserves to be remembered as Georgia Tech's founder and the creator of its tradition of promoting economic development through technological education."[69]

---

[65]"The Formal Opening," *Atlanta Constitution*, 6 October 1888, p. 2.

[66]Garrett, *Atlanta and Environs*, 170.

[67]Wallace, *Dress Her in White and Gold*, 17.

[68]"The Formal Opening," *Constitution*, 6 October 1888, p. 2.

[69]"Student's Family Discovers Tech Founder in Family Tree," *The (Atlanta, GA) Whistle*, 14 September 1998, p. 1.

6

GROWING PAINS

I sincerely congratulate you, and with all my heart I thank you for
your speech.

—J. F. Hanson to Henry Grady

AFTER THE FOUNDING of Georgia Tech, the Major continued to pursue
his forward-thinking vision—a vision that included a strong industrial
economy that employed a skilled workforce in Southern factories. The
Major never looked back, nor did he romanticize the days of the Old South.
His oratory and his writings always focused on a more vibrant and
diversified economic future for the South, a broad ideology often called the
New South movement. The term "New South" came into being after the
Civil War and referred to the vision of a new Southern civilization.[1] According to historian Paul Gaston, in his book *The New South Creed: A Study in
Southern Mythmaking*, the New South leaders favored industrialization as the
catalyst for diversified agriculture.[2] In many ways the Major fit the mold of a
New South spokesman in both his efforts to create a technological university
and his strong support of industrialization. He envisioned a more technically
proficient labor force that would supply a healthy local market for
agricultural products, which he had eloquently described in his testimony
before the state legislature when advocating for a technological school.

When the Major launched Bibb Manufacturing in 1876, manufacturing had been slowly increasing in the South after the Civil War. Historian
and author Broadus Mitchell pinpoints 1880 as the beginning of industrialism in the Southern states, which he describes as "the consciousness of a
new economic era, arising in the mind of a theretofore sluggish and perverse
South." Most importantly, he states, the "expression of this consciousness

---

[1]Paul M. Gaston, *The New South Creed: A Study in Southern Mythmaking* (New
York: Alfred A. Knopf, 1970) 4.

[2]Ibid., 67.

went far to create the development."[3] An example of this expression is the speech delivered by the Major's editorial rival, Henry Grady, at the New England Society of New York's annual Forefathers' Night in December 1886.[4] Grady, considered one of the leading New South spokesmen, delivered his speech immediately following William Tecumseh Sherman, who exited the stage to the musical strains of "Marching through Georgia." But Grady was not intimidated; on the contrary, he played well to his New York audience in a self-deprecating style that was both endearing and humorous. The sentiments Grady expressed that evening would forever place him in history as the man who made the South rise from its ashes, even as he poked good fun at the man who was responsible for the fires.

In this his most famous speech, titled "The New South," Grady described the region as filled with industrial promise, in harmony with the "negro," and sincerely interested in being a part of the Union. He described a Southern homeland that had "planted the schoolhouse on the hilltop and made it free to white and black." He encouraged Northerners to invest in the region, stating that "we wiped out the place where Mason and Dixon's line used to be, and hung out the latchstring to you and yours." And in contrast to the common image of a Southern civilization that supported the planter class that cracked the whip over their slaves, he boldly stated that Southerners "have fallen in love with work." According to Grady, Southerners had achieved "a fuller independence for the South than that which our fathers sought to win in the forum by their eloquence or compel in the field by their swords."[5] The *New York Times* wrote that "no speech on any recent occasion has aroused such enthusiasm in the city—and it aroused boundless enthusiasm, bringing every man in the room to his feet with waving handkerchief and sonorous cheers."[6] Grady may have expressed an overly optimistic view of conditions in the South, but it was music to the ears of the Major, who was hopeful that Grady's positive expressions would

---

[3]Broadus Mitchell, *The Rise of Cotton Mills in the South* (Columbia: University of South Carolina Press, 2001) 69.

[4]Harold E. Davis, *Henry Grady's New South: Atlanta, a Brave and Beautiful City* (Tuscaloosa: University of Alabama Press, 1990) 175.

[5]Joel Chandler Harris, ed., *Life of Henry W. Grady including His Writings and Speeches* (New York: Cassell, 1890) 88.

[6]"Greeting Grady," *Atlanta Weekly Constitution* (hereafter cited as *Weekly Constitution*), 28 December 1886, p. 7.

lead to increased Northern capital investment in Southern industries, which the South urgently needed. The audience that evening was composed of some of America's most influential capitalists, such as J. P. Morgan and Henry Flagler, along with shapers of American public opinion, including theologian and author Lyman Abbott and Nobel Peace Prize winner Elihu Root.[7]

Grady received many telegrams and letters of congratulations after his illustrious speech, but none surprised him more than the one he opened first: "I sincerely congratulate you, and with all my heart I thank you for your speech.—J. F. Hanson."[8] According to the *Atlanta Constitution*, Grady "appreciated deeply this generous message coming from one with whom he had so often been in political opposition."[9] The *Macon Telegraph* praised Grady's speech for giving "pleasure and satisfaction [not only] to his hearers, but to his fellow citizens of the South, who looked to the occasion not without apprehension."[10] In expressing his sincere admiration and gratitude to Grady, the Major put aside the verbal thrust and parry that had occurred between the two in the previous five years, for he realized that Grady had just delivered a most important speech to an audience who could help the Major realize his vision for a diversified Southern economy. The Major was well aware that the South remained far behind its Northern competition in the manufacture of textiles. In 1878, near the end of the financial panic of 1873, the South had a half million spindles in operation in its cotton mills, while New England had more than eight million.[11] However, according to the Southern historian C. Vann Woodward, Northern capital was slow in flowing southward,[12] even after the rousing speech delivered by Grady in New York, and the Major had to invest his own capital in order to move his vision forward.

The Major looked to invest in existing mills that needed more capital; he also advised them in more effective mill management and pricing

---

[7]Davis, *Henry Grady's New South*, 176.

[8]"Greeting Grady," *Weekly Constitution*.

[9]Ibid.

[10]"Mr. Grady's Speech," *Macon (GA) Telegraph* (hereafter cited as *Telegraph*), 26 October 1886, p. 2.

[11]U.S. Census Office, *Twelfth Census of the United States, 1900*, Manufactures Schedule 9, pt. 3: 54–57.

[12]C. Vann Woodward, *Origins of the New South, 1877–1913* (Baton Rouge: Louisiana State University Press, 1951) 134.

strategies. In 1889 the Major partnered with Oliver Porter, owner of Cedar Shoals Manufacturing Company in Newton County, Georgia, when Porter sold his interest in the company to the Major. The company was renamed Porterdale Mills, and Porter continued to serve as its secretary, while the Major became its president.[13] At the same time, the Major and his brother Newt purchased a half-interest in the Taylor Manufacturing Company of Potterville, near Reynolds, Georgia.[14]

In addition to purchasing existing mill operations, the Major established several new enterprises. One was the Macon Knitting Company, chartered in 1888. This new mill made hosiery for men and women on state-of-the-art equipment whose inventor was superintendent of the new mill and one of its stockholders.[15] One of the Major's riskiest investments was made in the fledgling town of Cordele, Georgia. The growth of new Southern towns exploded between 1880 and 1910, and the Major was willing to invest his own capital to support this expansion.[16] The town of Cordele was only a year and a half old in 1889 when the Major began construction of the new Cordele Manufacturing Company.[17]

In August 1889, shortly after construction had begun on the Cordele mill, the Major was invited to a Masonic celebration in the town. Governor John B. Gordon was also in attendance, along with more than five thousand people. Both the governor and the Major gave speeches that were met with enthusiastic applause, according to the *Atlanta Constitution*, although their words could not have been more dissimilar. Gordon harkened to the Civil War and rallied the audience around calls for sectional unity and sovereignty of the Southern states. The Major, who never missed an opportunity to press on an audience the merits of manufacturing, spoke about the industrial progress of the South, never mentioning the past. His address was applauded many times and was interrupted only when the platform fell from the rush of people trying to get close enough to hear the Major's words.[18] The

---

[13]Lucille Ivey Shaw, *The History of Porterdale*, accessed 29 June 2006, http://home.earthlink.net/~porterdale/porterdale/history/porterdale-history.htm.

[14]*History of Bibb Manufacturing Company*, 17.

[15]"Knitting Mills: How They Work," *Telegraph*, 3 December 1893, p. 9.

[16]Edward L. Ayers, *The Promise of the New South: Life after Reconstruction* (Oxford: Oxford University Press, 2007) 55.

[17]"No Game," *Milledgeville (GA) Union & Recorder*, 23 June 1889, p. 6.

[18]"Cordele's Great Day," *Atlanta Constitution* (hereafter cited as *Constitution*), 13 August 1890, p. 3.

enthusiasm expressed by the townspeople toward the Major's industrial vision was tangible. The Major was creating a reality out of the expression of one New Orleans newspaper editor who, in describing the new vigor for industrialization, noted that "the stagnation of despair has, by some magic transformation, given place to the buoyance of hope, of courage, of resolve. The silence of inertia has turned into joyous and thrilling uproar of action."[19]

While establishing and purchasing mills with his own funds, the Major was simultaneously purchasing competitors' mills using Bibb Manufacturing funds in what today would be termed a "roll-up strategy," whereby a company grows in value through the acquisition of other companies. He had begun this strategy only two years after establishing the Bibb Manufacturing Company, with the Bibb's acquisition of Macon Manufacturing in 1878. The Bibb also purchased stock in the Nelson Mill and Rogers Mill, both in Upson County, Georgia. The Bibb eventually merged the Macon Knitting Company, Taylor Manufacturing, Cordele Manufacturing, and Porterdale Mills into the Bibb operation in 1898, giving the Major and other shareholders Bibb Manufacturing stock in exchange.[20]

By the end of the 1880s, Bibb Manufacturing was strong and profitable, with an impressive group of Georgia stockholders that included W. G. Raoul, president of the Central of Georgia Railway; William Low, father-in-law of Juliette Gordon Low, the founder of the Girl Scouts; and William W. Gordon, Juliette's father.[21] At this point, only one Bibb stockholder was located outside the South, supporting Woodward's claim that Southerners were the primary investors in the Southern textile industry. By 1890 the Bibb owned or controlled nine textile mills in Georgia. Hugh Moss Comer could not have chosen a better man to run the affairs of the Bibb Manufacturing Company. His brother, Governor Braxton Bragg Comer of Alabama, credited the Major with "making an extraordinary success of [Bibb Manufacturing's] management and as the years passed by, he extended it to large proportions."[22] In less than fourteen years, the Major's growth-by-

---

[19]*New Orleans Times-Democrat*, quoted in Woodward, *Origins of the New South*, 112.

[20]*History of Bibb Manufacturing Company*, 20; Shaw, *History of Porterdale*.

[21]*History of Bibb Manufacturing Company*, 14.

[22]"Major J. F. Hanson Dies Suddenly," *Montgomery (AL) Advertiser*, 16 December 1910, p. 1.

acquisition strategy had crowned the Major and his investors the largest mill owners in the state.

Owning many mills brought with it the responsibility for the labor employed in those mills, a responsibility the Major took very seriously. Labor unions were beginning to organize in the early 1880s, and the Major's factories were not unaffected. Most Georgia mill owners had little interest in supporting an organized labor movement as it signaled a potential loss of unilateral control over their businesses and placed them at risk of walkouts and strikes in the event of a failure to agree to worker demands. Union affiliation, which was motivated by poor working conditions and low wages, gave laborers a unified voice with which to press their demands on management through collective bargaining.

Founded in 1869, the Knights of Labor—officially the Noble and Holy Order of the Knights of Labor—was the most important labor organization of the 1880s. By December 1885, seven Knights of Labor lodges existed in the city of Atlanta, with a combined membership of six hundred, excluding black members, who organized separately. The Knights were uniting to set up boycotts of certain businesses, among them the *Constitution*, which employed nonunion printers. To counter their moves, Atlanta manufacturers began firing employees they knew to be members of the Knights of Labor.[23]

The Knights of Labor organized a chapter of mill hands in Macon in March 1886, and by October there were five chapters in the city. According to labor historian Matthew Hild, who has written extensively about the Major and his relationship with the Knights of Labor in Georgia, the Major worked supportively with the group as evidenced by the fact that there was never a labor dispute or strike while the Major controlled the Bibb. In contrast, most Georgia mill owners were actively trying to crush the labor movement in their factories.[24]

The Major found solidarity on this issue with few of his peers, with the exception of James E. Schofield, son of James S. Schofield, who owned Schofield Iron Works in Macon. The younger Schofield was a partner in the family iron works and a member of the Knights of Labor. In July 1886, Schofield placed an ad in the *Macon Telegraph* announcing his intention to

---

[23]"The Georgia Knights of Labor," *New York Times*, 3 December 1885, n.p.

[24]Matthew Hild, "A Pro-Labor Industrialist in the New South? J. F. Hanson and the Knights of Labor," paper presented at the Tennessee Conference of Historians, University of Tennessee, Knoxville, 1998, p. 3.

be the "working-man's" candidate from Bibb County for the Georgia House of Representatives.[25] The Major tacitly encouraged Schofield's candidacy by publishing his announcement in the *Telegraph*. As the owner of the largest textile operation in the city and editor of its most influential newspaper, the Major could have easily used his position to discourage or disparage Schofield. Other newspapers in Georgia were hostile to labor candidates, often attempting to discredit them.[26] The Major and Schofield were unique among men at the time; a mill owner encouraging the Knights of Labor to organize in his mill was as unusual as an owner of a factory being a member of a labor union.

Schofield, successful in his bid for a seat in the house, wasted no time in introducing a bill in December 1886 that limited the workday to ten hours. In 1887 the House Committee on Manufactures held an informal session in the Speaker's room to discuss the bill, which the Major attended along with some of his colleagues. Unlike the other mill owners present, the Major surprised the committee by speaking in favor of the bill. Conversing in a familiar manner, the Major explained that he had already reduced weekly hours from seventy-two to sixty-five at the Bibb with plans to reduce them by three more hours. Enabling the workers to have more rest, he found, improved their productivity.[27] He was particularly in favor of reduced hours for the women and children who made up three-fourths of his labor pool, stating that "no mill manufacturing establishment, in which women and minors worked, should run more than ten hours a day," and adding that the ten-hour day had the further benefit of "weeding out inefficient labor."[28] Only one other mill owner in Georgia testified in support of the bill: Colonel R. L. Bloomfield, president of Bloomfield Cotton Factory in Athens. Bloomfield also had reduced his workweek but, according to Hild, only after the Knights of Labor had boycotted his mill.[29] Because the other mill owners in Georgia opposed the bill, the Major tried to make it more palatable by suggesting an amendment that would phase in the shorter

---

[25]"To the People," *Telegraph*, 17 July 1886, p. 7.
[26]Hild, "A Pro-Labor Industrialist," 9.
[27]"The Ten Hour Bill," *Constitution*, 30 July 1887, p. 2.
[28]"Major Hanson's Argument," *Augusta (GA) Chronicle* (hereafter cited as *Chronicle*), 31 July 1887, p. 2.
[29]Hild, "A Pro-Labor Industrialist," 11.

workday over a two-year period.[30] The original bill was defeated, however, and the house voted not to reconsider the amended bill.

At the same time that the legislature was considering a bill to reduce working hours, it was also considering a bill, introduced by Representative McCord of Augusta and supported by the Knights of Labor in that city, that would prohibit children under the age of twelve from laboring in the mills.[31] The Major joined with the Knights of Labor in support of this legislation. At the time, children under twelve years of age were often employed in the mills, particularly in the post-Civil War South where a high percentage of war widows needed the income of their working children to sustain the family. The Major argued in favor of the bill, stating that factory labor was "deleterious to children's health, stunting their growth and depriving them of education."[32] For the period, the Major was progressive in his outlook toward labor as represented by the fact that he was alone among the state's mill men in supporting the child labor bill. Nonetheless, this bill was also defeated.

While working with the Knights of Labor on the issues of child labor and the ten-hour workday, the Major supported Schofield's efforts to end the convict lease system.[33] This issue was one of the Major's arguments against General John B. Gordon's fitness for office during the gubernatorial campaign, which he had expressed in *Telegraph* editorials and stump speeches in support of Augustus O. Bacon in the early summer of 1886.[34] In July 1886 convict laborers mutinied at the Dade Coal Company in North Georgia, turning up the heat on the issue. The *Macon Telegraph*, in its second editorial on the topic, suggested that the company might be at fault for the revolt because of its "liberal use of the strap," stating that the "horrors of our convict system are sufficient without invoking any more."[35] The *Telegraph* went on record for a third time condemning the system during hearings at the state capitol in December, sensitively illuminating the racial implications of the issue by recognizing that "the preponderance of colored

---

[30]"Major Hanson's Argument," *Chronicle*.

[31]Hild, "A Pro-Labor Industrialist," 13.

[32]"The Ten Hour Bill," *Constitution*.

[33]"The Demands of Labor," *New York Times*, 22 November 1886, n.p.

[34]Ibid.; "The Campaign," *Macon (GA) Weekly Telegraph* (hereafter cited as *Weekly Telegraph*), 15 June 1886, p. 11.

[35]"The Convicts Again," *Telegraph*, 23 July 1886, p. 2.

convicts makes it a phase of the negro problem, and in its discussion wisdom, patience, and absolute fairness are required."[36] The *Macon Telegraph* was the only paper in 1886 and 1887 that took a consistent and vocal stand against convict leasing by the state.[37] It wasn't until 1908, when Hoke Smith became governor, that the legislature outlawed the convict lease system in Georgia, more than twenty years after the Major first campaigned for its abolishment.[38]

In addition to his support for the textile industry and its workers, the Major's vision for a strong industrial economy included a healthy system of railroads, on which he and other mill owners depended to deliver their products to the marketplace. The efficiency and cost effectiveness of transporting finished goods via the railway greatly outstripped the other available options, while opening access to the entire United States. However, Southern railroads needed to be financially sound and in good operating condition to move products in a timely and cost-effective manner. The Major understood this and did everything in his power to remove obstacles from the path of Georgia's railroads in order to encourage much-needed investment. The South trailed the North in all economic measures, including the railroad industry. Woodward describes the Southern railroad infrastructure after Reconstruction as either in deplorable condition or nonexistent, and with the exception of those run by Northern capitalists, the railroads were "barely passable for trains running ten or fifteen miles an hour."[39] The South understood the need for efficient railroad transportation, and between 1879 and 1890 a rapid expansion occurred.[40] During that period, the South saw a 108.6 percent increase in railroad mileage, and 180 new railroad companies opened for business.[41] With so many new railroads being launched, competition spurred monopolistic tendencies for survival while many rail lines opened only to fall into receivership within a few years.

In its formative years, the American railroad system was financed primarily by the private investments of individuals who formed boards of

---

[36]"The Convict Lease," *Telegraph*, 3 December 1886, p. 2.

[37]Hild, "A Pro-Labor Industrialist," 14–15.

[38]Dewey W. Grantham, Jr., *Hoke Smith and the Politics of the New South* (Baton Rouge: Louisiana State University Press, 1967) 174.

[39]*New York Tribune*, quoted in Woodward, *Origins of the New South*, 108.

[40]Woodward, *Origins of the New South*, 120.

[41]Ibid.

directors, sold stocks or bonds to finance construction, and operated without government assistance or interference. In Georgia many citizens from small towns and cities pooled their money and issued common stock in order to establish railroad lines that would connect their municipalities to larger lines in hopes of bringing economic prosperity to their towns. Some cities and individuals turned to investors outside their state and nation to garner enough money to build a railroad line.[42]

Construction of the railroads was unregulated in the South, both in the number of roads built in any one location as well as the size of the track used. A consistent standard gauge of track was not imposed on the nation's railroads until after the Civil War. It wasn't until June 1886 that more than eleven thousand miles of track in the South were converted to the standard gauge used by all other railroads in the nation, a costly undertaking for Southern railroad owners.[43] Before standardization, freight and passengers coming from the South would reach a logjam at the Ohio and Potomac rivers, where they would have to be loaded onto different rail cars to continue traveling northward.[44] Regulating the size of the track streamlined travel and avoided the time-consuming transfer of goods and people.

Long before the standard gauge track was imposed, the state of Georgia imposed its own regulations on the burgeoning industry. During the Georgia Constitutional Convention of 1877, the legislature mandated that a state railroad commission be formed to regulate the freight and passenger rates charged by the railroad industry. Inequities in both passenger and freight rates caused some citizens and farmers to complain vigorously that the railroads were taking unfair advantage of the public and creating monopolies in order to sustain their positions of power. Railroads often charged more per mile to transport goods over a shorter distance than over a longer one. The issue was one of economy of scale, but it placed small businesses and farmers at a disadvantage, and they made their dissatisfaction known to their representatives in the legislature. In response to this public outcry, the state created a railroad commission in 1879 with the authority to

---

[42]Alfred D. Chandler, Jr., "Patterns of American Railroad Finance, 1830–1850," *Business History Review* 28/3 (September 1954): 263.

[43]Achsah Nesmith, "A Long, Arduous March toward Standardization," *Smithsonian* 15/12 (March 1985): 176.

[44]Woodward, *Origins of the New South*, 123.

set passenger and freight rates, among other powers.[45] Georgia became the first state in the South to regulate the operations and rates of its railroads, and the first in the nation along with California.[46] General Robert Toombs defended the mandate to create a railroad commission, explaining that "all civilized nations have found it necessary to regulate by law the tolls of common carriers."[47]

The Railroad Commission of Georgia was to be composed of three commissioners appointed by the governor, with only one member to have any railroad experience, as dictated by the law.[48] Governor Colquitt chose James M. Smith, a former Georgia governor, as chairman of the commission because Smith was familiar with the law. Samuel Barnett, president of Washington Bank in Washington, Georgia, was chosen to represent the public interest. The third member of the committee, representing railroad interests, was Major Campbell Wallace, who had been superintendent of the Western and Atlantic Railroad, Georgia's only state-owned railroad, as well as manager and developer of several other state railroads before, during, and after the Civil War.[49]

The railroad commission's first semi-annual report, issued on May 1, 1880, remarked that having only one member with any previous railroad experience made the job difficult as the other two members of the commission were unfamiliar with the subjects being addressed.[50] This disclosure did not instill confidence among the managers and stockholders of the railroads, who were already nervous about the strong control being exercised by the state over their business affairs. In fact, a letter written to the *Macon Telegraph*, signed "Macon," assailed the state for passing a law

---

[45]"General Toombs on the Railroad Commission," *Weekly Telegraph*, 9 April 1880, p. 3.

[46]Arthur S. Link, "The Progressive Movement in the South, 1870–1914," in *Myth and Southern History*, vol. 2, *The New South*, ed. Patrick Gerster and Nicholas Cords (Urbana: University of Illinois Press, 1989) 70.

[47]"General Toombs on the Railroad Commission," *Telegraph*, 2 April 1880, p. 3.

[48]Railroad Commission of Georgia, *Semi-Annual Report of the Railroad Commission of the State of Georgia, Submitted to the Governor* (Atlanta: Constitution Publishing, 1881) 11.

[49]"The Railway Commission," *Weekly Telegraph*, 7 May 1880, p. 2; *The National Cyclopaedia of American Biography*, vol. 2 (New York: James T. White, 1892) 61; "The Railroad Commission," *Telegraph*, 26 May 1881, p. 2.

[50]"The Railroad Commission," *Telegraph*, 9 May 1880, p. 2.

that required all but one of its members to be ignorant of the industry on which they were to make regulations. "Macon" further expressed the opinion that the state was getting involved in an industry where no interference was necessary: "with special reference to their incompetency for the duties assigned them, and their consistent course in their official capacity— illustrates the reckless ignorance and folly, that have characterized the agitation of State interference with the railroads from the first inception of the question to the present time."[51]

In a second editorial, "Macon" defended the railroads in answering an individual from Fort Valley who complained about the disparities in hauling rates across the state. "Macon" pointed out that it cost just as much to build a railroad over a lightly used road as it did over one with a higher volume because wages to employees, interest payments on borrowed capital, and investment returns were the same in both cases. In order to prevent the railroads from losing money and defaulting on their interest payments on lightly traveled lines, freight rates were adjusted according to their ability to cover the operating costs of that line.[52]

In the same semi-annual report, the commission issued a new tariff schedule of three cents per mile for passengers. In commenting on the wisdom of the new tariff schedule, the *Augusta Chronicle* quoted the *Chicago Railway Age*, the transportation industry's oldest trade magazine, which questioned the soundness of the three-cent rate. The magazine cited the fact that "travel, both local and through, on most of the roads in Georgia is exceedingly light, and passenger trains are often run at an actual loss" in a state where few of the railroads "have been at all remunerative to their owners."[53] Further, in Illinois the passenger rate on only the wealthiest of railroads was as low as three cents per mile, and the magazine was certain that the "thinly peopled State of Georgia cannot afford to carry as cheaply as they."[54]

Farmers and citizens had legitimate concerns about railroad pricing, but the railroads had their defenders as well. The Major could easily have been the person who represented himself in the *Telegraph* as "Macon"; however, the pseudonymous writer turned out to be none other than Albert R. Lamar,

---

[51]Ibid.
[52]"The Railroad Commission," *Telegraph*, 14 May 1880, p. 2.
[53]Reprinted in the *Chronicle*, 21 December 1880, p. 1.
[54]Ibid.

the soon to be editor-in-chief of the *Macon Telegraph*, which may have contributed to the Major's decision to hire him.[55] In December 1881, within days of assuming ownership of the *Telegraph*, the Major had written his first editorial on the matter, suggesting that "the legislation aimed at railroads is the direct result of ignorance and prejudice, skillfully played upon by designing demagogues" and that he would do as much as he could "to soften the prejudice which exists and is manifested towards these corporations by the people of Georgia," which the Major described as "a humiliating reflection upon the intelligence and fair dealing of the inhabitants of the Empire State of the South."[56] It was the Major's opinion that a commission having the power to determine the earnings of the railroads without appeal was unjust. He did not advocate for the repeal of the law creating the commission, but he did advocate for an amendment so that the question of earnings and rates would be not "the subject of assumption by the commission but of proof before the courts." His feelings on the issue were revealed when he expressed in an editorial that "the railroads ought to be protected against outrage at the hands of the Railroad Commission: and if it isn't an outrage to take the management of the roads out of the hands of those who build and operate them, we can't understand the meaning of the term."[57]

The Major was certain that the arbitrary power of the railroad commission was responsible for halting investment in Georgia's railroads, in direct opposition to what the railroads, and by association manufacturing, needed in order to grow and thrive. He claimed that "railroad building in Georgia, as an enterprise and investment, ceased when the present Railroad Commission came into being."[58] The Major's claim was substantiated by a comparison showing that railroad development in surrounding Southern states without state controls exceeded that in Georgia by 13 percent during the first five years of the commission's existence, when the arbitrary rules of enforcement were in place. The Major, through his forceful editorials, created a statewide movement for reform of the railroad commission, resulting in a bill that passed in the senate on September 19, 1885, that would return control of the railroads to their owners. However, the bill was

---

[55] Harry Stillwell Edwards, "John F. Hanson—The Man," *Telegraph*, 18 December 1910, p. 6.

[56] "Our Position and Policy," *Telegraph*, 15 December 1881, p. 2.

[57] "News in Georgia," *Telegraph*, 19 June 1884, p. 3.

[58] "More Railroads for Georgia," *Telegraph*, 19 June 1884, p. 2.

defeated in the house, and the commission retained its control over Georgia railroads.[59] In response the Major declared, "We will never consent without protest to any statute that in its enforcement carries the confession of its injustice in an exemption from judicial scrutiny of the actions of agents created by its authority."[60] The Major and the railroad commission would spend much of the next two decades at odds with each other.

The Georgia legislature did what it could to promote railroad investment by placing few restrictions on those seeking a charter for a railroad line. The Major agreed with this philosophy and supported the policy in testimony he was asked to give before the House Committee on Railroads in December 1886. The legislature was considering requests from two different investment groups for charters for a railroad line that would run between Macon and Covington. The Major argued that the state was obligated by constitutional and statutory law to grant both charters and, further, that it was important to the vitality of the state to encourage railroad investment as much as possible. According to the Major, the right of citizens to invest in railroads or to be recipients of those investments "outweighs every consideration that can be invoked in a contest between rival corporations. It is a question that involves the future prosperity of the State, the future development of her railroads, and it is important that this committee and the Legislature should so consider it."[61] During a time when Georgia's railroads needed upgrades and improvements, the Major felt that the state should do everything it could to encourage the infusion of capital and then let the investors succeed or fail based on their own skills and financial expertise. It was not the business of the government to choose the winners and the losers. After the hearings of the House Committee on Railroads, however, the state legislature did choose a winner, granting the charter to the Covington and Macon Railway.[62]

As the proposed railroad would pass through Madison, the people of that town were quoted in their newspaper as wanting to "tender their most

---

[59]Ida Young, Julius Gholson, and Clara Nell Hargrove, *The History of Macon, Georgia* (Macon: Lyon, Marshall & Brooks, 1950) 336.

[60]"The Railroad Commission," *Weekly Telegraph*, 27 June 1884, p. 2.

[61]J. F. Hanson, "Speech of J. F. Hanson of the *Macon Telegraph*, before the House Committee on Railroads," 10 December 1886, Hargrett Rare Book and Manuscript Library, University of Georgia, Athens.

[62]"The Railroad to Florida," *Telegraph*, 10 December 1886, p. 5.

sincere thanks to Major J. F. Hanson, of the *Macon Telegraph*, for his gallant, able, and successful defense of the road before the special legislative committee in Atlanta this week. His defense on this occasion is the more appreciated because of it having been gratuitously made."[63] The newspaper was referring to the fact that although the Major may have been a customer of the railroads, he had no ownership stake in them. At the heart of his testimony was his broader interest in defending the investment climate in Georgia, which he thought would ultimately benefit the people and create a stronger railroad industry. The Major was reluctant to see the state interfere any more than it already had through the oversight of the railroad commission.

According to Woodward, the railroad industry "inflamed the imagination and hopes of whole states and regions."[64] An example of the exuberance and excitement generated by the railroads in communities across the nation can be found in the celebration held in Monticello after completion of a portion of the Covington and Macon Railroad line between Macon and Monticello, two-thirds of its projected distance. The town celebrated with a huge barbecue consisting of eighty carcasses of pork, ham, beef, and lamb with breads, cakes, and pickles and more than 2,500 people in attendance. Politicians, including Governor Gordon, Senator Colquitt, Congressman Blount, and Nathaniel Harris, lined the tent to partake in the hearty fare, with all of them making speeches, as did the Major. Not being a politician, the Major was invited in appreciation of his testimony before the legislature and because he was the publisher of one of the most influential newspapers in the state.[65]

After six years of advocating on behalf of the railroads, the Major made his first personal investment in the railroad industry in 1887, when he became a financial supporter of a new railroad venture intended to link Macon to Birmingham, Alabama. The Major powered his mills with Alabama coal from the Birmingham region to utilize Southern resources and reduce transportation costs, as coal would otherwise have come from Pennsylvania. He was quoted as saying that the Macon to Birmingham line would save

---

[63]*The Madisonian*, quoted in "The Georgia Press," *Weekly Telegraph*, 21 December 1886, p. 4.

[64]Woodward, *Origins of the New South*, 120.

[65]"Monticello and Macon," *Telegraph*, 4 June 1887, p. 5.

him three hundred dollars over his current line of access to Alabama's coal.[66] That access was via a rail line that ran from Birmingham to Atlanta and then to Macon. An alternative was the Montgomery route, which traveled from Birmingham to Montgomery, then to Opelika, Alabama, and to Columbus, Georgia, finally arriving in Macon. The new direct line between Macon and Birmingham would take seventy-five to a hundred miles off the length of the other two routes, providing a significant savings in transportation costs to Middle Georgia textile mills. In addition to his own funds, the Major pledged five thousand dollars of Bibb Manufacturing capital to the railroad venture. By 1891, construction had reached as far as LaGrange, Georgia, but the enterprise went into receivership two months after this segment opened.[67] The railroads were seen as the financial giants of the day, but not all were successful, and many people lost their investments in support of the burgeoning industry—the Major now among them.

Balancing the need for a beneficial investment climate with the clamor of Georgia's farmers and citizens for regulatory relief from the pricing policies and monopolistic tendencies of the railroads was not unique to Georgia. A national movement with the intent to create federal regulation of the railways was also gaining momentum. Discontented farmers, particularly in the Midwestern states, formed their own organization by uniting the local granges, or lodges, into a national organization called Grangers in order to speak with a greater voice. In the early 1870s the Grangers legally challenged the right of private enterprise to establish pricing policies, winning several cases in state courts. One particular case went to the Supreme Court in which Chief Justice Morrison Waite established the precedent for state intervention in the regulation of railroads with his decision, stating, "When, therefore, one devotes his property to a use in which the public has an interest, he, in effect, grants to the public an interest in that use, and must submit to be controlled by the public for the common good."[68] However, these early cases did nothing to settle the issue of pricing when railroads sent

---

[66]"On to Birmingham," *Weekly Telegraph*, 29 March 1887, p. 5.

[67]"Macon and Birmingham Railroad," *RailGa.com*, accessed 10 March 2014, http://railga.com/macbirm.html.

[68]*Munn v. Illinois*, 94 U.S. Supreme Court 113 (1876); Harold Underwood Faulkner, *American Economic History*, 5th ed. (New York: Harper & Brothers, 1924) 464.

goods across state lines. Further, a Supreme Court case in 1886 established that states did not have the authority to set rates beyond their borders.[69]

Eight years after the establishment of the Railroad Commission of Georgia, the federal government became involved in the regulation of railroads when the first Interstate Commerce Act was passed and signed into law by President Grover Cleveland in 1887. The act made it illegal for railroads to practice discrimination in their rates, such as giving preferred rates to heavy business users, politicians, and off-season travelers. The act contained a clause that made it illegal for railroads to charge more per mile for short hauls than for long hauls. It also established a five-member Interstate Commerce Commission with the power to investigate state railroad operations if complaints were filed, making the railroads the first industry in America to come under federal supervision. Although it technically superseded state authority, the Interstate Commerce Commission had to bring suit in federal court to enforce compliance.[70] This two-layered oversight of railroad operations was particularly vexing to the Major.

The Interstate Commerce Act drew such strong protests from manufacturers throughout the nation that it was suspended pending hearings to be held nationwide to gather input from businesses and railroads. The evening before the Atlanta hearing, on April 27, 1887, a group of Georgia businessmen met and decided that rather than speak they would "leave their memorial and argument in the hands of Major J. F. Hanson."[71] At the hearing the Major presented a forty-five-minute argument in support of both the railroads and the manufacturers when he called for a complete suspension of the fourth clause, the long-and short-haul clause of the proposed bill. Under the new law, the short-haul rates within Georgia would go down while the long-haul rates would increase. The Major argued that the short-haul rates were set as low as they could be while still allowing "the railroads to maintain themselves."[72] With respect to the increase in long-haul rates, he testified that the margins in cotton would not support an increase in the cost of transporting cotton goods to market without a price increase to the consumer. However, an increase in the price the Major charged for his cotton goods would have its own set of consequences. The Major sent his

---

[69]Ibid., 465.
[70]Ibid., 466–67.
[71]"The Railroad Commission," *Telegraph*, 28 April 1887, p. 1.
[72]"Long and Short Hauls," *Telegraph*, 29 April 1887, p. 1.

goods from the Bibb to thirty states, and that meant that they entered into competition with goods from the mid-Atlantic and northeastern states. The Major didn't feel he could charge more for his goods to pay for increased transportation costs and still remain competitive with other mills. He contended that the Northern mills had greater margins than he did because of the efficiency of their factories, and if Georgia mills had to charge more to cover their transportation costs, they would lose any competitive advantage they might have. The Major tried to make the case that circumstances were so varied nationally that it made no sense to set a uniform rule for hauling rates.[73]

Despite the Major's appeal, which the *Macon Telegraph* described as "a marvel of terseness...logical, clear and convincing," the address did not convince the Interstate Commerce Commission to suspend the fourth clause.[74] In June 1887 the Commission decided that the long-and short-haul clause would stand and that any departures from it would be judged according to individual circumstance.[75]

In his zeal to create an industrial revolution in the South, the Major had become an investor and promoter of Georgia's largest industries: textiles and railroads. He also looked to national and state politicians for help in growing an industrial economy for the South and found that neither political party was addressing the needs of the Southern business community. The Major expressed his frustration with post-Civil War Southern politics when he penned these simple words in the *Telegraph*: "Sentiment has more weight than ideas."[76]

The Major often decried the solid Democratic South in his editorials and speeches. Of Southern voters in the presidential election of 1872, 26 percent voted as Republicans and 23 percent voted as Democrats, with a 50 percent voter turnout. In the election of 1876, however, more votes were cast for the Democratic Party. A steady decline in Republican voters continued until 1904, when only 8 percent of the voting population cast Republican

---

[73]Ibid.
[74]"Major Hanson's Speech," *Telegraph*, 23 May 1887, p. 2.
[75]"The Long and Short Haul," *Weekly Telegraph*, 21 June 1887, p. 3.
[76]"As to Two Parties," *Telegraph*, 12 July 1887, p. 2.

ballots in the presidential election.[77] Although factions broke out within the Democratic Party after Reconstruction, such as the Independent Party movement in the 1870s and the Populists in the 1890s, from 1880 to 1920 the Democratic presidential candidate carried the South, while overall turnout declined from a high of 65 percent in 1876 to less than 29 percent in 1904.[78] This Southern voting trend toward a single dominant party concerned the Major because of the lack of diversity in thought fostered by a one-party system. He articulated this in an editorial, stating, "'In union there is strength,' but when it comes to the business of a country the opposite is true—in division and dissimilarity there is strength. A few men grow too rich, and the balance grow too poor, for the good of a country under a one-idea system, whether in business or politics. Competition and opposition rectify this."[79] The Major's words were predictive of the lack of interest and hope produced by the one-party system he feared. By the turn of the century, those who could cast a vote in a national election were disinterested, with disfranchisement of black males effectively eliminating their participation as well.

To address the solidity of the Southern landscape and its effects on economic and industrial progress, the Major wrote several editorials in summer 1887 that offered reform ideas. The Major was one of the few men of his time who thought that the strength of the Democratic Party in the South was becoming a liability to the region. He addressed this by suggesting ways "the Republican party could win strength and representation here." This was heretical thinking in the Major's day. The South was trying to weaken, if not destroy, the influence of the Republican Party in the South after Reconstruction. For the Major to be suggesting how the Republicans might reshape their approach to the South in order to become more influential went against most Southern political thought at the time. For the Major, though, a strong industrial economy was of the utmost importance, and he was beginning to cast his eyes toward the Republican Party and its policies to determine which party would be more beneficial to the economic growth of the South.

---

[77]J. Morgan Kousser, *The Shaping of Southern Politics: Suffrage Restrictions and the Establishment of the One-Party South, 1880–1910* (New Haven: Yale University Press, 1974) 12.

[78]Ibid.

[79]"The South and the Republican Party," *Weekly Telegraph*, 28 June 1887, p. 4.

The Major editorialized that Republicans "should drop the sectional torch, the bayonet and the bloody shirt and with olive branches for banners and business principles and measures for weapons come into the Southern States, if their lines were of steel rails and their forts factories nothing could stand before them."[80] The Major was not speaking just to a Southern audience. He was articulating his ideas for Northern Republicans when he stated, "Our efforts now are not alone to broaden and liberalize political thought and sentiment in the South but in the Republican North also."[81]

The Major's editorials fed right into the hands of Republican strategists who were considering ways to break up the solid Democratic South. Attempting to bring pro-business Southern Democrats into the Republican fold had become the new strategy of the Republican Party during the 1880s. The party was looking for men, exactly like the Major, who might align with their pro-business platform. Northern papers, such as the *Philadelphia Press* and the *Washington Republican*, read with interest the editorials in the *Macon Telegraph* and questioned the Major and his indictment of both parties. The *Telegraph* responded to the *Press* with this challenge: "We regret that the *Press* confines itself chiefly to efforts in justification of the attitude of the Republican party, and offers no practical suggestion touching the future."[82]

The Major blamed the Republicans for pushing Southern men of all persuasions into one party because of their fear mongering and adherence to a policy of placing race at the forefront of their platform. He editorialized on the issue at great length, stating in one editorial, "Because it is upon the defensive in the South, because opinions are subordinated to the necessity for union and resistance to outside pressure, because men of every political shade of opinion must rally round one standard to resist attack, the Democratic party is unable to meet the growing requirements of business and industrial development."[83] The Major presented to his readers the conundrum in which he found himself and the South: that the Republican Party played on "sectional prejudices" and that the Democratic Party "has not risen to an appreciation of the fact that the whole business system of the South has changed."[84]

---

[80]Ibid.
[81]Ibid.
[82]"The South and the Republican Party," *Weekly Telegraph*, 5 July 1887, p. 4.
[83]"Why Two Parties Are Needed," *Weekly Telegraph*, 5 July 1887, p. 3.
[84]Ibid.

7

THE TARIFF

We have no other object than the prosperity of this, our common country. We would not tear down Massachusetts to build up Georgia. The policy that is not suited for every section, we'll have none of.

—J. F. Hanson

SINCE HIS PURCHASE of the *Macon Telegraph* in late 1881, the Major had used the newspaper to expose political corruption within the state Democratic Party, to bring advanced technical education to Georgia, to advocate for fairer railroad oversight, and to lobby in support of labor—all components he believed were critical to a brighter economic future for Georgia. He also used the paper to address an issue outside his state: the protective tariff, which he described as "one of the earliest and most important that will engage the attention of the national legislature."[1] Throughout the nineteenth century, this tariff on foreign goods was constantly being considered for adjustment, particularly when a surplus existed in the federal treasury, which was the case when the Major purchased the *Telegraph*.

The first Congress of the United States, in 1789, authorized a duty on imported manufactured goods called a tariff. The tariff was the main source of revenue for the federal government from 1790 until 1914; it wasn't until 1913, with the Sixteenth Amendment to the U.S. Constitution, that the federal income tax was enacted. Not only did the tariff supply revenue for government operations, but when levied on certain goods it had the added benefit of protecting American factories and jobs from competition that came from low-cost imported goods; thus, the term "protective tariff" came into use.[2] In the eighteenth and early nineteenth centuries, a large portion of

---

[1]"Our Position and Policy," *Macon (GA) Weekly Telegraph* (hereafter cited as *Weekly Telegraph*), 15 December 1881, p. 2.

[2]Harold Underwood Faulkner, *American Economic History*, 5th ed. (New York: Harper & Brothers, 1924) 296.

finished goods in the United States was imported, and strong support for a protective tariff to promote American over British manufacturing was being led by Senator Henry Clay of Kentucky, who included the tariff as part of the "American System" of economic policies he promoted.[3] The protective tariff may have been part of Clay's American System, but many Southerners resented it because Britain was the South's primary market for its cotton. As the tariff reduced America's demand for Britain's textile products, Britain bought less cotton from the South.

This issue came to a head in the South after higher tariff schedules were passed in 1828 and 1832 while the nation was experiencing an economic downturn. South Carolina's economy suffered the most, and the state began advocating for the repeal of the tariff laws in the hopes that doing so would spur an increase in cotton sales and decrease the price South Carolinians paid for goods from abroad. In November 1832 the South Carolina legislature passed its own Nullification Ordinance declaring the 1828 and 1832 tariff laws null and void. In response, Congress passed the Force Bill, which authorized the president to use military intervention against South Carolina to enforce the tariff laws. A newly negotiated tariff bill, referred to as the Compromise Tariff, was passed in 1833 with the help of Senator Clay, which satisfied South Carolina and led to its repeal of the Nullification Ordinance.[4] The tariff issue, however, would continue to occupy Congress for most of the nineteenth century.

The South was struggling to define its new role in the nation after the Civil War, and the Major firmly believed that "the labor of the country produces its wealth and it is an imperative necessity to the South to diversify her labor and productions."[5] He felt strongly that the protective tariff was needed to give newly established manufacturing enterprises in the South a chance to compete. From this conviction he could not be dissuaded during his lifetime, but with nearly sixty years of Southern opposition to the idea of a protective tariff, the Major was waging an uphill battle with his fellow Southerners in garnering support for keeping a protective tariff in place. His purchase of the *Macon Telegraph* allowed him to present a fresh perspective on the issue using facts and figures rather than loyalty to old ideas.

---

[3]Ibid., 304.
[4]Ibid., 305.
[5]"The Tariff Discussion," *Weekly Telegraph*, 17 December 1881, p. 2.

On Christmas Day in 1881, just ten days after he assumed the reins of the *Telegraph*, the Major wrote about the impact of manufacturing on the wealth and prosperity of Macon. His professorial style was reflected in the title of his editorial: "Macon's Manufactures—What They Teach." The idea for his article required research, which the Major accomplished by sending one of his reporters on a four-day fact-finding mission to gather employment and wage statistics about the manufacturing industry in Macon. From this exercise the Major was able to inform his readers that, based on aggregate wages of the citizens, the manufacturing enterprises of Macon contributed five million dollars to the economic vitality of the city, a statistic that increased when money circulated more rapidly, as it did in Macon because of its large laboring class. The Major explained that the prosperity of a city lay in the strength of its laboring class because, in part, they spend their income on rent, clothing, food, fuel, supplies, doctor bills, contributions to churches, and other expenditures within the local economy, whereas the wealthy classes invested their money in stocks and bonds, essentially "hiding it" by keeping it out of circulation.[6] Manufacturing, according to the Major, was the economic backbone of any community and therefore should be protected from foreign competition in order to ensure its viability. The Major believed the vehicle with which to do that was the protective tariff.

With the state being heavily agrarian at the time, Georgia farmers were unable to see the value of a protective tariff policy, which they considered as benefiting manufacturing interests alone. The Major championed the protective tariff as an economic policy that was beneficial to the farm as well as the factory. He illustrated for his readers how manufacturing affects the farmer and land values when he became the third party in an editorial debate between two of his contemporaries in February 1882. Sidney Lewis of the *Sparta Ishmaelite* in Hancock County and John Shivers of the *Warrenton Clipper* in Warren County were engaged in a "journalistic set to," in the words of the *Telegraph*, over the protective tariff. Lewis was a free trader and Shivers a protective tariff man, and the Major took it upon himself to enter the fray and settle their differences, stating that "the farming country that sells its products of the soil to pauper labor, is the victim of pauper labor; the

---

[6]"Macon's Manufactures: What They Teach," *Weekly Telegraph*, 25 December 1881, p. 2.

country that sells its products of the soil to a protected labor is the beneficiary of protection." He demonstrated this point by comparing the poor granite soil of Massachusetts, whose farmland was worth $283 per acre, to the rich soil of Hancock County, Georgia, which was worth $10 per acre. He asked his readers how that could be. Manufacturing was his answer. The people in Massachusetts, a manufacturing-rich state, purchased goods produced by Massachusetts farmers with a purchasing power made stronger by the protective tariff. He warned, though, that if this labor pool were forced to compete with cheap foreign labor, wages would fall by 50 percent and "the land would dwindle in value until its products reached the level of purchasing power."[7]

The friction between the farmer and the industrialist over the tariff issue continued to fill column inches in the Georgia press. At the same time, the Major's consistent promotion of the tariff had made him a logical choice to serve as a Southern representative on a federal tariff commission being established by President Chester Arthur. When citing the fact that "Brother Hanson" was being considered for a position on the commission—an appointment that, despite rumors, did not come to pass—the *Constitution* told the Major that the cotton planters of Georgia were not making as much money as the cotton manufacturers. In his reply to the *Constitution*, titled "Put Up or Shut Up," the Major launched another duel of sorts between the two journals. He pointed out to his readers that *Constitution* editor-in-chief Evan P. Howell was probably well versed in the profits of cotton planting but didn't know as much about cotton manufacturing as he soon would as one of the owners of a cotton mill then being built at Oglethorpe Park in Atlanta. The Major predicted that if Howell ran his factory the same way that cotton planters ran their planting operations, it would "fall under the sheriff's hammer in three years!" In contrasting the two industries, the Major pointed out that agricultural labor is idle for 30 to 40 percent of the time that a cotton factory is in operation. If the same conditions of operation were applied to farming as are applied to cotton manufacturing, he believed that a greater profit could be made from farming than from cotton manufacturing. His challenge was not idle banter. The Major was willing to invest between five and ten thousand dollars in agriculture for three years, and he wagered

---

[7]"Protection and the Farmer," *Georgia Weekly Telegraph, Journal & Messenger*, 17 February 1882, p. 6.

that the investment would show larger profits than Howell would realize on an equal investment in stock of his company, "to be determined on actual cash earnings of farm and factory, without any reference to speculative profits in either."[8] The Major was attempting to show the people of Georgia that cotton mills are a difficult business worthy of protection and should not be positioned as an adversary of the farmer.[9] He published several more editorials and spoke many times on this subject in an attempt to persuade Georgia farmers that a protective tariff was also in their best interest.

The *Constitution* never accepted the Major's challenge to "put up or shut up." In fact, the *Constitution* continued to muddy the waters with regard to the protective tariff issue, making its stance difficult to ascertain; it was pro-business but liked to court the agrarian element as well. The *Telegraph* accused the *Constitution* of promoting the notion that the current tariff gave rise to "monopolies, robberies and subsidies," referring to the common claim by those opposed to a protective tariff that it promoted the formation of industrial monopolies, robbed the people in the form of higher prices for foreign goods, and subsidized industrial leaders whose enterprises benefited from the tariff on foreign competition.[10] The *Macon Telegraph* took the bait and challenged the *Constitution*: "If our contemporary is really suffering from the pressure of monopolies, robberies and subsidies, it would be a happy diversion for him to point out instances of such that have been developed under the tariff system. When he does this, he may feel sure of our aid in bringing about a wiser adjustment of the protective system." The *Constitution* never responded. The *Telegraph* stated that it was opposed to monopolies and would consider modifications to the tariff system, but only if it were done by qualified people and not by "ignorant and sectional politicians."[11]

What made the Major different from his contemporaries in selling the South as a place for industrial investment and development was his desire to build up the South without doing so at the expense of other sections of the country. Historian Patrick J. Hearden suggests that Southern cotton mill

---

[8]"Put Up or Shut Up," *Macon (GA) Telegraph* (hereafter cited as *Telegraph*), 28 May 1882, p. 2.

[9]Ibid.

[10]"The Constitution and the Tariff," *Telegraph*, 27 January 1882, p. 2; Abbot Kinney, *The Tariff: Protection vs. Free Trade* (n.p., [1883?]) 1–5.

[11]"The Constitution and the Tariff," *Telegraph*.

owners sought "revenge rather than reconciliation" with the North after the Civil War by "bringing the cotton factories to the cotton fields."[12] Hearden refutes the theory of historian Paul Gaston that Southern mill owners desired "sectional amity," pointing out that Gaston fails to recognize that Southern mill owners would espouse "sectional reconciliation rather than economic retaliation" outside the South, but voice anti-Yankee rhetoric at home.[13] An example of this rhetoric can be found in Southern newspapers of the period. The *Southern Recorder*, a Milledgeville paper, in commenting on the South's campaign to industrialize through the building of cotton mills, declared that the South would "beat the brains out of New England with the club she has so foolishly put into our hands." The *Montgomery Mail* predicted that the construction of cotton factories in the South would "shake to pieces the artificial power of our enemies."[14]

Of course, these very thoughts had occurred to the textile manufacturers of New England, who used their political might to thwart the post-Civil War mill-building campaign in the South. Hearden states that, among other strategies, New England politicians proposed tariff hikes on foreign equipment used in textile factories in order to make the start-up costs of mills prohibitive.[15] (This proposal may have been made to protect the milling equipment manufacturers in New England from foreign competition.) Despite protests from the South, in 1883 the New Englanders won an increase on the import tax on foreign textile equipment, further antagonizing the South in its attempts to industrialize and destroy New England's hold on textile production. The South continued to build despite the tariff on foreign equipment, and many Southern mill owners bragged that "the New South would overpower New England in the fight for dominance in the textile business."[16]

The Major was an exception to Hearden's assessment that Southern mill owners were antagonistic toward their Northern rivals. The Major

---

[12]Patrick J. Hearden, *Independence and Empire: The New South's Cotton Mill Campaign, 1865–1901* (Dekalb: Northern Illinois University Press, 1982) 37.

[13]Paul M. Gaston, *The New South Creed: A Study in Southern Mythmaking* (New York: Alfred A. Knopf, 1970) 84, 95; Hearden, *Independence and Empire*, 46.

[14]Hearden, *Independence and Empire*, 39.

[15]Ibid., 46.

[16]*Manufacturers' Record* (20 September 1884, p. 167) quoted in Hearden, *Independence and Empire*, 46.

looked at the industry in national, rather than sectional, terms. Speaking to a Southern audience in 1882, he emphasized, "We have no other object than the prosperity of this, our common country. We would not tear down Massachusetts to build up Georgia. The policy that is not suited for every section, we'll have none of."[17] It may have been the Major's positive experience with Cyrus Wakefield, who invested in the Major's wicker furniture business shortly after the Civil War, that helped shape the Major's business outlook and contributed to his feelings of national unity while some businessmen continued to harbor ill will toward the North long after the war was over.

In the first session of the forty-eighth Congress, the legislature again turned its eyes to the government surplus and looked to tariff reform for the answer. On February 4, 1884, William R. Morrison, a Democrat from Illinois and chairman of the House Ways and Means Committee, introduced the Morrison Tariff Bill. It called for a 20 percent reduction in the protective tariff with an extensive list of goods that would be exempt from any tariff, a measure that the Major simply could not support.

Interested parties to the tariff legislation testified before Congress, and a reporter from the *New York Tribune* who was in Washington expressed surprise that the "cotton and sugar men of the South were not there."[18] The only testimony from a Southern manufacturer was a letter addressed to Congress from William H. Young of the Eagle and Phenix Mill in Columbus, Georgia, in support of reducing, if not totally eliminating, the duty on cotton goods. He wrote that New England held a distinct advantage over England and that the Southern cotton mills made approximately seven dollars per bale more on raw cotton than did New England, implying that since the Northern and Southern textile industries were more profitable than their English competitors, protection was unnecessary.[19]

When the Major read of Young's testimony, he refused to let Young's views represent Southern mill owners. The Major wasted no time in getting to Washington. In March 1884 he testified before the House Ways and Means Committee against the Morrison Bill. He spoke not only as owner of Bibb Manufacturing but as the representative of a large body of Southern

---

[17]"Protection and the Farmer," *Weekly Telegraph.*

[18]*New York Tribune*, quoted in "A Tariff Talk from a Southern Man," *Telegraph*, 9 March 1884, p. 2.

[19]15 Cong. Rec. 2,585–87 (1884).

cotton mill owners in his role as president of the Southern Cotton Manufacturers' Association. In the Major's opinion, the Morrison Bill, if passed, would weaken the domestic textile industry.

The Major's appearance before the committee surprised Congressman Blount, the Major's congressional district representative and the one who had sunk the Major's capitol commission appointment the year before. According to the *New York Tribune*, Blount "looked rather uncomfortable this afternoon when he entered the room and found Mr. Hanson...explaining his views to the committee."[20] Blount, as a free-trade advocate, had assured the Ways and Means Committee that Southern manufacturers felt no need for the protective tariff, and until the Major came before the committee, Blount's assertion had gone unchallenged by the Southern industrial community. The Major testified to the House Ways and Means Committee that lowering the tariff would be detrimental to the American textile industry. Following his desire for national unity, he reiterated that anything that "injured the northern mills must necessarily hurt the southern mills." The Major was also asked to respond to the claim made by Northern mill owners that the North had higher labor costs than the South. He testified that "the hands in the Lowell mills might earn better wages than those in the Augusta mills, but when the pay-roll came to be divided up at the end by production, I doubt very seriously whether Augusta could show as good results as Lowell could."[21] The Major felt that the inexperienced labor in Georgia resulted in lower productivity than did the experienced labor available in the North and that this difference in productivity wiped out any of the advantages the South had over the North in cotton transportation costs or the price paid for cotton. The *New York Tribune* described the Major's testimony as "one of the clearest and most forcible arguments that has been heard against the Morrison Bill," adding that it had "corrected many misapprehensions in regard to the relative advantages and disadvantages of cotton manufacturers in the South as compared with their Northern competitors."[22]

The Major was not satisfied with presenting his views only to the House. He also sent a letter to the Senate, which was entered into the

---

[20]*New York Tribune* quoted in "Tariff Talk," *Telegraph*.

[21]William A. Russell, "The Tariff: Revenue for the Government, and Protection for All," speech, H.R., 48th Cong. (16 April 1884).

[22]*New York Tribune* quoted in "Tariff Talk," *Telegraph*.

Congressional Record, assailing Young's views. In it the Major exclaimed, "If Congress will support Mr. Young and shape the policy of the Government to correspond with his theories he will surely 'hoist himself with his own petard.'"[23] On the editorial pages of his own newspaper the Major also refuted Young's assertion that the South received a $7.34-per-bale price advantage over the New England mills. But rather than use his own data from Bibb Manufacturing, he used the experience of Dexter Converse, president of the Clifton and Glendale Mills in Charleston, South Carolina. Converse had written in an editorial to the *Charleston News and Courier* that although he paid less for cotton than mills in New York, the difference was $1.50 per bale, not the $7.34 claimed by Young. Converse also pointed out that when the freight on goods sent to market was taken into account, any price advantage ceased to exist and his mill products entered the market in competition with Northern spinners without any advantage whatsoever.[24] The Major may have been correct in his assertions that Young might "hoist himself with his own petard." The Eagle and Phenix Mills, once the largest cotton milling business in the South, went into receivership in 1896.

The Major received strong support for his testimony before the House eleven days later when a representative from Massachusetts delivered a stirring speech endorsing a protective tariff. William Augustus Russell echoed the Major's sentiment that the tariff could provide "revenue for the government, and protection for all." In Russell's testimony he presented evidence to support the Major's claims that Southern mill owners did not want a reduction in the tariff, as some representatives from the South had claimed. Russell presented the results of a questionnaire that had been distributed by a New York firm to Southern cotton mill owners asking whether they favored or opposed a decrease in the tariff on manufactured cotton goods. Of the sixty responses received, forty-six were opposed to any changes.[25] In the end, the Morrison Bill was not popular among Morrison's own party members and never came to a final vote.

In 1884 all eyes were on the presidency. Chester A. Arthur, who had become president after the assassination of James A. Garfield, was in

---

[23] 15 Cong. Rec. 2,585–87 (1884).
[24] "The Mills and the Cotton," *Weekly Telegraph*, 9 May 1884, p. 4.
[25] Russell, "The Tariff."

declining health and was not nominated again.[26] In August, Grover Cleveland became the Democratic Party's candidate for president, running against Republican candidate James G. Blaine, a former Speaker of the House and a senator from Maine who had served as secretary of state under President Garfield, resigning after his assassination. One of the elements included in the Democratic Party platform was recognition of the protective tariff as important for generating revenue and protecting American products and labor, a theme the Major had been espousing on the *Telegraph*'s editorial pages and in the halls of Congress. The party's platform was also against excise taxes—called internal revenue taxes at the time—which were levied by the federal government on certain products, such as whisky and tobacco. Because they were a direct tax on the people, they were deplored by many, including the Major, who in many editorials had advocated for "wiping the last vestige of the internal revenue laws from the federal statute books."[27]

The Major eagerly anticipated Cleveland's acceptance letter in order to read his pronouncements about the tariff portion of the party platform, but Cleveland was silent on the issue and during his campaign never clearly articulated his position. The Major considered "the silence of Governor Cleveland upon these points as very damaging to his prospects of election."[28] He also had concerns about Cleveland's electability, contending in an editorial that "a few active politicians had committed the party to an unsatisfactory platform, placed an inexperienced leader as its candidate, and had precipitated a hard and uncertain contest." In response to the Major's comments, Larry Gantt, editor at the *Athens Banner-Watchman*, replied, "That platform was framed and Mr. Cleveland nominated after a careful investigation of the field by the ablest and purest men in the democratic party. The idea of a little pin-hook Georgia editor putting his opinion in direct antagonism to such statesmen, is as egotistic as it is ridiculous." Gantt was dismayed with the Major not only because the Major voiced his concerns about the strength (or lack thereof) of the Democratic ticket, but because the Major's editorial comments were being picked up by Republican newspapers in the North as possible encouragement for a breakup of the solid Democratic South. Gantt complained about the Major's editorials

---

[26]"Presidents: Chester A. Arthur," White House website, accessed 24 February 2015, http://www.whitehouse.gov/1600/presidents/chesterarthur.

[27]"Plain Positions of Vital Issues," *Weekly Telegraph*, 5 September 1884, p. 4.

[28]"Telegraphic Sparks," *(Athens, GA) Banner-Watchman*, 9 September 1884, p. 2.

several times in his paper, claiming, "The leading republican organs of the North contain daily columns of extracts from the *Macon Telegraph*, as an illustration of how a leading (?) democratic paper looks upon the ticket of its party. And here is where the real harm comes in. It tends to weaken and discourage our support in the North."[29] In another editorial, Gantt lamented that "the republican party is making renewed efforts to regain its power in Georgia, and we attribute that ardor to nothing but the encouragement they are receiving from a certain weak-kneed democratic sheet."[30] Having already called the *Macon Telegraph* a "weak-kneed democratic organ" in a previous jab, it was clear to whom the *Banner-Watchman* editor was referring. The *Middle Georgia Times* also chimed in, complaining that the *Telegraph* was thwarting the nomination of Cleveland and his running mate, Thomas A. Hendricks. The Major replied that "constant applause" would not win the election for Cleveland and that a discussion of the "causes that operate for and against a candidate" would help in securing his election. "Is it treason to discuss the campaign coolly? Is it Republicanism to publish the news?"[31]

Despite what other newspapers thought about the Major's comments in the *Telegraph*, the Major supported the Cleveland nomination with personal funds and helped solicit donations from others in his city.[32] The Major's concerns about Cleveland's timid stance on the protective tariff notwithstanding, Cleveland held many of the same convictions as the Major. Both were pro-business and against bossism and corruption in politics. When Grover Cleveland won the presidency, the Major breathed a sigh of relief. He was right to have worried about the election. It turned out to be a very close contest, decided by the state of New York; Cleveland won that state by a margin of only 1,200 votes, and the entire election by fewer than 50,000.[33]

---

[29]Ibid.

[30]Ibid.

[31]"Cold Water vs. Common Sense," *Telegraph*, 30 August 1884, p. 2.

[32]"The National Campaign Fund," *Columbus (GA) Enquirer-Sun*, 7 October 1884, p. 1.

[33]"Campaigns and Elections," *American President: Grover Cleveland*, University of Virginia, Miller Center website, accessed 24 February 2015, http://millercenter. org/president/cleveland/essays/biography/3.

The South was jubilant. Cleveland was the first Democrat to win the office since 1856, and the South had high hopes for an administration free of corruption and influence, which the region had assigned to Republican administrations. Huge celebrations erupted in cities all across the South.[34] Macon saluted its new chief in a blazing celebration. An elaborate parade launched the festivities. Students from Mercer University marched in the parade wearing red sashes and carrying blazing torches, followed by a coffin bearing a skull and crossbones and containing an effigy of James G. Blaine, the Republican loser. The fire department joined in the celebration with decorated engines, piercing whistles, and fireworks bursting forth from their trucks. Macon's citizens shared in the exuberance by covering their homes with illuminated lanterns. The parade passed through a grand arch erected over Second Street consisting of "a framework twenty-five feet high and thirty-five feet wide." On either side of the arch stood life-size statues and above them an arch with a bas-relief of two figures clasping hands, one draped in the American flag and one draped in the Confederate flag. At each corner of the arch stood a flagstaff bearing clusters of hanging Chinese lanterns and a swag of lanterns hanging beneath. Once the procession passed underneath, fireworks were discharged from the arch, framing the Macon Confederate monument on the street and making a rousing display.[35]

After the fireworks, the parade proceeded to Mulberry Street where an august group of state and local dignitaries, including the Major, Evan Howell, Congressman Blount, and Governor McDaniel, made eloquent speeches. Henry Grady provided his own drama to the evening when a messenger handed Howell a telegram from Grady, who was in New York. When Howell read Grady's words confirming Cleveland's election, the crowd erupted into applause that the people on the podium were hardly able to contain.[36] Maconites went home that evening happy with their first Democratic presidential victory in twenty-eight years. The Major, however, would live to regret his vote for Cleveland.

During Cleveland's first term, the administration retained a surplus in the treasury, which the president wanted to eliminate by lowering the protective tariff. This turn of events was exactly what the Major had feared

---

[34]Edward L. Ayers, *The Promise of the New South: Life after Reconstruction* (Oxford: Oxford University Press, 2007) 47.

[35]"Macon Ablaze," *Atlanta Weekly Constitution*, 18 November 1884, p. 10.

[36]Ibid.

when Cleveland refused to make his position on the protective tariff clear during his campaign. The Major believed that lowering the tariff would put American businesses in jeopardy, and he thought that the surplus could be eliminated by abolishing the excise tax.[37] He also verbalized his frustrations with his representatives in Congress for supporting Cleveland's calls for tariff reform, which he felt was a betrayal of the well-stated plank of the party platform: "It is a sad reflection upon the intelligence of the Southern Congressmen that they have suffered themselves to be whipped into the support of these schemes which they had only to compare with the declarations of the convention at Chicago to ascertain that they did not pretend to carry out the wishes of the party."[38]

In his frustration with the party and the president, the Major began a campaign to inform the Georgia electorate about the merits of a protective tariff by expanding his reach beyond the *Telegraph* and taking his message directly to the people. The Major used one of his strongest assets, his oratorical skill, to explain how the protective tariff benefited all Southerners. Between March and August of 1887 he spoke in at least nine different cities, including Atlanta, Oxford, Eastman, La Grange, Cartersville, and Monticello. He even debated his good friend Congressman Charles Frederick Crisp at a barbecue attended by thousands in Montezuma.[39] It was an exhaustive exercise that showed the courage of his convictions in wanting his fellow citizens to understand the issues that he felt were critical to providing a better climate for industry.

President Cleveland met with no success in his attempt to lower the tariff, which came in the form of a reintroduced Morrison Bill in 1886. The Morrison Bill was destined for defeat, receiving opposition from within his own party again. Congressman Samuel J. Randall, a former Speaker of the House and a staunch Democrat protectionist from Pennsylvania, led the

---

[37]"The Tariff and Internal Revenue," *Weekly Telegraph*, 24 September 1882, p. 2.

[38]"The Tariff in Georgia," *Weekly Telegraph*, 25 January 1887, p. 4.

[39]"Gossip from the Gate City," *Columbus (GA) Enquirer-Sun*, 24 March 1887, p. 1; "The Towns around Us," *Telegraph*, 5 May 1887, p. 3; "Major Hanson at Eastman," *Weekly Telegraph*, 17 May 1887, p. 11; "Miscellaneous News Notes," *Augusta (GA) Chronicle*, 20 May 1887, p. 2; "The Great South," *(Atlanta, GA) Sunny South*, 21 May 1887, p. 7; "Montezuma Barbecue," *Weekly Telegraph*, 26 July 1887, p. 7; "Maj. Hanson's Speech," *Telegraph*, 7 August 1887, p. 2; "Major Hanson at Talladega," *Telegraph*, 9 August 1887, p. 4; "Monticello: Major Hanson's Address Excites Great Interest," *Telegraph*, 18 August 1887, p. 3.

opposition, and the bill never made it past the Ways and Means Committee. In December 1887 Cleveland again called on Congress to enact tariff reform legislation, which passed the House but died in the Senate. The Major was so frustrated by Cleveland's continual press for a lowering of the tariff that he sought the ear of Congressman Randall, who had once been a strong supporter of Cleveland. The two men spent an evening together riding through the streets of Washington in a carriage so that their conversation could not be overheard. The Major later shared the crux of their discussion with Harry Stillwell Edwards. After the Major's death, Edwards revealed that the Major had told him "Randall's denunciation of Cleveland was the most bitter expression he had ever heard from human lips." According to Edwards, "Randall never afterwards entered the White House."[40]

After desperately seeking Randall's counsel and being offered no hope that Cleveland could be counted on to adhere to the platform adopted in Chicago in 1884, the Major was left with a difficult choice in 1888 when Cleveland sought a second term and the Republican Party had become the standard bearer for protectionism. By the end of the 1880s the Major was recognized as a high-profile industrialist, a lifelong Democrat, and an independent thinker who supported only those candidates whose platform he could agree with or, in his own words, risk "self-stultification." Could he support Cleveland, a low-tariff advocate, over a Republican protectionist candidate? Could he switch parties and become a Republican based on that one issue? If he did, how could he face his supporters and his *Telegraph* subscribers, to whom he had fiercely defended his loyalty to the Democratic Party? Would he be vindicating every editor who had accused him of being a Republican? What would it be like to sit across the aisle politically from most of his peers? To be a Southerner in post-Civil War Georgia was to be a Democrat. According to Edward Ayers, author of *The Promise of the New South: Life after Reconstruction*, party affiliation determined one's marriage choices and, to a great extent, one's social and business circles.[41]

Because of the Major's firebrand approach to commenting on state and national politics, he had more than doubled the worth of the *Macon Telegraph* based on the strength of its subscriptions, which were then the

---

[40]Harry Stillwell Edwards, "John F. Hanson—The Man," *Telegraph*, 18 December 1910, p. 6.

[41]Ayers, *Promise of the New South*, 34.

highest in the paper's history.[42] It was at the height of this success that the Major sold the *Telegraph* to James H. Campbell, a Macon businessman and relative of Congressman Blount, in September 1887. Although the sale was voluntary, Edwards contended that the Bibb Manufacturing board of directors had urged the Major to sell the paper in order to concentrate more on the mill business.[43] Shortly after he announced the sale, seven men, including Edwards, presented the Major with a gift of a silver ladle, "elegantly chased and engraved," accompanied by a letter that expressed their love and esteem for him. In it they stated, "We admired your ability and independence, but we also loved you whom we ever found as kind and forbearing as a father, and as sociable as a boyhood companion."[44]

In commenting on the sale of the *Macon Telegraph*, most Georgia newspapers reported it as a news item, the *Atlanta Constitution* among them. However, the *Constitution* extended its coverage to its editorial pages, offering praise for its rival: "Major Hanson has undoubtedly been honest in his views, and has fought up to his convictions with marked ability and earnestness." The *Constitution* also accused the *Telegraph* of being "narrow and irritative" and decried that "a paper should be more than the personal convictions of its manager and should never carry his prejudices." The *Constitution* claimed that a good newspaper "should be impersonal in the sense of emphasizing the best general sentiment rather than in maintaining one man's pride of opinion, and of advancing the general weal rather than gratifying one man's preference or prejudices," forgetting that on many occasions it had allowed Grady and Howell to use its pages to satisfy their own "preferences and prejudices" while trying to keep their political cronies in office.[45]

Despite what the *Constitution* had to say about its strongest competitor, the record shows that during the Major's ownership the *Macon Telegraph* advocated for a technological school, a strong two-party system in the South, a protective tariff for industry nationwide, and Democratic Party reform against machine politics in Georgia. The *Telegraph* supported the limitation of the powers of the Georgia Railroad Commission, the abolishment of the

---

[42]"Telegraph Began 125 Years Ago in Swaddling Village," *Telegraph*, 11 November 1951, p. 34.

[43]Edwards, "John F. Hanson," 6.

[44]"Some Testimonials," *Telegraph*, 29 September 1887, p. 5.

[45]"The Sale of the *Macon Telegraph*," *Atlanta Constitution*, 26 September 1887, p. 4.

convict lease system, a reduction in the length of the workday, and the elimination of child labor in factories in Georgia. The Major was not afraid to take unpopular positions in what he believed to be the best interests of the people of the South, and he and the *Telegraph* often endured slings and arrows due to their editorial positions. Never discouraged, the Major "believed that the highest compliment paid the paper was expressed in the words of a distinguished Georgian of that period when he said, 'Every scoundrel in the state is found abusing it [the *Macon Telegraph*].'"[46] The *Philadelphia Press* may have summed it up best by stating that the *Macon Telegraph* during the Major's ownership had "done more than any other paper to broaden and liberalize political thought and sentiment in the south."[47]

---

[46]"Telegraph Began 125 Years Ago," *Telegraph*.

[47]*Philadelphia Press*, quoted in "The South and the Republican Party," *Weekly Telegraph*, 5 July 1887.

8

A SWITCH IN PARTIES

I regard the solid South as the greatest evil of the time.

—J. F. Hanson

ONCE THE MAJOR had sold the *Macon Telegraph*, he began to advance a more critical appraisal of the South while continuing to promote the causes he believed were central to future economic prosperity of the region, most especially the protective tariff and the need for a strong two-party political system. The candor with which he expressed his views began to pique the interest of Northern newspapers and manufacturing concerns, who sought interviews and speaking engagements with the Major. He intrigued these Northerners because his opinions on economic and racial issues— particularly on the ways racial issues impacted Georgia voting dynamics— differed from mainstream Southern ideology. The Major also believed that the South was thwarting efforts to support American manufacturing interests and that Republican Party strategists were ineffective in recruiting Southerners to the fold. He used these speeches and interviews to express his desire to break Southern solidarity, which he felt could be accomplished by persuading Republican Party leaders to change their Southern political strategy, as he had boldly outlined in the editorial columns of the *Macon Telegraph*. By the end of the 1880s, Northern politicians and industrial leaders were beginning to recognize the Major as an important industrial voice of the New South.

The Major had one of his first opportunities to address a Northern audience in April 1888 when he spoke to the Manufacturers' Club of Philadelphia, in a city where his editorial views had previously been aired on the pages of the *Philadelphia Press* and the *Philadelphia Inquirer*. He spoke frankly about the dynamics between politics and race that occurred after the Civil War when the Republican Party had, in the Major's opinion, "made the fatal mistake...of addressing itself solely to the negroes of the south, of looking to the negroes for party strength and support and relying upon them to give shape and directions so far as the influence of the South was concerned, to public affairs both local and general." The Major felt that this not only "drew the color line, but its [the Republican Party's] actions since, had done everything that could be done to make the race issue perpetual."[1] During and after Reconstruction, a solid Democratic majority had emerged to counter Republican efforts to interfere in Southern affairs. The Major wished to see the voting populace divide over economic policy issues rather than adhere to what he termed "perpetual sectional antagonism by the politicians," with the result that "in the formulation of our public policies, partisanship is stronger than patriotism, and reason and judgment are silenced by passion and prejudice."[2]

Because the Democratic Party now supported a low-tariff policy, the Major feared that the South's Democratic voting strength would destroy the policy of protection. Some Southern states, such as Georgia and South Carolina, overstated the number of eligible voters for the allocation of the nation's Congressional seats and then denied many of these voters access to the ballot box through disfranchisement, complicated registration procedures, or a poll tax. As a result, a larger number of Southern representatives were serving in Congress than was reflective of the actual number of voters. In fact, one Georgia vote was worth as many as five votes in other states in the country.[3] This gave the South extraordinary influence in determining the outcome of national legislation. Referring to the region's voting strength, the Major told his Philadelphia audience that "if the cause of protection shall fail…it must fall and die at the hands of the solid South," but he also warned that "the people of the North will not be blameless." If the Republican Party altered its strategy, he predicted that "both black and white races…will blend with the other in political considerations founded upon great principles rather than the sentiments and prejudices which so long and successfully solidified them against each other." He believed that "when the Republican party comes to this attitude in absolute good faith the solid South will dissolve like a rope of sand."[4] He also assured his Northern audience that he

---

[1]"A Great Tariff Speech," *Augusta (GA) Chronicle* (hereafter cited as *Chronicle*), 19 May 1888, p. 1.

[2]Ibid.

[3]Edward L. Ayers, *The Promise of the New South: Life after Reconstruction* (Oxford: Oxford University Press, 2007) 50.

[4]"Great Tariff Speech," *Chronicle*.

advocated for economic policies that were advantageous to both North and South, stating, "I advocate for no policy for Georgia, that I would not advocate for Pennsylvania" and that what he most wanted was "two great political parties divided upon questions of national policy, rather than sectional issues."[5]

Within a week of his speech in Philadelphia, the *Boston Daily Advertiser* interviewed the Major, addressing similar themes. When the Major was asked about the causes of poverty in the South, he attributed it to the South's failure to recognize the "double value of home over foreign products, and the fact that we have always relied upon purchasing with one staple crop articles of consumption which we should have produced." He explained to the reporter that when a crop is raised and used to purchase necessities made elsewhere, the money leaves the state and lines the pockets of producers elsewhere, whether foreign or domestic, instead of benefiting the home economy. He described this as a "free trade policy" that "demonstrates its own folly in the condition of our people, whether this was produced by buying from other states...or abroad." The Major believed that not only would a free-trade policy not improve conditions for the people of the South, it would also "drag other sections of the country down to our level of poverty."[6]

His most surprising statement was given in answer to the question, "How about the solid South?" The Major replied, "Personally, I regard the solid South as the greatest evil of the time." Again blaming the Republican Party for forcing most Southern white males into the Democratic Party, the Major suggested that Republicans adopt a "policy toward the white people of the South that would break up this solidity. When that is done it stands to reason that a division of the white men into two parties will result in a division and an absorption of the black men by both parties."[7] Voting on principles rather than along color lines was a conviction he had espoused on the editorial pages of the *Telegraph*; now he was using his voice and the pages of other newspapers to deliver his message outside the Southern region in his strategy to crack the solid South and maintain a protective tariff.

---

[5]Ibid.
[6]"Protection South," *Boston Daily Advertiser*, 16 April 1888, p. 5.
[7]Ibid.

In commenting on the Major's speech to the Manufacturers' Club, the *Philadelphia Press* suggested that his sentiments might indicate a possible divide in the South on the tariff issue. The *Atlanta Constitution* picked up on this remark, replying, "Bosh! The south will be solid against the republican party as long as the republican party exists.... When it comes to a choice between the two parties in this section, the tariff question and the surplus don't amount to a snap of the finger.... The great issue is the necessity for democratic success."[8] While the South was still clinging to post-Reconstruction reactionary thinking, as suggested by the *Constitution's* response, the Major was advocating for economic policies that would benefit the nation as a whole.

The Major continued to press his views on Southern issues, not only with regard to the tariff but on the subject of emancipation as well. Not long after his speech before the Manufacturers' Club of Philadelphia and his interview with the *Boston Daily Advertiser*, the Major wrote a letter to the editor of the *Philadelphia Inquirer* in response to an *Inquirer* article titled "The New Conspiracy." His letter was chosen to be published in the paper from among "numerous communications." The editor felt that the Major had handled his reply "in a business and also a statesmanlike manner, as one thoroughly familiar with Southern sentiment, Southern politicians, and the aspirations and desires of the 'New South' in its relation to questions of political economy and tariff revision."[9] Among several topics discussed in the original article was the opinion that there existed a conspiracy in the South to control the Supreme Court in order to undo the constitutional amendments granting emancipation and enfranchisement to blacks. In his letter, the Major denied that any such conspiracy existed, stating that Southerners regarded "the questions of emancipation, of negro suffrage, and the loss of the money value of slavery as irrevocably settled." He did, however, believe that "justice to the South...would have resulted from payment, by the federal government, of fair compensation for the slaves emancipated." The Major stated that the nation had a moral obligation to emancipate and enfranchise blacks, and it should be bound by the same responsibility "to compensate those who had vested rights in slavery,

---

[8]"Democratic Success," *Atlanta Constitution* (hereafter cited as *Constitution*), 18 April 1888, p. 4.

[9]"Conspiracy Denied," *Philadelphia Inquirer*, 4 July 1888, p. 7.

acquired under the sanctions of federal law." In short, he felt—and likely wasn't alone in this feeling—it was unfair that Southerners bore the entire financial burden of emancipation.[10]

Another topic addressed in the *Inquirer*'s original article was the Mills Tariff Bill, which had been introduced by Roger Q. Mills, a Democratic congressman from Texas, and had passed the House in April 1888. The Major described the Mills Bill as one that pitted North against South because it provided for a small tariff reduction on sugar and rice, which gave some protection to Southern interests where those products were grown while removing protection from wool and lumber, which was to the detriment of Northern interests. Mills was not necessarily interested in protecting sugar and rice. The Major asserted that Mills had drafted the bill with the intent of making the legislation palatable to Southern interests, who held voting power in Congress, thus the concession to sugar and rice producers. The Major described Mills as a "free trader in everything except sugar and rice" and suggested that "Mr. Mills who is inconsistent in nothing but his ignorance and inconsistency on this question, proposes…to secure free trade in one section and on some products through protection in another section and on other products, while the Representatives whose votes he desires to capture propose to secure protection at home by voting for free trade in other sections." As long as some products were to be protected while others were not, he saw no hope for an end to sectionalism. He believed that the tariff issue could never be dealt with until sectionalism died, declaring that "every consideration of public and private interest, which must be affected by any line of public policy, demands a broad spirit of nationalism in the treatment of this and all public questions."[11]

Based on the 1886 midterm election results in other states, most notably in Illinois and Oregon, the Major predicted in his letter that a low-tariff candidate—a term that was often synonymous with the label "free-trader"—would be defeated by a protective-tariff candidate in the upcoming 1888 presidential election. "I cannot account for the increased Republican majorities in these states upon any other hypothesis than that the people are alarmed at the course of the Democratic President and the Democratic majority in the House of Representatives," he wrote, referring to the party's

---

[10]Ibid.
[11]Ibid.

continual movement away from protectionism toward a low tariff. He closed his letter to the editor by predicting that the issue in the next election would be "free trade vs. protection" and that if the Republican Party were to stay away from sectional issues and choose a protection candidate, "they will win."[12]

The Republican Party was already keenly aware of the Major's political strategy. As the presidential race drew near, the party came to two conclusions: first, that it was most important to focus on the broader issues of jobs and the economy, which would benefit both blacks and whites, and second, that to regain the White House it needed to provide the nation with a pro-business high-tariff candidate who could bring Southern protectionist Democrats like the Major into the Republican fold. The Republican platform of 1888 offered a clear referendum on the issue of a protective tariff, just as the Major had predicted in his letter to the *Philadelphia Inquirer*. And as the Major had also predicted, the election was decided over the protective tariff, with Benjamin Harrison, a high-tariff advocate, defeating Cleveland in a very close election.[13] Although Cleveland won the popular vote, Harrison won the Electoral College by a wide margin. Harrison also received more Southern ballots than any other Republican presidential candidate had since the end of Reconstruction.[14]

Shortly after the election, the Major was asked to speak at the Augusta Exposition to an audience composed of thirty-nine cotton mill owners from four states, representatives from several cotton exchanges, and members of other commercial organizations.[15] As a prominent spokesman of the New South, Henry Grady also delivered a speech at the Augusta Exposition, although the two men could not have been more diametrically opposed to one another. Grady hearkened back to the Civil War, invoking the names of Calhoun and Stephens and describing soldiers with "hand clasped in hand, heart locked in heart, standing undaunted in the desolation of defeat." Far

---

[12]Ibid.

[13]"A Life in Brief," *American President: Benjamin Harrison*, University of Virginia, Miller Center website, accessed 10 December 2014, http://millercenter.org/president/bharrison/essays/biography/1.

[14]Stanley P. Hirshson, *Farewell to the Bloody Shirt: Northern Republicans and the Southern Negro, 1887–93* (Bloomington: Indiana University Press, 1962) 167.

[15]"A Most Significant Speech," *(New York, NY) Tariff League Bulletin* 2/24 (14 December 1888): 277.

from looking forward and painting a picture of a New South, Grady spoke of the one-party South as essential for the region, even into the future, and described it as a reality "not dreamed of in antebellum days." He seemed to relish the idea that the region's 153 electoral votes could be "hurled as a rifle-ball into the electoral college," substantiating the fears expressed by the Major to his Philadelphia audience about the solid South wielding its power against the nation's tariff policy. Grady used fear mongering on the racial issue, stating that if the solid South were divided, "it will debauch its political system, destroy the defenses of its social integrity, and put the balance of power in the hands of an ignorant and dangerous class."[16]

The Major's speech not only contrasted sharply with Grady's but marked a turning point for him. The Major spoke of a future of national unity and against the solid South, predicting that "a spirit of nationalism is developing in all parts of the country, and…will succeed the spirit of sectionalism which has cursed us for fifty years."[17] Rather than fearing the black vote, as Grady did, the Major told his audience that he viewed their enfranchisement positively, because in voting for the Republican Party—the party for which blacks were inclined to vote—they supported the "American policy of protection" and voted "against the perpetuation of permanent internal federal taxation."[18] The Major also stated that he would always vote for the party that represented what he considered a sound fiscal policy for the nation—an admission that in the recent election he had voted for Harrison, a Republican.[19] Because this was the first public declaration of his switch in party affiliation, the Major's Augusta speech was seminal: it confirmed his conviction that his economic aspirations for the future of the South, and the nation, could be realized only through the Republican Party. To declare himself a Republican was a very courageous admission at a time in history when being a Republican in the South was generally akin to committing political and social suicide.

The Major's speech also focused on cotton manufacturing, taking full advantage of the opportunity to address an audience of industrialists from the region. He described the growth of the textile industry in the South in

---

[16]Joel Chandler Harris, ed., *Life of Henry W. Grady including His Writings and Speeches* (New York: Cassell, 1890) 125.

[17]"Do We Divide?," *Chronicle*, 3 December 1888, p. 4.

[18]"A Most Significant Speech," *Tariff League Bulletin*.

[19]Ibid.

the previous seven years as having doubled in production capacity, from 700,000 spindles in 1880 to 1,400,000 in 1887. He felt that the industry was better positioned to double its growth in the next ten years than it had been in 1880, and he asked his audience to consider the consequences of such growth, as the South was already seeing prices decline due to overproduction. The solution, he felt, was for the South to export its cotton to foreign markets. He warned his audience that "the rapid growth of our cotton mills brings us face to face with a serious problem," and to avert a crisis, Southerners needed to find "more consumers, new demand, new outlet" for their products. "Naturally we turn to the countries south of us—to Mexico, Central and South America and the West Indies...the trade is ours by natural laws, and a wise and liberal policy on the part of our Government will secure it."[20] Hearden describes Southerners as having been devoted to the idea of exporting their products, stating that Southern cotton manufacturers "attempted to influence the conduct of American diplomacy during the last three decades of the nineteenth century."[21] Further, historian Joseph A. Fry characterizes the South as being adamant in its pursuit of overseas markets during the late nineteenth century, more so than any other part of the country.[22]

As a leading Southern advocate of this policy, the Major attempted numerous times, beginning with this speech, to persuade the federal government to assist manufacturing interests through diplomatic means. The Major felt that Latin America was the logical partner with which to establish a trading relationship, although he didn't think the American private sector could compete with subsidized European shipping, stating that "there is no adequate remedy except in government subsidies to American shipping." He even went so far as to suggest that a "double track railroad down the backbone of the continent from the border of Texas to Cape Horn" would be a national expenditure worthy of the country's support.[23] At the close of the Major's speech, a resolution was passed to inform Congress of the Major's proposition that the federal government

---

[20]"A Most Significant Speech," *Tariff League Bulletin.*

[21]Patrick J. Hearden, *Independence and Empire: The New South's Cotton Mill Campaign, 1865–1901* (Dekalb: Northern Illinois University Press, 1982) xiii.

[22]Joseph A. Fry, *Dixie Looks Abroad: The South and U.S. Foreign Relations, 1789–1973* (Baton Rouge: Louisiana State University Press, 2002) 110–11.

[23]"A Most Significant Speech," *Tariff League Bulletin.*

begin "subsidizing steamship lines from Savannah and other Southern ports, for the purpose of establishing trade with the great republics of South America and the Empire of Brazil." Later, on January 28, 1889, Senator Joseph E. Brown of Georgia entered the resolution into the Congressional Record.[24]

In his speech at the Augusta Exposition the Major had clearly defined himself as a unique standard bearer of the New South. Paul Gaston describes the spokesmen of the New South as being "unmindful of paradoxes" who "subscribed with ardor to the mythical conception of the Old South."[25] The Major never looked back nor did he romanticize the days of the Old South; rather, he championed a new economic vision for the South and the hope of national unity, while Grady often perpetuated the sectional flame of Bourbon Democracy, more closely fitting Gaston's profile of a New South spokesman. Historian David Carlton suggests that Gaston "neglects the entrepreneurial activity that was actually attempting to realize the [New South] Creed in brick and mortar" and that was "far heartier than the promotional froth emanating from Grady" or other New South spokesmen of the time.[26] Carlton used Daniel Tompkins, a contemporary of the Major who owned the *Charlotte Observer* and established three cotton mills in North Carolina, as one example of this entrepreneurial spirit, but he could have been describing the Major. However, according to Carlton, most apostles of the New South Creed did not focus on regional economic vitality but rather concentrated their efforts on their own local enterprises.[27] Although the Major was certainly interested in strengthening Bibb Manufacturing and Macon's economy, he thought in broad regional and national terms, advocating for upgrading the textile industry throughout the South, expanding the markets for American goods, and establishing economic and political policies that advanced the entire nation. In commenting on the Major and his new party affiliation, the *Philadelphia*

---

[24]15 Cong. Rec. 2,585–87 (1884).

[25]Paul M. Gaston, *The New South Creed: A Study in Southern Mythmaking* (New York: Alfred A. Knopf, 1970) 173.

[26]David L. Carlton, "Carlton on Gaston," review of *The New South Creed*, by Paul M. Gaston, H-South, H-Net Reviews (January 2003), https://networks.h-net.org/node/512/reviews/685/carlton-gaston-new-south-creed-study-southern-mythmaking.

[27]Ibid.

Press touted him as "one of the brightest journalists and most energetic businessmen of the South since the war. It needs a rare combination of talents to enable a man to edit a newsy, piquant paper and at the same time build up one of the biggest cotton manufacturing establishments in his section." In referencing his switch to the Republican Party, the *Press* stated, "He has always been too progressive to belong to the Democratic party."[28]

The disparity in the messages of the two orators at the Augusta Exposition did not go unnoticed. The editor of the *Augusta Chronicle* observed that Grady had appealed for a continuance of the solid South, while the Major spoke in "bold antithesis" to Grady. The same editor predicted that the Major's words would "attract attention and invite discussion North and South," and he could not have been more correct.[29] A columnist for the *Manufacturers' Record*, a leading industrial journal published in Baltimore, referred to the Major's address as "one of the most practically eloquent he had heard in 20 years."[30] These comments along with the Major's speech were printed in the *Tariff League Bulletin*, a publication of the American Protective Tariff League in New York, an influential organization of manufacturers and politicians who supported protectionism. In fact, the group was so intrigued by this Southerner who spoke so fervently about the protective tariff, foreign markets, and American shipping subsidies that they invited the Major to speak at their annual dinner at Delmonico's, in New York City, in January 1889. He was billed as a "representative Southern Protectionist" and appeared with a distinguished group of men that included Congressman William McKinley of Ohio, a staunch protectionist who later became president; Chauncey Depew, an attorney for the Vanderbilts' railroad interests and president of the New York Central Railroad; and Warner Miller, a former U.S. Senator from New York.[31] The demand for seats at the dinner far exceeded expectations. Perhaps many were enticed by the Major's topic, "The Southern Industrial Growth, the Strongest Bond of Union and Peace"; in any case, Delmonico's was prepared for a capacity crowd. The iconic New York restaurant was accustomed to

---

[28] *Philadelphia Press*, quoted in "Major J. F. Hanson," *Chronicle*, 13 January 1889, p. 4.

[29] "Do We Divide?," *Chronicle*.

[30] "A Most Significant Speech," *Tariff League Bulletin*.

[31] "A Notable Dinner," *(New York, NY) Tariff League Bulletin* 2/26 (28 December 1888): 303.

handling America's men of mark. Its location on Beaver Street in the heart of Manhattan's financial district made it the perfect choice for the annual dinners of America's leading industrialists.

The Major had proclaimed his support of the Republican administration in his speech at the Augusta Exposition, but being in the presence of the captains of the high-tariff movement in America vitalized his oratory. He began by praising the Union, to assure his Northern audience that he did not sympathize with the lost cause. With formalities addressed, the Major wasted no time in getting to his point of protection versus the low tariff—or free-trade advocacy, as it was sometimes referred to at the time—that predominated in the South. Adopting a free-trade policy by eliminating the tariff on imports would have demanded that the federal government find another means of deriving its operating revenue, since the only other revenue generator at the time was the internal revenue tax, the federal excise tax on whisky and tobacco.

The Major felt that support for a free-trade policy in the South was the direct result of slavery. The South favored free trade when slave labor was the predominant source of labor for planting and harvesting its main commodities. Slaveholders paid no wages and therefore were unconcerned about competition from cheap foreign products. The Major couldn't have been more deliberate in his condemnation of the free-traders when he exclaimed that the country had been in jeopardy when a policy predominated that "was conceived in the womb, nurtured at the breast, dandied upon the knee and rocked in the cradle of free trade." He referred to slavery, succession, and free trade as the "trinity of errors" that led to the Civil War.[32] The Major claimed that the recent political campaign for the presidency was the first in the nation's history that had allowed the people to decide whether they favored a protective tariff policy for the financial administration of the nation's affairs or a free-trade policy with a permanent internal revenue system levied on them. By electing President Harrison, the Republican protective-tariff candidate, the Major asserted that the American people had cast their votes for the customs house as the income generator for the country, which he described as "duties so adjusted as to give ample protection to American capital and labor."[33] He criticized the federal excise

---

[32]"Major Hanson's Speech," *Constitution*, 18 January 1889, p. 3.
[33]Ibid.

tax as being in violation of the spirit of the Constitution and blamed the Democrats—"the party to which I have always acted"—as the perpetrator of this scheme on the American people, who he said were "as ignorant of the effects of such a policy as were the leaders of the party." The Major called on the administration to "cut up the internal revenue system by the roots and secure the permanency of the American policy of protection."[34]

The Major's boldest statements criticized a Southern political agenda that, he said, sought to destroy the American system of protection through its artificial voting power in Congress. As he had done in his speech to the Manufacturers' Club of Philadelphia eight months earlier, the Major told his Tariff League audience that Southern representation in Congress was disproportionate to the number of actual voting citizens, something not many Southern politicians would admit. The Major stated that the South had "secured representation in congress far beyond that in which we are entitled upon the basis of population represented by that portion of our people participating in and deciding our congressional elections," which "gives us abnormal power in deciding the legislation of the country."[35] The Major "did not believe in a solid south for the purpose of controlling federal fiscal policies in opposition to the majority sentiment of the people of the north." He stated that the "political south" was intent on destroying the protective system and that "the man or party who will save the political south from itself, and save the country from the political south, will best promote the interests of the south and the country."[36] Though he was not aware of it, this speech revealed the Major himself as the man who was trying to "save the political south from itself," although he would find that cracking the solid South was a daunting task.

The Northern press took note of such unorthodox words coming from a Southerner and were generous in their commentary. The *Daily Inter-Ocean* of Chicago quoted the *New York Press*'s comments about the Major's speech, titling the article "The Trinity of Errors"—a direct quote from the Major. The *Press* had taken particular note of the Major's wish that a fear of blacks at the ballot box could be overcome because he believed that "many more southerners would take the ground he does and boldly support the

---

[34]Ibid.
[35]Ibid.
[36]Ibid.

Republican party, but race prejudice has made cowards of those who believe in protection, and the free traders continue to misrepresent even manufacturing districts of the industrial south," referring to Congressman Blount's 1884 testimony in support of the Morrison Bill assuring Congress that Southern manufacturers didn't see the need for a protective tariff. The *Press* article praised the Major as a man of "intelligence and business sense" and expressed that it was "gratifying to find now and then a Southerner who sees the South and the so called Southern statesmen as others see it and him."[37] The *San Francisco Bulletin*, *Oregonian*, and *Evening Star* in Washington, D.C., took particular note of the Major's comments about the solidarity of the political South being used to destroy the American system of the protective tariff, quoting liberally from that portion of his speech.[38] John T. White, editor of the *People's Choice*, a publication for blacks, and himself a leading black Republican, foretold the national implications of such a speech, stating, "Major Hanson has a national reputation because of his pronounced views on the tariff, and there is an under current of very strong sentiment in administration circles to encourage such men as he to come to the front...and...make the advocacy of the protection principle paramount and obliterate old party lines by bringing representatives of the New South to the front."[39]

Not surprisingly, the Southern press disagreed wholeheartedly with almost everything the Major had to say in his speech at Delmonico's. The *Macon Telegraph* denounced the Major's position, claiming that "he can no longer stand among Southern men in full sympathy with their traditions, their sufferings and their hopes" and concluding that the Major "will use his rare gifts of intellect and energy in thwarting their [Southern men's] desires and weakening their political power."[40] The *Charleston News and Courier* accused the Major of being an "extremist among the extreme apostles of Protection, and every one of his assertions as to the political sentiment and

---

[37]*New York Press*, quoted in "The Trinity of Errors," *Chicago Inter-Ocean*, 30 January 1889, p. 7.

[38]"Tariff League Banquet," *(Portland) Oregonian*, 18 January 1889, p. 2; "The Tariff League," San Francisco *Bulletin*, 18 January 1889, p. 4; "A Southern Protectionist," *(Washington, DC) Evening Star*, 18 January 1889, p. 6.

[39]"He Talks on Harrison," *Macon (GA) Telegraph* (hereafter cited as *Telegraph*), 18 March 1889, p. 6.

[40]"Major Hanson's Speech," *Telegraph*, 18 January 1889, p. 4.

purposes of the South proves him to be utterly out of sympathy with the people for whom he claimed the right to speak." The *News and Courier* predicted that the Major would "carry but few of the thinking men of the South with him in his new departure" and that when the voters were next asked to cast their approval at the ballot box for a protective tariff the outcome would be very different than that of the 1888 election.[41]

Emphasizing the opposition the Major faced from his Southern peers, the *New York Times* published in its entirety the colorful response to the Major's speech by the editor of the *Montgomery Advertiser*. The editor of that paper branded the Major a heretic among his own people, exclaiming, "For abject getting down into the dirt and kissing the feet of the powers that are to be, commend us to Major J. F. Hanson of Macon, Ga. In his speech before a select circle of Republican magnates, millionaires, and monopolists in New York, he went to the extent of vilifying the history, traditions, and habits of the people among whom he was born and raised." In a fever pitch of poor taste, the editor continued, "It would not be at all surprising to hear of his declaring that the Southern pastime had always been the roasting of negro babies, induced thereto by the doctrine of free love." He concluded that "the people of the South are not to be bound hand and foot by tariff monopolists, and the Georgia Major speaks for a small number of men when he makes such declarations as those that fell from him at the Belshazzar feast in New York last Thursday night."[42]

The Major could not let his critics go unanswered. He responded to them in a letter to Patrick Walsh, a Democrat, a lifelong friend of the Major's, and the editor of the staunchly Democratic *Augusta Chronicle*. The Major stated that he had "no apologies to offer with reference to my conclusions or principles, beyond the supreme conviction in my own mind that I am right." His letter to the editor outlined a history of the Democratic Party's failure to understand the importance of a protective tariff to the nation and to the party's chances for success. He denounced those who criticized him and other Democratic protectionists for asking the Democratic Party to adhere to the protectionist portion of the Chicago platform and blamed them for Cleveland's defeat in 1888.[43] Walsh wrote his

---

[41]"Crazy on Protection," *Charleston (SC) News & Courier*, 19 January 1889, p. 4.

[42]"An Editor Who Is Excited," *New York Times*, 19 January 1889, n.p.

[43]"Major J. F. Hanson: His Reply to Criticisms upon His Recent Speech," *Chronicle*, 28 February 1889, p. 2.

own editorial aimed at the Major's critics, admonishing them to "become accustomed to allow men to challenge party views and to criticize public men without calling them traitors. Intolerance is a blight to any section and...we must expect differences among ourselves and always respect honest dissent."[44] Despite the harsh reaction the Major received from his Southern peers, his speech at the American Protective Tariff League dinner became the catalyst that would place him in the national political spotlight for many years to come.

In December 1889, less than one year after the Major had made his most important speech to such a prominent national audience, Henry Grady, whose own New York speech had electrified a Northern audience just three years earlier, passed away at the age of thirty-eight, in the prime of his career. He died after suffering from bronchitis, which developed into pneumonia during his travels to Boston for a speaking engagement. His death was a shock to the entire state, which mourned his passing with tributes in the state press, among many other accolades.[45]

Macon honored Grady by holding a memorial service at the Academy of Music on December 26. Men representing the Macon city government, the chamber of commerce, the Macon press, Macon's University of Georgia alumni, and the Chi Phi fraternity all paid tribute to the state's most eloquent orator.[46] The Major was asked to address the assembly on behalf of the chamber of commerce. It was a difficult speech for the Major; he and Grady had not seen eye to eye on many issues concerning the advancement of Georgia's citizens and the politics of the day. The Major was both honest and reverent in his appraisal of Grady's legacy. He told his audience that Grady's speeches would define his role in history, predicting that they would "constitute the record upon which must rest his claim to statesmanship." And indeed Grady is well known today for his speeches and less so for his editorials. Despite the solemn occasion, the Major questioned Grady's methods of achieving racial supremacy, stating that "in these matchless efforts to maintain the supremacy of the Anglo-Saxon in the public affairs of this section, there are differences of opinion with reference to the methods,

---

[44]"Major Hanson's Letter," *Chronicle*, 28 February 1889, p. 4.

[45]Harold E. Davis, *Henry Grady's New South: Atlanta, a Brave and Beautiful City* (Tuscaloosa: University of Alabama Press, 1990) 7.

[46]"Grady Memorial Meeting," *Telegraph*, 27 December 1889, p. 6; Harris, *Life of Henry W. Grady*, 385–86.

which, by implication at least, he was supposed to have approved, for the accomplishment of this purpose." But he predicted that "the people of the South will keep his memory green, whatever the opinion of the world may be with reference to this question." The Major also understood that Grady's legacy was his beloved city of Atlanta, whose growth "was due to the broad liberality and supreme confidence in its future with which he inspired the people of Atlanta." The Major acknowledged that Grady had not reached "the meridian of his powers" but that he died "in the fullness of a great fame."[47]

In contrast to the Major's restrained tribute, his Macon neighbors were effusive in their praise and reverence. Judge Emory Speer, like Grady a graduate of the University of Georgia, described Grady's life as "one long protest against narrowness of partisanship and sectional bigotry"—this in stark contrast to the Major's view of Grady as a partisan politician and hearty supporter of "sectional bigotry," especially when he was exciting the flames of the Confederate cause in supporting the solid South as a political tool to be used to thwart the rest of the nation.[48] A fraternity brother of Grady's likened him to "Moses who led the Southern people through a wilderness of weakness and of want at least to the Pisgah whence, with prophetic eye, he could discern a New South true to the traditions of the past as was the steel which glittered on the victorious arm, at Manassas."[49] The Major's oration reflected the relationship he had with his most well-known editorial rival, whose death he marked with respect and little sentimentality.

A year after Grady's passing, the Major was no less outspoken in his views. When the Major was in the nation's capital on business, a reporter from the *Cincinnati Enquirer* interviewed him and was "surprised at the novelty of his sentiment with reference to southern questions," among them the issues of blacks and their voting rights and power. The Major, unlike his Southern peers, supported "federal supervision of all congressional and other federal elections." He further declared, "There are some negroes...who are just as qualified to cast the ballot as a good many white men, and I cannot see how the black man is to take care of himself, to protect himself without

---

[47]Harris, *Life of Henry W. Grady*, 397–98.
[48]Ibid., 403.
[49]Ibid., 412.

the ballot box."[50] The biggest driver of post-Reconstruction Democratic solidarity was the fear of renewed federal intervention in Southern affairs. The fact that the Major was in favor of federal-election oversight to prevent disfranchisement was a stunning proclamation from a Southerner. And in a nation that believed in the supremacy of the white race, it was a brave declaration to state that (some) blacks were as qualified to cast a ballot as (some) white men.

It may have been his candid interview with the *Cincinnati Enquirer* that resulted in the Major receiving an invitation from the E. S. Jones Post of the Grand Army of the Republic in Macon to speak at a most unlikely celebration: a Federal Memorial Day ceremony at the Andersonville Civil War prison site and cemetery on May 30, 1891. More than 45,000 Union prisoners had been held at the facility during its fourteen-month existence. Its extreme conditions and death toll of nearly 13,000 men made it one of the most infamous prisoner-of-war camps of the Civil War. Its commander, Captain Henry Wirz, the only Confederate officer tried for war crimes, was convicted and hanged on November 10, 1865.[51]

The celebration of a memorial day, initially called Decoration Day, began in Charleston, South Carolina, in 1866. Other Southern states soon followed South Carolina's lead, selecting different dates on which to memorialize their dead. Georgia chose April 26, the day General Joseph E. Johnston surrendered to General William T. Sherman. Confederate Memorial Day is still recognized in the South, in addition to the national holiday on the last Monday in May. In 1868, two years following its advent in the South, the Grand Army of the Republic established the first Federal Memorial Day (also called Decoration Day) on May 30.[52]

In the early years after the war, Andersonville Cemetery had been the site of Emancipation Day observances in January, organized by blacks and Northern white missionaries. These were solemn affairs of reverence and prayer, complete with the decorating of graves, because the "freedman

---

[50]*Cincinnati Enquirer*, 21 December 1890, quoted in "Gath and Hanson," *Augusta (GA) Chronicle*, 30 December 1890, p. 2.

[51]Raymond F. Baker, *Andersonville: The Story of a Civil War Prison Camp* (Washington, DC: National Park Service, 1972) 15.

[52]David W. Blight, *Race and Reunion: The Civil War in American Memory* (Cambridge: Belknap Press of Harvard University Press, 2001) 69–71.

considered the dead prisoners as their liberators and treated them as such."[53] Over the years, as Reconstruction came to an end and Northern missionaries returned home, blacks marked the celebration of emancipation in their own way, moving their celebration to the Federal Decoration Day observance on May 30. Rather than a reverent display of remembrance for the fallen men of the Union, the celebrations became a day of parades, picnics, revelry, and "excessive drinking and violence."[54] By the late 1880s the number of blacks descending on the cemetery at Andersonville had swollen into the thousands, and the white population in Andersonville and nearby Americus had become unnerved by this annual throng.[55] In response to this, the city of Andersonville pressed the Grand Army of the Republic, who had purchased the prison site from the federal government in 1890, to close the cemetery to blacks and orchestrate the first all-white celebration of the Federal Decoration Day at the site in 1891.[56]

In this newly organized affair, whites were seated within a fenced area of the cemetery in front of the speaker's podium, while blacks, including several black military companies, were relegated to the surrounding countryside. The ironic staging of the celebration pushed blacks to the periphery of an event that had been exclusively black since the early days of Reconstruction. Attendance was estimated at between ten and twenty thousand, nine-tenths being black. It was to this crowd that the Major, the "orator of the day," spoke.[57] It was also the first time an ex-Confederate was asked to give a Memorial Day speech on such hallowed ground for Northern sympathies. As a man who advocated the healing of the sectional wounds that remained from the conflict, and one who was interested in putting the Civil War behind him in order to advance the state of Georgia economically, the celebration at Andersonville was an opportunity for the Major to define for himself, if not for his generation, the reasons for the South's failure in the Civil War and the implications for the region's future.

---

[53]Christopher Barr, "The High Watermark of Slavery: Andersonville as a Monument to Emancipation" (paper presented at the biennial meeting of the Society of Civil War Historians, Baltimore, June 2014) p. 5.

[54]William H. Wiggins, Jr., *O Freedom! Afro-American Emancipation Celebrations* (Knoxville: University of Tennessee Press, 1987) 27.

[55]Barr, "High Watermark of Slavery," 8–10; "Decoration Day," *Americus (GA) Times-Recorder*, 31 May 1891, p. 8.

[56]Baker, *Andersonville*, 18; Barr, "High Watermark of Slavery," 10.

[57]"Decoration Day," *Americus Times-Recorder*.

He began his speech in a conciliatory tone, praising the Confederate soldiers and describing their valor and patriotism as having cast "luster upon the Union as the common heritage now of all the people of a peaceful and united country."[58] He criticized the war, however, blaming it on "mischievous and aggressive minorities" that had prevailed when the issues were imminently solvable via peaceful and lawful settlement.[59] He made note of the fact that in the South's efforts to wage the war, Jefferson Davis had urged a conscription law on the Confederate Congress, which the Major considered an indictment of the cause for which the South was fighting. The Major maintained that the war was not worth waging if no one was willing to fight, criticizing the Confederate government: "If statesmanship had ruled the counsels of the Confederacy, the war would have ended the moment conscription became necessary." He was no less critical of the law "that exempted from military service, in a war for the defense of slavery, every man who owned twenty slaves." He was appalled that the men who had the most to lose financially by emancipation and for whom the war was being waged were given an exemption, calling it the "crowning infamy of the century."[60]

The Major addressed the issue of disfranchisement openly, admitting that "the negro was disfranchised in many states of the South," a fact that many Southerners denied—and that even the Major had denied when he spoke to Northern audiences just two years earlier at the American Protective Tariff League banquet at Delmonico's. It was the Major's contention that in "denying him [black men] the right to vote, the Democratic Party assumes his representation, not by his will, but against his will." The Major was adamant that this unfairly gave the Democratic Party "the political power and influence in the electoral college and in Congress" to be used against blacks and "the Republican party, the party to which he [blacks] naturally desires to vote"; he had espoused these convictions in speeches and interviews in Philadelphia, Boston, and New York. He stated that the Democratic Party unfairly gained strength from disfranchisement, which he described as "a fraud upon the negroes and white men of the South, and upon the people of the country at large." The Major felt that the

---

[58]J. F. Hanson, *A Memorial Address* (Macon: News Publishing Company, 1891) 4. Hanson's address was published by the News Publishing Company as a twenty-four-page pamphlet, a copy of which is in possession of the author.

[59]Ibid., 6.

[60]Ibid., 18.

effort to disfranchise blacks was "destroying the integrity of the ballot box, and breeding contempt for the law" and that "we cannot preserve our institutions unless the ballot box, the supreme arbiter of all public questions, is kept pure."[61] He appealed to his audience "to make the future a future of implicit obedience to law, always remembering that upon the integrity of its citizens rests the safety of the State."[62]

In his speech the Major was attempting to crack the solid South's efforts to disfranchise blacks, a strategy that was becoming increasingly overt at the time. In maturing, the Major had developed a more tolerant view of blacks than most of his contemporaries, placing him in the liberal wing of the New South movement as described by Paul Gaston.[63] While Henry Grady had been telling his fellow white Georgians that blacks would never be more than domestic servants or unskilled laborers, the Major advocated for training that would allow blacks to make a living wage.[64] A reality of the Southern cotton mill was that blacks were excluded from the textile industry or, if employed, worked outside the factory in unskilled jobs such as cleaning the cotton and loading materials onto rail cars for shipping.[65] Historian Lewis Nicholas Wynne notes that "industrialization was to be the exclusive domain of whites; there was no place for blacks."[66] The Major may have been an exception. Only anecdotal information about the initial hiring practices of the Bibb Manufacturing Company remains, but from its earliest days, the Major had what was referred to by the *Macon Telegraph* as a "black attaché" in the factory, who had once defended the Major's life in an altercation with a knife-wielding employee. At the Bibb Mill No. 2 in Macon, three black men were in charge of the critical responsibility of maintaining the steam engines that powered the mill and starting the engines each morning, evidence that he employed some blacks in more than

---

[61]Ibid., 23.

[62]Ibid., 24.

[63]Gaston, *New South Creed*, 143.

[64]Davis, *Henry Grady's New South*, 134; Ida Young, Julius Gholson, and Clara Nell Hargrove, *The History of Macon, Georgia* (Macon: Lyon, Marshall & Brooks, 1950) 415.

[65]"The Southern Textile Industry," part 3, *Work 'n' Progress: Lessons and Stories in Southern Labor History*, GSU Library Research Guides, Georgia State University Special Collections and Archives, accessed 23 July 2014, http://research.library. gsu.edu/WorknProgress.

[66]Lewis Nicholas Wynne, *The Continuity of Cotton: Planter Politics in Georgia, 1865–1892* (Macon: Mercer University Press, 1986) 91.

the menial, dirty jobs to which most were relegated.[67] Both Grady and the Major held the view common to most Americans of the period that whites were superior to blacks, but the Major differentiated himself from most of his Southern peers by encouraging blacks to become skilled laborers. Whereas Grady thought that blacks should be "pinned to the soil,"[68] the Major thought advancement for both poor whites and poor blacks could be achieved through factory labor, which the Major saw as an important contribution to the American way of life that would bring improved economic conditions to the people of Georgia. This support manifested itself in his encouraging black and white chapters of the Knights of Labor to organize in his factories and his push for the training of blacks to be more than tenant farmers.[69]

The Major was also supportive of the women who worked in his factory. In 1891, when an article about Southern female mill workers written by Clare de Graffenried portrayed them in an unflattering light, he came to their defense in what became known as the De Graffenried Controversy. As an investigator for the U.S. Bureau of Labor, de Graffenried was given the assignment to write an article about "wage-earning women and children."[70] De Graffenried, a Georgia native, penned an article titled "The Georgia Cracker in the Cotton Mills," which was published in the well-known *Century Magazine*. The article was unflattering to the mill owners and employees alike and "was cited as an authoritative statement of the condition of southern textile workers" by the Northern press.[71] It received criticism from a wide array of journals in the South, including the *Manufacturers' Record* and the *Wool Hat,* a Georgia Populist party paper; both of these publications disputed de Graffenried's claims. One of de Graffenried's most disturbing characterizations of the mill women described them as being morally loose and taken advantage of by lazy and shiftless men. She described the living conditions as "whole families huddled together

---

[67]"Difficulty in East Macon," *Telegraph*, 11 September 1878, p. 4; "A Horrible Fate," *Macon (GA) Weekly Telegraph*, 6 May 1881, p. 8.

[68]Mills B. Lane, ed., *The New South: Writings and Speeches of Henry Grady* (Savannah: Beehive, 1971) 102.

[69]Young, Gholson, and Hargrove, *History of Macon*, 415.

[70]LeeAnn Whites, "The De Graffenried Controversy: Class, Race, and Gender in the New South," *Journal of Southern History* 54/3 (August 1988): 449.

[71]Ibid.

irrespective of sex or relationship," adding that "moral distinctions are unknown."[72] The Northern mill industry feared its loss of domination and was bolstered by the Northern papers that seized on the article and spread it widely in an attempt to discredit the Southern mills.[73] The Major refused to let de Graffenreid's characterization of the mill women stand without refutation. For this he turned to Rebecca Latimer Felton. It was the Major's contention that a response to de Graffenried's article should come from Felton because "it seems appropriate that this work of a woman should be undone by one of her own sex, not to say state."[74]

Felton and her husband had led a movement of Independent Democrats in the late 1870s and early 1880s when the Major owned the *Macon Telegraph* and opposed Alexander Stephens's run for the governorship. Although the Major didn't support their political ambitions, including the Independent movement and Rebecca Felton's work with the Georgia Woman's Christian Temperance Union, he nonetheless hoped she could help him to right what he considered an injustice to female mill workers. In a letter to her, the Major admitted that the extreme cases illustrated in de Graffenreid's article might exist in some places, but that "these exceptions do not represent either the conditions for which southern mill owners are responsible, nor the moral conditions prevailing among the operatives, most of whom are virtuous, and a large percentage intelligent."[75]

Felton was more than willing to do battle in the press for the women of the Georgia mills; as she stated to an audience of mill workers in Roswell, "I was willing and ready before I was requested to reply to these unjust— untrue—and ungenerous statements."[76] She wrote her rebuttal to *Century Magazine*, but the magazine declined to publish it, describing her arguments as merely opinions without weight.[77] With more than half of Georgia's mill operatives working in Augusta, Felton published her article in the *Augusta Chronicle* instead. She defended the mill women as "industrious, honest,

---

[72]Ibid., 451.

[73]Ibid., 455.

[74]J. F. Hanson to Rebecca L. Felton, 14 April 1891, Rebecca Latimer Felton papers, ms 81, Hargrett Rare Book and Manuscript Library, University of Georgia Libraries (hereafter cited as Felton papers).

[75]J. F. Hanson to Rebecca L. Felton, 3 March 1891, Felton papers.

[76]Whites, "De Graffenried Controversy," 456–57.

[77]Ibid., 457.

virtuous, well behaved, law-abiding and God-fearing," refuting the claim by de Graffenried that they were "too indolent to dress modestly and too indifferent to moral law to seek a divorce before exchanging husbands."[78] Her arguments, while genuine and heartfelt, were supported by little concrete evidence. However, the *Augusta Chronicle* substantiated Felton's statements by conducting interviews with "local mill superintendents, school teachers and ministers" who backed up her sentiments with, in the paper's words, "actual facts."[79]

Ninety-seven years later, historian LeeAnn Whites published an article titled "The De Graffenried Controversy: Class, Race, and Gender in the New South" that confirmed the Major's and Felton's assessment of the female worker in Georgia mills as honest, industrious, and virtuous. Whites's research of the Georgia mill industry in the 1880s demonstrates that families stayed together, disputing de Graffenried's appraisal of mill families as degraded. The 1880 census data for Augusta shows that of the 364 mill-working households only three were listed as single-parent homes with a child or two. Further, only six women were listed as married while living without husbands, and sixteen divorced women were living in the community, most with their family of origin. Whites disputes de Graffenried's contention that the mills contributed to the dissolution of the family structure: "the census data indicates the remarkable extent to which the family persisted as the basis of social organization in the community." She notes that of all the mill-working households in the city, only two were "entirely composed of nonkin members."[80]

Whites describes the Major's reaction to de Graffenried's article and his motives for coming to the defense of his female mill workers as an act of "paternalistic noblesse oblige," an appraisal that could be applied to the Major's management style as a whole. In addition to allowing the Knights of Labor to organize inside the Bibb, he supported the labor movement by advocating in the halls of the legislature for a shorter workday, and he spoke many times on the subject of elevating the status of the laborer in the eyes of the public. He recognized that in some Southern states the mill owners were not as good to their employees—or "operatives," as he called them—"where

[78]Ibid., 458.
[79]Quoted in Ibid.
[80]Ibid., 459.

long hours, poor pay, and 'pluck me' stores enforces a system of abject slavery upon the poor mill operatives."[81] In contrast to the "pluck me" stores, where employees' pockets were figuratively plucked by avaricious mill owners, the Bibb company store was more genial. The Major paid his workers in cash so that the money could flow back into the community. Many textile operations paid their workers in scrip that was good only at the company store, where the mill owners controlled the prices. In further evidence of the Major's more generous employment practices, at one time during a mill shutdown of seven or eight months, the mill workers continued to make purchases at the Bibb commissary. When the mill went back into operation, the workers were concerned about the huge debts they had incurred, which would take years to repay. When the situation was brought to the Major's attention by one of his supervisors, the Major immediately wrote an "order to wipe out every account on the books against them."[82] Harry Stillwell Edwards, after the Major's death, wrote of the Major's relationship with his employees: "Hanson's hold upon the laboring classes has always been a very strong one. They understood each other perfectly and their confidence in him was perfect."[83]

While the Major defended female mill workers and labor unions, and advocated for enfranchisement for blacks, it was his zeal for a high protective tariff coupled with his lobbying for broader economic opportunities for Southern industry that would launch him into the national spotlight, where he could more effectively advance his goals for the South and for the nation as a whole.

---

[81]Ibid.

[82]"One Act of Major Hanson's Kindness Not Forgotten," *Telegraph*, 18 December 1910, p. 8.

[83]Harry Stillwell Edwards, "John F. Hanson—The Man," *Telegraph*, 18 December 1910, p. 6.

9

THE NATIONAL STAGE

Four hundred years ago a man was wandering about the capital of
Spain asking assistance from the government to enable him to extend
its riches and glory and power....He was called a subsidy beggar...but
his persistence and patriotism succeeded and America was discovered
from the deck of a subsidized ship.

—J. F. Hanson

BY THE LATE 1880s the Major had earned a reputation in Georgia for being
an outspoken leader in the industrial community—one who held strong
opinions about the financial policies of the United States, advocated for
improving trade with Latin America, and urged the establishment of a merchant marine. His determination to create a healthy climate for business began to garner attention from the highest circles of the Republican Party. As
a result, men of influence within the party offered the Major opportunities
to take various leadership roles in shaping national and international policies
with regard to trade and other areas of American commerce. At the dawn of
the new decade, the Major would find himself serving on the first Pan
American Conference and on the executive committee of the International
Monetary Commission while also becoming a confidant of one of America's
most popular presidents. These opportunities allowed the Major to influence
decisions made by the federal government that he believed would stimulate
further economic progress in the South and in the nation as a whole.

In spring 1889, two months after his Augusta and New York speeches,
the Major's call to expand trade relations with Latin America was heard in
the White House. President Benjamin Harrison asked the Major to serve as
a delegate to the First International Conference of American States to be
held in Washington, D.C. Commonly referred to as the Pan American
Conference, it was the first gathering of its kind to bring North and South
American nations together to discuss trade, communications, transportation,

and other commerce issues.[1] The Senate confirmed the Major's nomination on April 3, 1889, "after a short fight made against him by certain Democratic Senators" who had accused the Major of being a mugwump, a term used at the time to refer to someone who had abandoned his party.[2]

The idea for a Pan American Conference was first proposed by James G. Blaine, in 1882, when he was serving as secretary of state during the Garfield administration. Garfield's assassination and the subsequent change in cabinet ministers made by his successor, Chester A. Arthur, prevented the idea from coming to fruition. But Blaine never gave up, reviving the concept when he became secretary of state once again, under President Harrison. One of Blaine's reasons for convening such a conference was to improve economic relations with Latin America.[3] In Blaine the Major had found a kindred spirit. The Major had also been speaking about the need for U.S. commercial interests to cultivate markets outside the U.S. and for subsidies for American shipping, most recently in his speech before the Augusta Exposition in 1888. The Major saw that the enormous costs of international shipping and steamship service hindered their development in the United States. As he had told his audience, "It is folly for us to anticipate that private capital will afford us facilities which in other countries it is found cannot be secured except by Government aid."[4]

When the Major arrived at the conference, he was already well educated about foreign markets and international trade, having researched the topics extensively. He was a member of the American Shipping and Industrial League and had served as a delegate to its annual convention in Washington, D.C., in January 1889.[5] The organization represented the shipping and manufacturing interests of America's top industry leaders and served to educate, promote, and advocate for a stronger merchant marine

---

[1]"At the Capitol Today, Nominations in the Senate," *(Washington, DC) Evening Star*, 30 March 1889, p. 5.

[2]"The Senate's Work Ended," *New York Times*, 3 April 1889, n.p.; "Editorial Glimpses," *Milledgeville (GA) Union & Recorder*, 9 April 1889, p. 6; "Nominations under Fire," *Macon (GA) Telegraph* (hereafter cited as *Telegraph*), 2 April 1889, p. 1.

[3]James Gillespie Blaine, *Foreign Policy of the Garfield Administration: Peace Congress of the Two Americas* (Cambridge, MA: Harvard University, 1882) 1.

[4]"A Most Significant Speech," *(New York, NY) Tariff League Bulletin* 2/24 (14 December 1888): 277.

[5]"American Shipping League," *(Washington, DC) Evening Star*, 30 January 1889, p. 5.

and enlarged shipping opportunities for American vessels. It is hard to imagine a period when American shipping lines did not ply the global waters, but at the time of the Pan American Conference very few American flags were seen flying from ships in foreign ports. U.S. trade exports were almost nonexistent. In 1860, more than 65 percent of America's imports and exports were carried in American ships, a number that had dropped to less than 10 percent by 1890. This decline coincided with the rise of the industrial age in America, the growth of the mining industry, and the development of the American railroad system, which proved to be more profitable for investors than the high seas.[6]

In addition to the American Shipping and Industrial League, the Major was a founding member of the Spanish-American Commerce Union, having attended its organizational meeting in New York on March 29, 1889, only days after being nominated as a delegate to the Pan American Conference. The Commerce Union represented bankers, manufacturers, and merchants in the mutual interest of stimulating trade between the United States and Latin America. Two other delegates to the Pan American Conference, Charles R. Flint and Cornelius Bliss, both from New York, were founding members of the Commerce Union as well.

The Major was on the forefront of the war for trade expansion and was leading an uphill battle that he wouldn't give up. Knowing that the job of promoting international trade is an important role of the secretary of state, the Major also presented his arguments to Secretary of State Blaine in a seventeen-page letter.[7] The letter, written in July 1889, reveals a man who had made a thorough study of American and foreign commerce. In it, the Major quoted statistics from foreign consular reports and State Department records as well as the book *Our Merchant Marine* by Charles S. Hill of Washington, a resource on which the Major relied to bolster his push for foreign steamship subsidies.[8]

---

[6]Harold Underwood Faulkner, *American Economic History*, 5th ed. (New York: Harper & Brothers, 1924) 642.

[7]"Duties of the Secretary of State," U.S. Department of State, accessed 20 November 2014, http://www.state.gov/secretary/115194.htm.

[8]John F. Hanson to James G. Blaine, 20 July 1889, RG 43, Records of U.S. Participation in International Conferences, Commissions, and Expositions, National Archives and Records Administration, Washington, DC.

The Major's letter focused on the imbalance of trade between the United States and other nations and how it might be overcome. Among the statistics he quoted, the value of manufacturing in the U.S. at the time was over five billion dollars, but only 2 percent of that value reached foreign markets, according to a State Department study completed in 1888. In a breakdown of these figures, the Major determined that "our unsatisfactory sales to Spanish America constitute the weak point in our foreign commerce...and...our failure to export our manufactures is the most serious result of our foreign commerce, as it affects domestic conditions." At the time the Major wrote his letter, the United States paid ninety million dollars in gold annually to Latin America because of the trade imbalance, reflecting the fact that the U.S. imported more from these countries than it exported to them. The Major suggested that the United States could solve this imbalance by "improving our inadequate and uncertain means of communications" through improved mail and transportation facilities to be on a par with Germany, France, and England, whose trade with Latin America far exceeded that of the United States. The Major's research into European superiority in the export of manufactured goods revealed that their success was made possible by the subsidies paid by those nations to their shipping industries, which made it "impossible for American merchants to compete with European merchants for this trade. Hence, the trade upon which our steamships must rely for patronage to make them profitable, or even self-sustaining cannot be established." He also suggested in his letter that an American silver dollar be established as the preferred coinage of the Americas. According to the Major, "the Latin American merchant who buys goods in Europe is forced to pay for them in gold or its equivalent, for which he pays a premium of about 30% in silver." By establishing a separate currency, which the Major called an international American silver trade dollar, U.S. products would be 30 percent cheaper than European goods. The Major was optimistic about the success of a silver coinage act, maintaining that most of the Latin American states, as "large producers of silver," were interested in sustaining its value.[9] The Major was also aware that it would please American silver producers and banks in the West. His thorough knowledge on issues of American foreign commerce would be an important asset to the conference.

---

[9]Ibid.

The Pan American Conference convened in Washington, D.C., at the State Department, on the morning of October 2, 1889. Attendees were divided into committees, each tasked with analyzing specific issues involved in developing a stronger relationship between North and South America. The committees included Communication on the Atlantic, Communication on the Pacific, Railway Communications, Customs Regulations, Patents and Trade Marks, Sanitary Regulations, Weights and Measures, Extradition, Banking, International Law, and General Welfare. The Major was assigned to the Committee on Communication in the Gulf of Mexico and Caribbean Sea, whose purpose was to recommend actions that would improve trade in the gulf ports.[10] The committee members discussed such topics as the lack of postal and cable communications and the need for government subsidies for increased steamship service. Experts addressed the committee while other groups, such as the Chicago Board of Trade and several chambers of commerce, submitted reports with suggestions for improving their ability to more cost effectively ship from Southern ports than they were able to do from New York.[11]

In reporting the activities of the conference delegates, the *Evening Star* of Washington, D.C., described the Major, who hosted a dinner at the Arlington Hotel for twenty conferees, as "very popular with his colleagues."[12] The *New York World* called him "the handsomest man in the Pan American Congress…a tall, well-built man, in the prime of life and wears a military moustache and imperial" and that he dressed "more like a New Yorker than a Georgian." Among the frivolity, the *World* painted a vivid picture of the Southerner in reporting that the conference attendees called the Major "Mr. Hansom."[13]

At the conclusion of the business sessions, the Major drafted "The Report on Communication on the Gulf of Mexico and the Caribbean Sea."[14] He summarized his committee's findings, recommending that mail and

---

[10]"Pan-American Congress: A Full List of Committees Announced Today," *(Washington, DC) Evening Star*, 13 December 1889, p. 6.

[11]Committee on Communication on the Gulf of Mexico and the Caribbean Sea, p. 11, RG 43, A1 11, box 1, National Archives and Records Administration, Washington, DC.

[12]"Social Matters," *(Washington, DC) Evening Star*, 24 February 1890, p. 15.

[13]*New York World*, quoted in "The Big Week," *Chronicle*, 30 November 1889, p. 4.

[14]"The World's Markets: A Southern Man's View," *Telegraph*, 16 January 1898, p. 1.

passenger transport be improved and that subsidies to build ships be granted by the various countries in the Gulf region.[15] In a summation of all the committee reports, nineteen recommendations emerged from the conference, including many of the Major's ideas, such as an intercontinental railroad, subsidies to steamship lines, and the establishment of an American coin.[16]

As an outcome of the Pan American Conference, Blaine was able to secure reciprocity agreements between the United States and eight Latin American nations and Spain.[17] These agreements resulted in reduced tariff duties on items exported from those countries to the United States and reduced the duties on American imports to those same countries. Although a high-tariff advocate, the Major felt that the reciprocal agreements were an equitable arrangement for both the United States and its trading partners. President Harrison was impressed by the Major's report and, in a message to Congress, referred specifically to his recommendations for government subsidies for American shipping.[18]

Eighteen countries participated in the Pan American Conference, laying the foundation for what is today called the Organization of American States, or OAS, which has been in continuous operation since that first conference. Many of today's reciprocal trade agreements, extradition treaties, and arbitration agreements with Latin America arose from this original meeting and forged "a shared system of norms and institutions."[19] Shortly after the conference, Representative Henry Bacon of New York introduced the International American Bank Bill in the House to incorporate an international bank to stimulate trade among the participating countries, naming the Major as one of the commissioners along with Andrew Carnegie of Pennsylvania, Cornelius Bliss of New York, and Marshall Field of

---

[15]International American Conference, *Reports and Recommendations, together with the Messages of the President and the Letters of the Secretary of State Transmitting the Same to Congress* (Washington, DC: Government Printing Office, 1890) LCCN 01023417.

[16]Pan American Union, *Fifth International Conference of American States: Special Handbook for the Use of the Delegates* (Washington, DC: Government Printing Office, 1922) 6–8.

[17]"Blaine and Pan Americanism," U.S. Department of State, accessed 5 January 2015, http://future.state.gov/when/timeline/1866_timeline/blaine_pan_amism.html.

[18]"The World's Markets," *Telegraph*.

[19]"Our History," Organization of American States, accessed 8 January 2015, http://www.oas.org/en/about/our_history.asp.

Chicago, among others.[20] Although this effort failed, the initiative was realized sixty-seven years later, in 1959, under the Organization of American States with the formation of the Inter-American Development Bank.[21]

With his speech to the American Protective Tariff League and his service to the Pan American Conference, the Major was developing a reputation that drew him increasingly to the national stage. So it was no surprise when in spring 1891 he was invited to address the largest and most influential gathering of his career at another dinner in New York for the American Protective Tariff League, an organization on whose board of managers he now served.[22] The venue, however, was not Delmonico's. Instead, he would be speaking to five hundred protectionists—the who's who of the national Republican Party—in the banquet hall of Madison Square Garden. The Major was seated at the head table among an influential group of men: Cornelius Bliss, the evening's master of ceremonies and one of the nation's most successful industrialists; Vice President Levi P. Morton; Congressman William McKinley from Ohio, the keynote speaker; and Senator Nelson W. Aldrich from Rhode Island and Secretary of the Interior John W. Noble, both leaders of the Republican party.[23] It was clear from the invitation to speak that the party leadership held the Major in high regard and expected him to enlarge the influence of the Republican Party in the South.

The Major was given an opportunity that few Southern industrialists of his time were afforded: to speak on national issues to the most influential people of the majority party in Congress and the White House. He was given the following topic to address: "The New South, the Effect, and

---

[20]"The International American Bank," *(Washington, DC) Evening Star*, 30 January 1892, p. 6; Ida Young, Julius Gholson, and Clara Nell Hargrove, *The History of Macon, Georgia* (Macon: Lyon, Marshall & Brooks, 1950) 334; Pan American Union, *Fifth International Conference: Special Handbook*, 6–8; Thomas B. Paton, ed., *Journal of the House of Representatives of the United States, 1892* (Washington, DC: Government Printing Office, 1893) Index, p. 8.

[21]"History of the Inter-American Development Bank," IADB website, accessed 24 March 2015, http://www.iadb.org/en/about-us/history-of-the-inter-american-development-bank,5999.html.

[22]"Report of the American Protective Tariff League Banquet," *American Economist* 7/18 (1 May 1891): 273.

[23]"The Tax Eaters' Banquet," *New York Times*, 30 April 1891, n.p.; "The Protective Tariff League Dinner," *New York Herald-Tribune*, 20 April 1891, p. 3.

Destined to Become the Bulwark of Protection." He began by telling his audience how difficult it was to be a protectionist in the South. "I occupy a peculiar position, as I am without home, or party, or section in this question. The doctrines expressed here tonight are doctrines that I have to maintain in the face of great opposition."[24]

The Major continued by praising the progress of the United States, declaring that the country was living in "the golden age of the Republic" and regaling his listeners with a litany of facts and statistics to support this claim. He also praised the principle of protection, which he felt contributed to the fact that American labor was "regularly employed...better paid...and live[d] better than the labor of any other country," making the United States the "greatest manufacturing nation of the world." As always, he didn't employ sectional rivalry but rather linked the success of Southern manufacturers to their counterparts in the North: "We are beginning to understand that the iron interests of Alabama and Pennsylvania, and the cotton manufacturing of Georgia and Massachusetts, must stand or fall together."[25] In defense of the 1890 McKinley Tariff Act, which established an average import duty of 50 percent on foreign products, the Major criticized those who had misrepresented both "its purposes and its effects," causing people to rush to purchase foreign and domestic goods for fear of a large spike in prices once the law passed. Regarding the outcome of the law, the Major told his audience that "if the testimony of merchants in the columns of the daily press are to be credited, goods have declined instead of advancing, and are cheaper now than prior to the enactment of this law," an opinion not shared by all.[26]

As one of the Southerners who wore the mantle of leadership on the issue of foreign trade, the Major couldn't resist lobbying his captive audience to recognize the need for government subsidies to the American shipping industry to foster a strong merchant marine and expand overseas markets for American manufacturing. In addition to his typical fact-based arguments, he also looked to the nation's history to reinforce his point, comparing subsidies for the shipping industry to the voyage of Christopher Columbus by noting that "four hundred years ago, a man was wandering about the capital of

---

[24]"Tariff League Banquet," *American Economist*, 273.
[25]Ibid.
[26]Ibid.

Spain asking assistance from the government to enable him to extend its riches and glory and power.... He was called a subsidy beggar...but his persistence and patriotism succeeded and America was discovered from the deck of a subsidized ship." He challenged this influential group "to commemorate the close of the fourth century of American civilization by recovering control of a commerce that belongs to us by reason of geographical and political associations."[27]

Many more toasts and speeches were given that evening, but the most rousing applause came when Congressman McKinley rose to speak on protectionism as America's preferred policy of both raising revenue for the government and protecting American industry, a position he carried with pride after having successfully passed the McKinley Tariff Act into law. At the end of McKinley's speech, Chairman Bliss closed out the toasts by stating, "The man whose name was a household word in America would be triumphantly elected Governor of Ohio next Fall"—an exclamation followed by three more cheers.[28] After serving in Congress since 1876, McKinley was staging a run for the Ohio governorship.

Wanting to be sure that Bliss's toast came true, the Major became one of McKinley's campaign voices in Ohio, speaking at rallies and encouraging Ohioans to vote for him. McKinley was keenly aware of the Major's position on the protective tariff and recognized him as one of the strongest protectionist voices in the South, having frequently consulted the Major when framing his tariff legislation.[29] McKinley could not have had a stronger campaign supporter than the Major.

The Major often began his Ohio stump speeches by admitting that he was a native Georgian who had fought for the Confederacy, and then declaring that as a Georgia manufacturer doing business with Ohio, he felt that he was an Ohio businessman as well. This never failed to make him an appealing figure to his audiences. The Major was candid about his switch from the Democrat Party, stating that after Cleveland had become a free trader, "no man who entertained the views I had, and desired to maintain the integrity and best interests of the country, could conscientiously vote for Mr. Cleveland." In describing one of the Major's campaign speeches, the

---

[27]"Tariff Talk," *Philadelphia Patriot*, 30 April 1891, p. 1.

[28]"Tax Eaters' Banquet," *New York Times*.

[29]"Hanson's Chances Are Good," *Atlanta Constitution* (hereafter cited as *Constitution*), 13 December 1896, p. 16.

Cleveland Leader deemed it "one of the best Republican speeches that has ever been heard in this city."[30]

After having worked with McKinley on his tariff legislation and vigorously campaigning for him for the Ohio governor's seat, a race in which McKinley prevailed, the Major and McKinley had become good friends. According to the *American Economist*, which commented on the Major's willingness to campaign for McKinley, "The strong personal and political friendship thus cemented endured unbroken until the death of President McKinley in 1901."[31]

After serving two terms as Ohio's governor, McKinley was poised for a run at the White House, and he chose Marcus Alonzo Hanna as his campaign manager. Hanna was a longtime friend who had managed McKinley's bid for Speaker of the House in 1889, a campaign he lost to Thomas Brackett Reed of Maine.[32] As part of his presidential campaign strategy for McKinley, Hanna encouraged the formation of the National Association of Manufacturers in order to support the Republican Party's agenda of industrial growth for the nation and to increase support for the party in areas like the South that were solidly Democratic.[33] The National Association of Manufacturers promoted ideas and laws that would benefit manufacturing on a national scale.

With his firm ideas about market growth and the protective tariff, the Major was a perfect candidate to become a member of this new association. Working with Hanna during the McKinley campaigns for governor had afforded the Major an opportunity to get in on the ground floor of the organizational meetings of the fledgling association. On January 23, 1895, the Major met with a convention of organizers in Cincinnati to discuss its formation. He was chosen as a regional vice president and helped formulate its objectives: "the extension of domestic and foreign markets, reciprocal tariffs, the Nicaragua Canal, expansion of the merchant marine, and

---

[30]"A Southern Orator," *Cleveland (OH) Leader*, 28 October 1893, p. 8.

[31]"Major John F. Hanson of Georgia," *American Economist*, 30 December 1910, p. 319.

[32]Herbert David Croly, *Marcus Alonzo Hanna: His Life and Work* (New York: Macmillan Company, 1912) 150.

[33]Cathie Jo Martin, "Sectional Parties, Divided Business," *Studies in American Political Development* 20/2 (Fall 2006): 160.

expansion of waterways," most of which the Major had long advocated.[34] By its 120th anniversary, in 2015, the National Association of Manufacturers had become the leading advocacy group for U.S. manufacturing interests, representing eleven thousand manufacturers and twelve million producers of American-made products.[35]

One year after the initial meeting of the National Association of Manufacturers, Hanna organized an informal trip to Thomasville, Georgia, renting a beautiful Victorian home there as a winter retreat and unofficial headquarters for a Southern campaign strategy session. McKinley made plans to join Hanna in February 1896, although ostensibly he was traveling to South Georgia for his wife's health.[36] The Major, aware of the trip to Thomasville, invited McKinley to stop in Macon. McKinley, reluctant to appear as though he were campaigning, replied, "Would it not be better for you to join me at Macon and run over to Thomasville with me? I cannot get the consent of my mind to do anything that places me in the position of seeming to seek an office and anything I might say or do would be at once interpreted as an effort in that direction."[37]

At McKinley's invitation, then, the Major became a participant in McKinley's Southern campaign strategy. He withdrew his offer to have McKinley come to Macon and instead met with him when he stopped to spend a night in Atlanta. The Major was among those who attended an informal gathering at the Aragon Hotel in Atlanta, arranged by Hanna, for men of the party who wanted to meet Governor McKinley and pay their respects. Political scholar Olive Hall Shadgett speculates that more than merely socializing with McKinley, the Major was one of the men with whom Hanna and McKinley conferred on their stop in the Gate City.[38] From Atlanta the Major went on to Thomasville to spend more time with

---

[34]Ibid., 166.

[35]"Why Join the NAM?" National Association of Manufacturers, accessed 26 January 2015, http://www.nam.org/Membership/Benefits/.

[36]Lucian Lamar Knight, *A Standard History of Georgia and Georgians*, vol. 3 (New York: Lewis, 1917) 1289.

[37]William McKinley to J. F. Hanson, 27 February 1896, reel 16, McKinley Papers, Manuscript Division, Library of Congress, Washington, DC.

[38]Olive Hall Shadgett, *The Republican Party in Georgia from Reconstruction through 1900* (Athens: University of Georgia Press, 1964) 130.

McKinley, helping to formulate his campaign strategy for the 1896 presidential election.[39]

The Major's contribution to the plan was to ensure that McKinley received as much support from Georgia as he could personally muster. To accomplish this, the Major became involved in state Republican politics for the first time. The field that year contained numerous candidates in addition to McKinley. Speaker of the House Thomas Reed eventually became McKinley's strongest contender for the party's nomination, but Matthew Quay, Republican "boss" of Pennsylvania; Levi Morton, the New York governor and a former vice president; and several others had thrown their hats into the ring.[40] The Major's main objective was to make sure that a majority of Georgia delegates chosen to attend the national Republican convention in St. Louis would cast their votes for McKinley. The national Republican Party was just as anxious for the Major to play a significant role at the state level, not only as a delegate at the convention but also as a recruiting tool. The Republicans hoped the Major would attract other Southern businessmen who were disenchanted with the Democratic Party. According to Shadgett, it was the McKinley wing of Georgia Republicans that was most interested in seeing the Major rise to prominence in the Georgia party; she contends that the "party planned to push the new recruit as fast and as far as possible to make political capital of his prestige and prominence in order to attract to the party other men of the same type."[41]

Many in the party thought that the Major would bring national credibility to the Southern wing of the party if he represented Georgia as a delegate. The *Atlanta Constitution* weighed in on the matter, describing the Major as "one of the brainiest men in the south, a man of high social and commercial standing, and a gentleman of culture and fine appearance. He will be the most prominent man in the St. Louis convention from the south."[42] Serving as a delegate is a prestigious role in the party and not one usually offered to a neophyte such as the Major. Shadgett notes that "the effort to promote a newcomer to such a position of leadership met with bitter opposition," and a "backlash against his candidacy as a delegate

---

[39] Ibid., 126.

[40] "It's the Field against McKinley," *Constitution*, 23 February 1896, p. 14.

[41] Shadgett, *Republican Party in Georgia*, 130.

[42] "Buck and Hanson," *Constitution*, 23 March 1896, p. 3.

developed quickly."[43] Black party leader William Pledger declared "violent warfare against Major Hanson" as a possible delegate, claiming that "they will leave nothing undone to defeat him; that he is a usurper in the ranks of republicanism and they swear to have his scalp before the state convention."[44] White party leader Alfred E. Buck was surprised to see Pledger coming out against the Major because Pledger had been an early supporter of his admission into the inner circle of the state Republican Party, and "especially since he [the Major] is the friend of the black man."[45]

The press, in its zeal to cover the Major's entrance into Republican politics, also got ahead of itself in promoting him as anything other than a newcomer to the process. The *Constitution* reported that the party would be nominating the Major as the next Republican candidate for governor and that even "among the colored politicians...sentiment has crystallized in favor of Major Hanson and there is no doubt but that he will be their choice if he permits his name to be used."[46] The *American Economist* concurred on the Major's fitness for office: "He is a man of the highest character and courage, of the finest executive ability, and would make Georgia one of the best Governors she ever had." Still, the journal did speculate on the Major's willingness: "We don't believe he [the Major] would care to lead the forlorn hope of a Republican campaign against the Georgia Democracy."[47] The Major put it in even stronger terms when he told a *Savannah Morning News* reporter that he "cared nothing for the governorship and would not have the office if he could get it."[48]

By the time the state convention met on April 29, district delegates had been selected, leaving only the four delegate-at-large positions to be filled. In a contentious forum, a slate consisting of Buck, the white leader of the party, and three black delegates was presented and elected. Black party members felt this configuration represented their majority within the party.[49] And thus the newcomer to the state political process, who many thought

[43] Shadgett, *Republican Party in Georgia*, 130.
[44] "Factions Are Fierce," *Constitution*, 21 February 1896, p. 5.
[45] "Fierce Fight Will Follow," *Constitution*, 22 February 1896, p. 7.
[46] "Major Hanson for Governor?," *Constitution*, 25 February 1896, p. 5.
[47] "A League Defender Named," *American Economist*, 31 January 1896, pp. 55–56.
[48] Quoted in "Hanson Not in It," *Constitution*, 26 February 1896, p. 3.
[49] Shadgett, *Republican Party in Georgia*, 133.

was the best person to represent Georgia at the St. Louis Convention, was not chosen to attend.

Being excluded from the convention was of no consequence to the Major. He hadn't entered state politics for his own aggrandizement. His only interest in the process was to secure Georgia's delegates for McKinley. The *Savannah Tribune*, a black-owned newspaper, printed the contents of a letter from the Major written to Buck in May after the Major had learned that some in the party were upset that he had not been made a delegate. In it, the Major stated, "I beg to assure you that personally I am more than satisfied with the situation, as I wanted something done to prevent a contesting delegation, and that would secure the largest practicable number of McKinley delegates."[50] About the Major's reaction, Shadgett writes, "Although rejected by the party at the state convention and, to all appearances, 'sold out' even by the men who had been most diligent in seeking his acceptance, the Macon man evidently understood the political facts of life in Georgia and was willing to continue in the effort to build up the party in the state."[51] More pointedly, the Major was less interested in party politics at the state level than he was in cracking the solidity of the Southern Democratic Party.

Despite being overlooked as an official delegate, the Major was asked to attend the National Convention in St. Louis to serve as one of Buck's "chief lieutenants." Then, when one of the delegates became ill, the Major was asked to cast his vote for him, serving as a delegate after all. The party also called on the Major to help coax delegates to vote for McKinley, and he successfully converted a number of delegates to the McKinley camp with the result that the Georgia delegation cast twenty-two votes for McKinley and two each for Quay and Reed.[52] When on June 18, 1896, William McKinley received his party's nomination for president, one of the many congratulatory telegrams sent to McKinley came from the Major in which he told McKinley simply, "I am with you to the end."[53]

On July 25, at a secret meeting of the Georgia central committee convened in Macon, an all-white slate of electors was chosen to cast Georgia's votes for president in the Electoral College, including the Major

---

[50]"Major Hanson," *Savannah (GA) Tribune*, 16 May 1896, p. 2.
[51]Shadgett, *Republican Party in Georgia*, 134.
[52]Ibid., 132.
[53]"Rush on Canton Wires," *New York Times*, 20 June 1896, n.p.

and Confederate General James Longstreet, a longtime Georgia Republican. Although it was not unusual to have an all-white slate, a black man would usually have been included as a matter of policy. For that year's Electoral College, however, Pledger had convinced the black committeemen to accede to the all-white slate as he had been informed that "Northern Republicans thought it would secure accretions from the Democratic Party."[54]

Shortly after he was chosen as an elector, the Major was asked to speak at a meeting of the Georgia Republicans in Rome to officially ratify McKinley's nomination. Because the Major and other Republicans of the day perceived some in the Democratic Party to be working with socialists and anarchists, the Major tried to show that the Republican Party was the party of the people who wanted good, honest government, not radicalism, and made one of the most stunning declarations heard from a white man in Georgia politics:

> I had rather trust the government of my state and the country, the interests of my children who are to live after me, to the Negroes of Georgia and the South than trust them to the forces that [John Peter] Altgeld controls and leads, and for whom the Democratic platform speaks. The Negro is not a socialist; he is not an anarchist, he is not an enemy of property, or capital, or money.... [H]is ambitions point to a fireside and a home that he may call his own. I thank God in the interests of my country, and in the negroes' behalf, that thousands of them are property owners. Where this is the case they plead for the best men for office and for good government. Shall I refuse to do my duty to the country because the Negro is true to the country? No, I will vote with the negro when he votes right, and will refuse now and here after to vote with the white man when he votes wrong. I do not prophesy, but the time may come when the Negro will constitute the great conservative element in southern politics.[55]

In referencing John Peter Altgeld, the Major was referring to the governor of Illinois, who was considered to be a radical Democrat with socialist leanings.[56] It was the Major's opinion that the Democrats of Georgia had more to fear from the radical socialist influence on the

---

[54]Shadgett, *Republican Party in Georgia*, 135.

[55]"Major Hanson's Stirring Speech," *Savannah (GA) Tribune*, 22 August 1896, p. 2; Clarence A. Bacote, "Negro Office Holders in Georgia under President McKinley," *Journal of Negro History* 44/3 (July 1959): 218.

[56]See Waldo R. Browne, *Altgeld of Illinois: A Record of His Life and Labor* (New York: B. W. Huebsch, 1924).

Democratic Party than from the influence of blacks on the Republican Party. The Major's interest in sound fiscal policies at the federal level, which he thought were best represented by the Republican Party, superseded any fear of blacks having a political voice, a concern that drove most Southern voters.

After McKinley received the party's nomination, the Major began campaigning in earnest on his behalf, traveling throughout Georgia speaking on national issues, particularly sound money—an issue over which the two parties were in opposition and one that emerged as the pivotal issue of the 1896 campaign. "Sound money" was the term used by the McKinley ticket to describe the policy of using the gold standard for U.S. currency. McKinley actually preferred a policy of bimetallism, which supported the unrestricted currency of both gold and silver, but his advisors urged him to commit to the gold standard, which became part of the Republican Party platform presented at the St. Louis convention.[57]

The Coinage Act of 1873 had demonetized silver, placing the United States de facto upon the gold standard, along with most of the Western world. This act hurt banks in the Western U.S. that were heavily invested in silver; it also had a detrimental effect on the silver mining industry and reduced the supply of money.[58] Over time, with the increased productivity of the United States as a whole and a reduction of currency in the marketplace, the price of goods declined while the value of the dollar increased. This helped those who were invested in dollar-based assets, but it made life difficult for borrowers such as farmers and small-business owners who watched their incomes decline while their debts had to be repaid with money that was now worth more than when they had borrowed it.[59] Financial firms with overseas investments fared much better under the gold standard.

Ultimately, farmers and laborers who were struggling financially wanted a stronger voice in the economic decisions of their collective states. They united in the final decades of the nineteenth century to oppose the strength of the industrialists, forming numerous regional political alliances

---

[57]"William McKinley," The Gold Standard Now, Lehrman Institute, accessed 26 January 2015, http://www.thegoldstandardnow.org/mckinley.

[58]Milton Friedman, "The Crime of 1873," *Journal of Political Economy* 98/6 (December 1990): 1163.

[59]Jean Strouse, *Morgan: American Financier* (New York: Random House, 1999) 304.

to further their aims. A national People's Party, also known as the Populists, emerged from these regional alliances in the early 1890s and tried to win legislative races, sponsoring anti-corporation bills and stronger railroad regulations, among other initiatives. In Georgia the Farmers' Alliance became a dominant political force, controlling the Democratic Party in the state by 1891.[60] By 1892, the Farmers' Alliance in Georgia had become the state People's Party, though it met with limited long-term success as entrenched Southern Democrats were reluctant to leave their party.[61] Those who did switch allegiances, however, came largely from the Democratic Party.[62]

The federal government wasn't indifferent to the problem created by the Silver Coinage Act, and in order to placate the nation's silver interests, Congress had passed the Sherman Silver Purchase Act in 1890, authorizing the government to buy back silver. But when silver rose from $0.98 an ounce to $1.26 an ounce in three years, the buy-back policy caused a serious reduction in gold reserves, prompting President Cleveland to repeal the act and return the United States to the gold standard.[63] Because of this, the Democratic Party abandoned Cleveland and backed William Jennings Bryan as the party's nominee. Bryan stood staunchly for a silver standard and campaigned on nothing else.[64] He also received the support of the Populist Party.

The Major, like McKinley, preferred bimetallism to either a gold or silver standard. In an interview with a *New York Tribune* reporter in May 1896, before the Republican convention in St. Louis, the Major had said, "I do not doubt that the maintaining of the gold standard is going to help the great financial companies and other organizations of a similar character, but I sincerely believe that the best thing for the people is a more extensive use of silver."[65] In the Major's opinion, bimetallism would increase the amount of money in circulation, thereby helping farmers and laborers while also

---

[60]Kenneth Coleman, *A History of Georgia* (Athens: University of Georgia Press, 1977) 223.

[61]Robert C. McMath, Jr., *American Populism: A Social History, 1877–1898* (New York: Hill & Wang, 1993) 160, 148.

[62]Coleman, *History of Georgia*, 223.

[63]Faulkner, *American Economic History*, 505.

[64]Strouse, *Morgan*, 359.

[65]"The McKinley Enthusiasm," *New York Tribune*, 25 May 1896, p. 2.

appeasing big business and overseas markets. He did not see the wisdom of a silver standard, as advocated by Bryan, and instead compromised his personal opinion and supported the Republican platform of a gold standard, to which McKinley was also wed.

The Major was optimistic that the South would show strong support for McKinley, telling a *New York Times* reporter that sound money would likely get "a big vote throughout the South." He expressed frustration with the sound-money Democrats of Georgia, whom he felt would be enough to "carry the state for McKinley if they would only come out and vote. They are still afraid of being 'read out' of the party down there. But that time is passing rapidly, and men will soon vote according to their convictions." Even if he wavered on whether McKinley would carry Georgia, the Major was certain that McKinley would carry several Southern states as well as the nation, telling the reporter that "if I felt that we were going to have four years of Bryan Democracy I should close out and leave the South, for business would be ruined."[66]

The Major campaigned in earnest to promote McKinley in Georgia, and at one of his campaign stops in October he found himself speaking to a rather hostile crowd in Columbus. The Major enjoyed the challenge of trying to convert his audience to his way of thinking, but from the moment he approached the podium he faced hissing, yells, and calls of "Rah for Bryan!" The audience became very annoyed at the persistent heckling and questions, many of which were shouted from the floor in the midst of the speech. But the reporter for the *Columbus Daily Enquirer* noted that the Major was not "disconcerted to any great extent, but made an address which was highly complimented by many."[67]

The Major explained the folly of the opposition's claim that the U.S. economy could sustain a silver policy. In his treatise on the Coinage Act of 1873, renowned American economist Milton Friedman explains, "By 1896 it was too late to undo the damage. Bryan was trying to close the barn door after the horse had been stolen. The gold standard world was entering into an inflationary episode; loosening a flood of silver as money could only intensify inflation in the gold standard countries, while releasing it full force

---

[66]"A Strong Sound-Money Vote" *New York Times*, 10 September 1896, n.p.

[67]"Major Hanson at Opera House," *Columbus (GA) Enquirer*, 30 October 1896, p. 5.

on the United States"—an outcome the Major wanted to avoid.[68] Indeed, referring to Bryan's silver policy, the Major told his audience that a candidate who put it forward as his platform "does not know enough to be made President of the United States."[69]

In an interview with the *New York Tribune* during McKinley's campaign, the Major suggested that the Georgia Populists should align with the Republicans in the state to help carry Georgia for McKinley. Despite the fact that the national Populists were backing Bryan and strongly in favor of silver over gold as the currency standard, the Major felt that the Populists in Georgia were disenchanted with the Democrats and thus might unite with the Republicans.[70] But even though he hoped for an alliance with the Populists to break the solid South, he felt that some of the Populist party's anti-corporation, anti-capital rhetoric was casting a negative light on both manufacturing interests and anyone with wealth. In the Major's opinion, the Populists were trying to divide the country along class lines by placing rich and poor in adversarial roles. In his Columbus speech, the Major had spoken directly to the young men in the audience, telling them that "he had known every degree of poverty and he had found the friendship of the men who possessed money as the most valued." He admonished them to be wary of "demagogues…who always tried to array the poor against the rich"—which is a "grievous wrong"—and emphasized that "the road to success was open to every worthy man of intelligence, sobriety, honesty and industry."[71]

In November, William McKinley was elected the twenty-fifth president of the United States, receiving more Republican votes in Georgia than any Republican candidate had since Reconstruction.[72] The Major had reason to be proud of his efforts in the state, and the Republican Party was most certainly pleased with the Major's influence on voters. With the election of his good friend as president, the Major would find himself in a position of political strength in his state, even though he belonged to a party that had no political influence in Georgia. By December, rumors were flying that he

---

[68]Friedman, "The Crime of 1873," 1177.

[69]"Major Hanson at the Opera House," *Columbus (GA) Enquirer*, 30 October 1896, p. 5.

[70]"McKinley Enthusiasm," *New York Tribune*, 25 May 1896, p. 2.

[71]"Major Hanson at Opera House," *Columbus (GA) Enquirer*.

[72]Martin, "Sectional Parties, Divided Business," 170.

was being considered for a cabinet position, as secretary of the interior.[73] The *New York Tribune* described the Major as one of the strongest contenders from the South for a cabinet position, calling him "a man of uncommon vigor, decided executive ability, very considerable culture, and possessed of a keen knowledge of politics."[74] The *Boston Daily Advertiser* referred to the Major as an "intimate friend of Maj. McKinley, and the latter would like to see him at his cabinet table."[75] The *Worcester Daily Spy* in Massachusetts reminded its readers that the Major first drew public attention when Secretary of State Blaine chose him to be a member of the Pan American Conference, and though he was once a Democrat, "his strong protection ideas forced him to break loose from his old party and to avow himself a Republican." The paper was quick to point out that the Major's change in political affiliation had not cost him the esteem of his fellow Georgians, "who recognize him as one of the ablest and most influential business men, and as an earnest, practical worker for its [the state of Georgia] uplifting on all lines of progress and development."[76] The *Washington Post*, on the other hand, seemed to have no idea who he was: "Every few days the Georgia papers make an effort to thrust a man of the name of Hanson into the McKinley cabinet. Anybody know Hanson?"[77] In fact, the Major was offered a position in McKinley's cabinet, presumably the secretary of the interior, as speculated by the press. Continuing his pattern of refusing invitations to serve in public office, however, he declined.[78]

Although he refused the appointment, the Major's status as an influential Republican meant that the president looked to him to recommend Georgians who could fill federal appointments in the state. The Major specifically recommended only two individuals: Harry Stillwell Edwards as postmaster of Macon and his daughter's father-in-law, Joseph Simpson Garrett, as postmaster of Columbus. President McKinley appointed both. The Major also became embroiled in controversies over several appointments of black Georgians, which were opposed by white citizens because of the race of the appointees. The Major was aware that

---

[73]"Major Hanson Is Indorsed [sic]," *Telegraph*, 8 December 1896, p. 1.
[74]"Cabinet Possibilities," *New York Tribune*, 30 November 1896, p. 1.
[75]"McKinley's Choice," *Boston Daily Advertiser*, 7 December 1886, p. 5.
[76]"Major McKinley," *Worcester (MA) Daily Spy*, 12 January 1897, p. 4.
[77]Quoted in "No," *Charlotte Observer*, 9 February 1897, p. 2.
[78]"Major John F. Hanson of Georgia," *American Economist*, 319.

McKinley had received more white Democratic votes in the South than any Republican candidate had since Reconstruction. He also feared that placing black candidates in public offices would send many white McKinley supporters back to the ranks of the Democrats—which is exactly what happened in some areas, an effect that was contrary to the Major's efforts to crack the solid South.[79] The Major took his concerns directly to the White House and met with the president to discuss several contested black appointments. What resulted was a compromise, with some of the Major's objections to black candidates being rejected by the president while others were upheld, such as the appointment of Judson W. Lyons as postmaster of Augusta. Instead, McKinley offered Lyons the position of "Register of the Treasury" in Washington, which he accepted, much to the relief of the Major. In the end, with the Major's help in Georgia, McKinley appointed more blacks to federal positions than any president before him.[80]

Because so much of the 1896 election had revolved around issues of currency, in January 1897 a monetary convention was convened in Indianapolis at the behest of Morgan and Rockefeller financial interests. It became known as the Indianapolis Monetary Convention. So as not to appear to be a gathering of elite Wall Street financiers, the organizers deliberately chose Indianapolis as the location and invited three hundred businessmen to investigate the banking and currency laws of the United States with an eye toward their revision.[81] Of these three hundred men, the Major was one of fifteen chosen to serve on an executive committee that recommended to the president that a monetary commission be formed to investigate the currency and banking affairs of the United States and laws relating to them.[82] The Major served on the committee along with such prominent men as ex-governor E. O. Stannard, of Missouri; George Foster Peabody, of New York; and John P. Irish, a California Democrat who had broken from William Jennings Bryan to support the gold standard as promoted by the McKinley ticket.

A bill to create the recommended monetary commission was formu-lated later that year, passing the House but dying in the Senate. Rather than

---

[79]Bacote, "Negro Office Holders," 220, 223.

[80]Ibid.

[81]Murray N. Rothbard, *A History of Money and Banking in the United States: The Colonial Era to World War II* (Auburn, AL: Ludwig Von Mises Institute, 2002) 188.

[82]"For Monetary Reforms," *New York Times*, 3 April 1897, n.p.

let the idea die with Congress, the Major and the executive committee created a monetary commission, choosing the delegates themselves.[83] They chose the name Indianapolis Monetary Commission because the idea for it had originated at the large gathering in that city in January. The eleven-member commission was chosen from a cross-section of America's leading businessmen and financiers, many with ties to J. P. Morgan's financial empire.[84]

The Indianapolis Monetary Commission sent out questionnaires to several hundred business and financial leaders across the country, soliciting their opinions on monetary issues. The commission met from October through mid-December 1897, sifting through the questionnaires, writing replies, and collating the information to be published as part of their final report to the executive committee. In January 1898, the executive committee organized a second and final gathering of the Indianapolis Monetary Convention, in Indianapolis. At the convention the report of the commission was ratified and served as a call for banking and monetary reform, including the establishment of a central bank of the United States. Although the report had no authority in its recommendations, many of the changes in banking that were later instituted in the country—at the turn of the century and beyond—had their genesis in the Indianapolis Monetary Commission Report of 1898, including the Gold Standard Act passed on March 14, 1900, which held until President Richard M. Nixon took the U.S. completely off the gold standard in 1971.[85] The commission's work has been described as "the first thoroughly organized movement of the business classes in the whole country directed to the bringing about of a radical change in national legislation."[86]

While the Major was working with the Indianapolis Monetary Commission, he also found time to pursue his principal political objective: to crack the solid Democratic hold on the South. The Major initiated a strategy to bring Populists into the Republican camp, hoping to gain the

---

[83]Robert Taylor, "Currency Reform," *Century* 55, New Series 33 (November 1897–April 1898): 628.

[84]Ibid.; Rothbard, *Money and Banking*, 188.

[85]Charles A. Conant, *The Plans for Currency Reform* (New York: Bankers, 1906) 1.

[86]F. M. Taylor, "The Final Report of the Indianapolis Monetary Commission," *Journal of Political Economy* 6/6 (June 1898): 322.

majority in several Congressional districts.[87] The mid-term Congressional elections were in full swing in 1898, and the Major campaigned for Republican candidates in several Congressional district races in Georgia, contributing five hundred dollars of his own money to the Republican campaign fund.[88] The *Columbus Daily Enquirer* reported that the Major, as a member of the Republican National Committee, recognized that more Republicans than Democrats were registered in the Eleventh Congressional District, in South Georgia, and that he hoped to capitalize on that Republican strength "to break the solid south."[89] The Major campaigned for J. M. Wilkinson, the Republican candidate in the district "making a bold and vigorous attack on democratic principles and policy," particularly with regard to the idea of protection. The Major emphasized the need for protective duties on timber, wool, and Sea Island cotton, appealing to the local economy. To encourage them to join the Republicans in "common cause against the democrats, alluring baits" were dangled before the Populists, financed by the Republican Congressional Campaign Committee, such as promises that delinquent taxes would be paid so that many who had not been able to vote in over ten years would be eligible to do so.[90] In the First and Eleventh Districts, strong black majorities along with Populist strength renewed the Major's hope that Republicans could be sent to Congress from Georgia.[91] However, despite heavy funding from the Republican Congressional Campaign Committee, the First and Eleventh Districts returned their Democratic incumbents to Washington, dashing the Major's hopes of cracking the solid Georgia Democracy in this election cycle.

The most challenging event of McKinley's presidency—and one that would cause him to once again seek advice from the Major—was the United States' war with Spain. Cuba's fight for independence from Spain had been going on for decades, but it wasn't until the sinking of the U.S.S. *Maine* in Havana Harbor on February 15, 1898, that U.S. intervention became a

---

[87]"Maj. Hanson's Idea," *Columbus (GA) Enquirer*, 23 September 1898, p. 5.

[88]"Congressional Contest Rumored," *Chronicle*, 16 October 1898, p. 5.

[89]"Effort to Break the Solid South," *Columbus (GA) Enquirer*, 24 September 1898, p. 5.

[90]"Maj. Hanson's Idea," *Columbus (GA) Enquirer*; "Storm Center Has Shifted," *Columbus (GA) Enquirer*, 9 September, 1898, p. 6.

[91]"Effort to Break the Solid South," *Columbus (GA) Enquirer*.

probability. President McKinley wanted to avoid a war and solicited the Major's opinion on the subject. The Major replied in a telegram to the president: "Our people opposed to war. Have found no man who proposes to go to Cuba to fight. Think they will volunteer very reluctantly. The masses sustain you overwhelmingly."[92] Although the Major and President McKinley both felt that war should be avoided, the president was feeling pressure from the Democrats in Congress to declare war. McKinley sent an ultimatum to Madrid to relinquish its control of Cuba, which resulted in Spain declaring war on the United States; the United States immediately followed with a formal declaration of war against Spain. After just ten weeks, the United States prevailed, in August 1898, crushing the Spanish Empire by wresting control of Cuba, Guam, and the Philippines, casting McKinley in the role of an empire builder.

At the conclusion of the war, McKinley launched a tour of the nation to celebrate and solidify support for the terms of the peace treaty in Paris. The Major had supported McKinley in his efforts to formulate strong protective-tariff legislation, stumped for him in two gubernatorial campaigns, and worked diligently to secure his nomination and election to the presidency. It was a gesture of gratitude to the Major that the president's national tour included a stop in Macon. McKinley's visit was the first by a U.S. president to the city of Macon, and the people were thrilled to receive him, even though, as the press noted, the South had not supported McKinley in the recent elections.

The crowds at Macon's Union Depot and along the sidewalks were estimated to be ten thousand strong, as cheap fares were advertised to bring people into the city. The president and his entourage disembarked from the train into carriages that awaited them at 8:30 a.m. Fifteen carriages in total carried the president and his party to the reviewing stand on Second Street. The president's opening comments addressed the recent war and its successful execution and conclusion. But his most prolonged ovation came when he said, "I congratulate my country on one other fact—we have not only triumphed over our enemy, but we have triumphed over our own prejudices and are now a united country."[93]

---

[92]J. F. Hanson to William McKinley, telegram, 16 April 1898, reel 3, McKinley Papers, Manuscript Division, Library of Congress, Washington, DC.

[93]"Welcomed the Nation's Chief," *Telegraph*, 20 December 1898, p. 1.

A Ladies' Reception Committee greeted the women in the presidential party, and because of the Major's friendship with the president, the committee chose the Major to present Mrs. McKinley with a large bouquet of roses and calla lilies, described by the press as "mammoth and greatly admired by all who saw it." As the parade continued through the streets of downtown Macon, it passed some of the most beautiful homes in the city, which were decorated with patriotic bunting and banners. Many people stood on their porches waving American flags as the president passed by. According to the press, one of the homes that attracted the most attention belonged to the Major. Cora Hanson had made sure that it was patriotically dressed in honor of her husband's good friend.[94] After a brief visit of two and a half hours, the president and his party boarded the train and departed the Union Depot for Augusta, leaving the Major and the city of Macon in their euphoria.[95]

---

[94]Ibid.
[95]Ibid.

IO

NEW INDUSTRIES

I have never done anything in my life that I did not think was for the best interests of Georgia.

—J. F. Hanson

HAVING A FRIEND and business ally in the White House, whose policies he anticipated would create a healthy climate for industrial development in America, gave the Major confidence in the economic future of the nation and fueled his investment strategies into the twentieth century. The Major differed in one fundamental way from the tactical and transactional businessmen and entrepreneurs who were building their own enterprises: his focus. He was developing a structural foundation for growth that would benefit all businesses and their consumers, not just the companies over which he had control. His strategic visions would bring him to the pinnacle of his business career as the leader of four enterprises simultaneously in which he enhanced the mobility of people and products, supplied the energy needs of business and the public, and stimulated the future expansion of manufacturing in the region.

In his optimism about the commercial prospects of the country, the Major launched two new enterprises, both in Columbus: a mill, the largest expansion in the history of Bibb Manufacturing, and a dam and power plant, his entrée into the production of electricity, an industry that was in its infancy at the time. With the rate of industrialization that was occurring in the state, the need for fuel was paramount. Electricity was considerably cheaper than steam power, and while cotton manufacturing was operating with such thin margins, mill owners wanted all the advantages they could secure.[1] Although the Major intended to power his new Columbus mill with

---

[1]"Progress Being Made by the Columbus Power Co.," *Columbus (GA) Enquirer*, 3 March 1898, p. 3.

this hydroelectric facility, his plans also incorporated the future power needs of the city of Columbus and other enterprises in the area.[2]

The Major began these new ventures in 1897 when he investigated a site on the outskirts of Columbus called Lover's Leap that consisted of a series of hills culminating in a high bluff overlooking the Chattahoochee River. The North Highlands Company owned the land and planned to develop the property into a residential community. The Major—along with a minority partner, G. Gunby Jordan of Columbus, who was a Bibb Manufacturing Company board member and a friend—eventually purchased the entire parcel. The site's location along the Chattahoochee made it ideal to house the dam and power plant, with ample land on which to build a large mill. That same year the Major received a charter from the state for the Columbus Power Company, granting him the right to supply "water, light, electricity, heat and power to municipalities, corporations, partnerships and individuals."[3]

The Major and Jordan partnered in the construction of the dam and power plant in 1899. The Major chose William States Lee as the project's chief engineer. Most noted for his work with James B. Duke in 1904 that led to the establishment of Duke Power, Lee credited his success on that project to his earlier work on the Major's facility.[4] Columbus already boasted a power plant that was running the city's streetcars and providing light to homes and businesses, but it was operating at capacity. The Major's new hydroelectric facility would enhance the city's ability to attract more industry to the region. In anticipation of its opening, community boosters capitalized on its potential by making plans to advertise Columbus as "The Electric City of the South" at the upcoming state fair in Atlanta in 1899 so that the city

---

[2]Columbus Historic Riverfront Industrial District, reference no. 78000995, National Register of Historic Places, item no. 8, p. 9; Hydroelectric Power Development North Highlands, survey no. GA-12, Historic American Engineering Record, Historic Preservation Division, GA Dept. of Natural Resources, Atlanta (hereafter cited as HAER).

[3]"In Re. Petition for Charter, Columbus Power Company," *Columbus (GA) Enquirer*, 24 July 1897, p. 3; Columbus Historic Riverfront Industrial District, National Register of Historic Places, p. 9; Hydroelectric Power Development North Highlands, HAER.

[4]Columbus Historic Riverfront Industrial District, National Register of Historic Places, p. 9.

would not "lose such an opportunity to advertise her advantages to the general public."[5]

In addition to planning for the new mill and power plant, the Major purchased the Chattahoochee Knitting Company of Columbus in March 1900 using his own capital, with some portion of the stock also being owned by Jordan. The enterprise had been closed for several years and the equipment sold. The Major purchased the building and resurrected it under the same name for the purpose of making a middle-grade cotton cloth, in contrast to the new Columbus mill, which would be using Egyptian and American long-staple cotton in the manufacture of a higher quality yarn.[6] The Major, who by now had a history of attracting outside investors, demonstrated his willingness to risk his personal capital in the pursuit of his vision, much as he had done in the 1880s when rescuing failing mills and establishing new ones throughout the Middle Georgia region.

Also in March 1900, three years after founding the Columbus Power Company, the Major and Jordan sold the operation to Bibb Manufacturing in exchange for Bibb stock in the amount of $300,000.[7] This placed the Bibb Manufacturing Company in the electric energy business, a strategy that today would be classified as vertical integration: owning the source of power assured the Bibb a steady supply of electricity at favorable rates, thereby reducing costs. The Major continued to be heavily involved in both enterprises. He supervised the construction of both the new Bibb Manufacturing facility, completed in 1901, and the Columbus Power Company dam and hydroelectric facility, completed in 1902, as well as secured contracts to sell power to other businesses, such as the Chattahoochee Falls Co. and the Columbus Railroad Company.[8]

---

[5]"Columbus—'The Electric City,'" *Columbus (GA) Enquirer*, 5 May 1899, p. 4.

[6]"Big Deals Made at Columbus," *Atlanta Constitution* (hereafter cited as *Constitution*), 11 March 1900, p. 6; "Egyptian Cotton for Georgia Mill," *Macon (GA) Telegraph* (hereafter cited as *Telegraph*), 12 June 1901, p. 1.

[7]*History of Bibb Manufacturing Company, 1876–1929* ([Macon]: n.p., 1937) 25–26. There is a copy at Middle Georgia Archives, Washington Memorial Library, Macon, GA.

[8]Bibb Company (Columbus Plant), survey no. GA-12, HAER, p. 1; Columbus Historic Riverfront Industrial District, National Register of Historic Places, p. 9; John F. Hanson and George Johnson Baldwin, correspondence, George Johnson Baldwin Papers, Southern Historical Collection, Manuscripts Department, Wilson Library, University of North Carolina at Chapel Hill.

The new Bibb Manufacturing facility in Columbus was the largest of all the Bibb mills, and in a continuing pattern of noblesse oblige, the Major also constructed a mill village on the North Highlands parcel, much of which is extant today. He commissioned the Atlanta architectural firm of Robert & Co. to design the 101 homes, which were set on forty-foot-wide lots and varied in size with three, four, or ten rooms. Each house was painted white with black trim and had a front and rear porch. The Major also erected a twenty-five-room hotel for women, which is no longer standing.[9] In addition to housing, the Major built a wooden schoolhouse on the Chattahoochee River that was operated by the mill during its first year of instruction; it then became part of the Muscogee County School District.[10] Completed in 1903, the village formed the nucleus of what became known as Bibb City and was incorporated in 1909 in response to Columbus's attempts to annex it.[11] Although mill villages were a common feature of the textile industry, "none of the Columbus mills seem to have attained the influence, nor generated the cohesive community, in evidence at Bibb City," which can be attributed to the Major's interest in establishing a social infrastructure for the benefit of his employees.[12] At its peak in the 1920s, the mill employed 2,500 workers and stood as the largest cotton mill in the United States, operating more than 125,000 spindles in a building that had been expanded to 650,000 square feet.[13] The mill remained active for ninety-six years, closing its doors in 1998.[14]

---

[9]Bibb City Historic District, reference no. 10000037, National Register of Historic Places, pp. 4, 12–13.

[10]Bibb Company, HAER, p. 14.

[11]Ibid.

[12]Ibid., 13.

[13]Columbus Historic Riverfront Industrial District, National Register of Historic Places, p. 9.

[14]Bibb City was incorporated into the city of Columbus in 2000, two years after the mill closed. Sadly, the massive Bibb mill building that was begun in 1900 burned to the ground in 2008. The cause of the fire has not been determined, but the impressive façade and portions of the mill, along with the homes of the original Bibb City village remain as a legacy of the Major's textile empire and contribution to the Southern economy. In East Macon the abandoned Bibb Mill No. 1 stands over the footprint of the original structure (purchased in 1876 by the Major, Newt Hanson, and Hugh Moss Comer), which had been expanded at some point during the Bibb Mill's history. The Major's legacy in Porterdale has fared much better. The extant Porterdale Mill, a National Register property, was converted to residential and retail space in 2006 ("About the Mill,"

Having established the power plant on solid footing, the Major announced at a board meeting of Bibb Manufacturing in January 1906 that he had sold the Columbus Power Company to George J. Baldwin for one million dollars. He had also secured a long-term contract to purchase low-cost electricity from the new owner. Although his association with the power industry had come to a close, the Major's undertaking served Columbus for years to come, becoming a major supplier of wholesale electricity to the city of Columbus.[15] The power plant also served as the catalyst for industrial expansion throughout the region: "The pioneering development of the Bibb dam marked the beginning of the large-scale application of hydroelectric power to textile mills in this area of Georgia and Alabama." Because of the availability of power from the Columbus Power Company, five new mills were built in the city and "all of the existing mills continued to expand through World War II." With the success of the Columbus Power Company, other new hydroelectric projects were initiated and, "within a twenty-one mile stretch north of the Bibb, three more dams were built."[16] The Columbus Power Company's facility was the largest hydroelectric power plant in the South at the time, and the North Highlands dam, as it is called today, still functions as part of the Georgia Power Company.

While overseeing his ambitious plans in Columbus, the Major was forging a leadership role in another industry. Transporting his mill products to the marketplace gave the Major a vested interest in the most exciting corporate enterprise in Georgia at the time: its railroads. In the early 1890s he was given a voice in their operation when asked to serve on the boards of several regional rail lines. Railroads were the key to economic growth in the state, encouraging business and agricultural development along its rail lines. With his extensive business experience, not to mention his influence at the highest levels of state and national politics and his access to outside capital, the Major would have been an attractive addition to any railroad board.

In 1893 the nation was in a stock market panic that precipitated one of the worst depressions in U.S. history. Banks and industrial firms failed, crop

---

Porterdale Mill Lofts website, accessed 19 January 2015, http://www.porterdalemill.com/about.html).

[15]Bibb Company, HAER, p. 3; Bibb City Historic District, National Register of Historic Places, p. 29.

[16]Hydroelectric Power Development North Highlands, HAER, p. 1; Columbus Historic Riverfront Industrial District, National Register of Historic Places, p. 9.

prices already in decline continued to plummet, and railroads were hit particularly hard, resulting in the bankruptcy of seventy-four railroads, one-third of the nation's rail lines.[17] This launched what has become known as the "Morganization" of the railroads. J. P. Morgan was America's banker, a prominent financier who quite literally propped up the American economy with his own wealth and prevented the country's financial bankruptcy several times during the nineteenth and early twentieth centuries. He concluded that consolidation of the railroads was the only thing that could save the nation's track lines from lying fallow. Morgan began buying the railroad lines out of bankruptcy, restructuring their debt, lowering their fixed costs, and consolidating lines for greater efficiency, all of which earned him the title of America's "railroad Bismarck."[18]

The South saw the nation's first Morganization efforts with the reorganization of the Richmond and West Point Terminal and Warehouse Company. This particular conglomerate consisted of rail lines that connected Washington, D.C., Richmond, Atlanta, Birmingham, and New Orleans, including the Central of Georgia, whose stock had been acquired by the company in 1888.[19] The Richmond and West Point Terminal was a prime example of egregious management of a railroad, where owners had sacrificed growth and stability in order to maximize profits. The company's situation also helps to illustrate how government and public distrust of speculators and stock manipulators contributed to the anti-railroad and anti-corporation backlash of the nineteenth century. By 1892, after playing speculative games with their stock, the owners of the Richmond and West Point Terminal found themselves on the verge of bankruptcy and approached J. P. Morgan for help. Through his firm of Drexel, Morgan & Co., Morgan formed the Richmond Terminal Reorganization Committee to financially restructure the company and consolidate all the profitable lines. He then renamed the new consolidated railroad the Southern Railway. The

---

[17]Harold Underwood Faulkner, *American Economic History*, 5th ed. (New York: Harper & Brothers, 1924) 504; Burke Davis, *The Southern Railway: Road of the Innovators* (Chapel Hill: University of North Carolina Press, 1985) 26; Jean Strouse, *Morgan: American Financier* (New York: Random House, 1999) 320.

[18]Strouse, *Morgan*, 320.

[19]Ulrich B. Phillips, "Railway Transportation in the South," in The South in the Building of the Nation, vol. 6, *Southern Economic History, 1865–1909*, ed. Thomas E. Watson (Louisiana: Pelican, 1909) 312.

Central of Georgia Railway was not a part of this restructuring, however.[20] It had been so badly mismanaged that the courts dealt with it separately, placing it in receivership in 1892 with Hugh Moss Comer named as the receiver.[21] The 42,200 shares of Central stock owned by the Richmond and West Point Terminal Company became part of the new mortgage on the Central and were held by the Richmond Terminal Reorganization Committee's stock trustees.[22]

Originally called the Central Railroad and Banking Company when it was founded in the early 1830s, it was renamed the Central of Georgia Railway when it was purchased out of receivership in 1895 by Samuel Thomas and Thomas F. Ryan of New York, who paid two million dollars, of which fifty thousand was paid in cash and the rest financed through consolidated mortgage bonds sold to outside investors.[23] According to Ulrich B. Phillips, the foremost Southern historian in the early twentieth century, the Central of Georgia Railway "emerged [from receivership] as a separate company" in July 1895, financed heavily by first, second, and third income bonds.[24]

The former Drexel, Morgan & Co., now reorganized as J. P. Morgan & Co., purchased $500,000 of the Central's new bonds.[25] With the purchase and restructuring of the Central, Comer was retained as president, and in November 1895 the Central of Georgia Railway sold $15 million in 5 percent, fifty-year bonds in order to pay its old bonded debt and increase the company's capital reserves to make improvements to the road and acquire other railroad lines in the region.[26] J. P. Morgan & Co. purchased $2.5 million worth of bonds in the November offering.[27] However, the days of

---

[20]Stuart Daggett, *Railroad Reorganization* (Boston/New York: Houghton Mifflin, 1908) 179.

[21]"The Central's Fate," *Constitution*, 22 March 1895, p. 8; Carl Snyder, *American Railways as Investments* (New York: Moody, 1907) 140.

[22]Daggett, *Railroad Reorganization*, 176, 187.

[23]Richard E. Prince, *Central of Georgia Railway and Connecting Lines* (Salt Lake City: Stanway-Wheelwright, 1976) 23, 42.

[24]Phillips, "Railway Transportation in the South," 313.

[25]Strouse, *Morgan*, 334; J. P. Morgan & Co. syndicate books, 1:55–56, 1:197–98, 2:151–52, 4:183–84, Morgan Library & Museum, New York.

[26]Snyder, *American Railways as Investments*, 141.

[27]J. P. Morgan & Co. syndicate books, 1:55–56, 1:197–98, 2:151–52, 4:183–84, Morgan Library & Museum.

financial mismanagement by the Richmond and West Point Terminal would haunt the Central well into the first decade of the twentieth century, not only because of its new debt structure, but because the Central had suffered "extreme neglect" under the company's ownership that now required large capital investments to rectify.[28] C. Vann Woodward attributes the precarious financial state of the Central and the "deterioration of the road's physical condition" to the Richmond and West Point Terminal's "scandalous mismanagement."[29]

Before its purchase by the Richmond and West Point Terminal, the Central consisted of over 2,700 miles of track, a portion of which was leased from the Georgia Railroad. The Central lost the lease when it defaulted on its payments while under the ownership of the Richmond and West Point Terminal Company, reducing the Central to 1,520 miles of track. Under Comer's leadership, however, the railroad acquired two additional lines and began the task of modernizing the Central's tracks, engines, and roadbeds.[30]

The purchase of the Central of Georgia Railway also included the Ocean Steamship Company, a wholly owned subsidiary of the Central located in the port of Savannah. The steamship company got its start in 1872 when Colonel William Wadley, president of the Central Railroad and Banking Company of Georgia, purchased the Empire Line with its six steamships and renamed it the Ocean Steamship Company under a charter allowing the company to transport passengers and freight between New York and Savannah. This acquisition connected all of the Central of Georgia rail lines with the city of New York and gave rise to the description of Wadley as "the unquestioned railroad genius of the south."[31] Wadley also purchased 276 acres of the pre-Revolutionary War Vale Royal Plantation along the Savannah River, just north of the city, to use for a terminal for both the railroad and the steamship line.[32] Before the advent of the trucking industry and airlines, rail and water transportation were the only viable

---

[28]Daggett, *Railroad Reorganization*, 180.

[29]C. Vann Woodward, *Origins of the New South, 1877–1913* (Baton Rouge: Louisiana State University Press, 1951) 123.

[30]Prince, *Central of Georgia Railway*, 42.

[31]Edward A. Mueller, *The Savannah Line: The Ocean Steamship Company of Savannah* (New York: Purple Mountain/Providence RI: Steamship Historical Society of America, 2001) 15.

[32]Ibid., 16.

options for moving people and freight. To have a rail line that connected the interior of the Southern region to a major port, and therefore to the world, placed the Central of Georgia Railway in an enviable position as the only rail line with direct access to the port of Savannah. All other railroads had to transfer their cargo onto Central rail cars in order to access the port.[33]

After the newly consolidated Southern Railway was restructured, its stock was placed in the hands of a voting trust, consisting of J. P. Morgan, Charles Lanier, and George Baker, that oversaw operations and appointed Samuel Spencer president. Spencer was an experienced railroad man who had been vice president of the Baltimore and Ohio Railroad and president of the Elgin, Joliet and Eastern. About him the *New York Times* said, "There was no man in the country so thoroughly well posted on every detail of a railroad from the cost of a car brake to the estimate for a terminal."[34] The Southern Railway began to consolidate other railroads in the South; one of its acquisitions was the Georgia Southern and Florida, on whose board the Major was already serving and continued to serve after its purchase. The Major could not have had a better mentor than Samuel Spencer, who has been credited with turning the Southern Railway into a "smoothly functioning regional system" and tripling its profits over a ten-year period.[35]

Amid the growth and reorganization of the nation's railroads, the Major was serving as a director of the Wrightsville and Tennille, the Alabama and West Point, the Western of Alabama, and the Georgia Southern and Florida railroads when, on July 20, 1896, Comer offered him a place on the board of the Central in a simple telegram: "Board of Directors Central of Georgia to be enlarged. You are offered place. Please attend meeting Aragon Hotel Atlanta on Wednesday, twenty second, two o'clock."[36] And with those unceremonious words the Major began a fourteen-year association with the Central of Georgia Railway and the Ocean Steamship Company. For Comer, serving as president of both, it was a natural extension to invite the Major, his business partner in Bibb Manufacturing, to join the board. Having watched the Major direct their

---

[33]Craig W. Kessler (director of breakbulk and bulk operations, Georgia Ports Authority), interview by author, 1 February 2013.

[34]Quoted in Strouse, *Morgan*, 320.

[35]Ibid.

[36]Central of Georgia Railway Collection, vol. 3, 1362AP-55, Georgia Historical Society, Savannah.

manufacturing business and grow it into one of the largest mill operations in the Southeast, Comer knew that the Major would contribute valuable leadership and business acumen—which he did, until Comer succumbed to throat cancer on February 26, 1900. At the age of fifty-eight (two years younger than the Major), one of the South's leading industrialists and financiers was dead. As the Major's most important business ally and financial advisor, Comer had supported the Major's dream of a textile mill in Macon, opened doors for him in the railroad and shipping industries, and supported his growth strategy for Bibb Manufacturing. His death ended not only an important business relationship that had lasted over twenty-five years, but also a friendship that had developed into an almost brotherly affection between the two, an intimacy that is revealed by the fact that the Major was the only non-family member present during Comer's final hours.[37]

The Bibb Manufacturing board immediately elected the Major to take Comer's place as president.[38] He was a majority stockholder, a founder of the business, and its manager for twenty-four years; the choice was a foregone conclusion. The title of president had little effect on the Major's operational control of the business, however. Long before his death, Comer had placed his full confidence in the Major by giving him the reins of the Bibb.

Because of the Major's many years of active service on multiple railroad boards, including the Central of Georgia, leading up to Comer's death, rumors began to circulate that he would be chosen to succeed Comer as the president of the Central of Georgia Railway and the Ocean Steamship Company. Indeed, many of the Major's friends were putting pressure on the board to name him as the successor.[39] However, at the April 9, 1900, board meeting, six weeks after Comer's death, the board elevated Vice President John Egan to the presidency, a move not unexpected within the railroad industry.[40] Egan had been hired some time before the death of Comer to help him with the management of the Central of Georgia Railway. Egan had moved to Savannah from Chicago, where he had held responsible

---

[37]"President Comer Is Dying," *Constitution*, 25 February 1900, p. 1; "Hugh M. Comer Surrounded by His Family Dies," *Constitution*, 27 February 1900, p. 1.

[38]*History of Bibb Manufacturing Company*, 25.

[39]"Many Men Mentioned for Presidency," *Constitution*, 2 March 1900, p. 5.

[40]"Egan Is President of the Central of Georgia," *Constitution*, 10 April 1900, p. 1.

positions with the Northern Pacific and the Canadian Pacific railroads. He was touted as one of the most knowledgeable railroad men in the business and by all accounts was an effective vice president under Comer's leadership.[41] Because Egan was already serving as an officer at Comer's right hand, the choice to promote him was a natural one—but an unusual move by the board shows that its members may have been conflicted. On the same day the board named Egan president, it also created the new position of chairman of the board and appointed the Major to fill it.[42] In this role the Major was given executive powers, while Egan, as president, was responsible for the day-to-day management of the company. Board member—and former editor of the *Atlanta Constitution*—Evan P. Howell described the Major's new function as being the financial head of the system, the same role that Comer had fulfilled. He said that the Major "was closer to Mr. Comer than any man in the state; is well acquainted with the financial condition having served on the executive committee of the board for three years or more. I don't think the directors could have found a safer man for the place."[43] Howell also uttered a warning for the Major with his assessment that the weight of the presidency of the Central of Georgia Railway had contributed to Comer's death: "I believe Mr. Comer would be alive today if he had been relieved sooner of the very heavy load he was carrying."[44] The Major would find that Comer's stress was now his own.

Not long after the Major became chairman of the Central Railway and the Ocean Steamship Company, his son Walter, who had been working at Bibb Manufacturing since graduating from Emory at Oxford in 1885, tendered his resignation and announced that he and his family would be moving to Point Loma, California. The Major and the board had been grooming Walter for the job of president of the Bibb. Walter had a quick mind, recognized leadership and oratory skills, and engineering proficiencies that made him an outstanding candidate to succeed his father at the helm of

---

[41]"John M. Egan Out; Central Railway Loses President," *Constitution*, 23 November 1903, p. 1.
[42]*Fifth Annual Report of the Central of Georgia Railway Company*, 7 September 1900, Central of Georgia Railway Collection, 1362AP-30, Georgia Historical Society, Savannah; "Egan Is President," *Constitution*.
[43]"Central Railroad in Good Condition," *Constitution*, 11 April 1900, p. 7.
[44]Ibid.

the enterprise the Major had spent his whole life building. His son's decision was a grave disappointment to the Major.[45]

After suffering his friend's death and his son's decision to move to California, the Major had more distressing news. On September 6, 1901, an assassin's bullet ended the life of President McKinley while he was visiting the Pan American Exposition in Buffalo, New York, elevating Vice President Theodore Roosevelt to the presidency. Even though the Major had lost a political friend, he did not lose his position as the go-to man for patronage in Georgia. The *Atlanta Constitution* announced on December 27, only three months after McKinley's assassination, that the Major was being chosen as President Roosevelt's "advisor and referee" in Georgia.[46]

With his many corporate responsibilities, however, the Major was left with little time to concentrate on anything else. He was never as involved in politics after the death of President McKinley, a blow from which it would be difficult to recover. But most importantly, he had little time in his schedule for political stumping. He controlled nine mills, a railroad and steamship line, and a power company that all required his constant attention. Official site visits, board meetings, and travel to New York to meet with agents and investors filled his days, not to mention the day-to-day management of each enterprise.

Comer had inherited a railroad that had suffered from years of neglect. Although he had placed the Central of Georgia on a more profitable footing and began the task of modernizing the line before he died, much still needed to be done once the Major became chairman. He wasted no time in continuing Comer's acquisition strategy by purchasing four rail companies in 1901—three smaller interstate lines and the Chattanooga, Rome and Southern Railroad—which provided those cities with direct access to the port of Savannah for the first time.[47] The Major's strategy for improving the Central was an aggressive one. In one year he had purchased twice as many rail lines as Comer had in the five years he served as president. The Central's expanded reach allowed it to become less dependent on feeder railroads that were at risk of being undercapitalized and unreliable.

---

[45]"Suit for Divorce," *Telegraph*, 15 September 1909, p. 7.

[46]"Republicans to Meet Saturday," *Constitution*, 27 December 1901, p. 10.

[47]"Central Gets the Road," *Telegraph*, 2 June 1901, p. 9; "New Road Opens a New Territory," *Constitution*, 30 June 1901, p. 4; Prince, *Central of Georgia Railway*, 4, 43.

With the acquisitions made by Comer and the Major, traffic on the Central of Georgia increased considerably, presenting a challenge to the Central's neglected and outdated infrastructure. A report commissioned by J. P. Morgan during reorganization of the Richmond and West Point Terminal Company had recommended replacing the "light and ineffective" engines in use on Southern rail lines, which had gradually been replaced in other parts of the United States.[48] By the close of 1901, the Major had purchased eleven new engines; five were placed on the Birmingham division, and the other six were used on the Savannah-to-Atlanta passenger run.[49] The new and heavier engines would allow the Central to pull longer trains and move more freight per trainload, thus improving efficiency, but they also created their own problems for the Central. The Southern roadbeds had been laid with little or no ballast or aggregate beneath, which allowed the rails to sink under the weight of the trains and made it difficult to transport goods with the new generation of locomotives. Solid roadbeds were replacing the older beds in the rest of the United States, but this upgrade had not been done on the Central lines when it was purchased out of receivership. Many of the rails in the South were iron and needed to be replaced with modern steel rails, increasing the number of improvements the Major needed to make.[50] By 1904 the Major would acquire thirty-three freight locomotives and five passenger locomotives as well as erect new depots along the line, reinforce bridges, and fill in forty-five trestles.[51]

As chairman of the board of the Central, the Major became involved in another project at the beginning of the century that would enhance passenger travel through Atlanta and make a significant contribution to the city's architectural environment for seven decades. In 1901, during the administration of Governor Allen D. Candler, the Georgia state legislature appropriated $500,000 and a parcel of state-owned land for the construction of a new railroad terminal in Atlanta, providing it met with the approval of the railroads. At the time Atlanta was the most active railroad terminus in the South, and a new terminal was badly needed. The Southern Railway, Central of Georgia, Western and Atlantic, and Seaboard Airline all expressed an interest in the new terminal. Governor Candler requested that

---

[48]Daggett, *Railroad Reorganization*, 180.
[49]"Eleven New Engines for Central," *Constitution*, 18 December 1901, p. 5.
[50]Daggett, *Railroad Reorganization*, 180.
[51]"Central of Georgia," *Telegraph*, 30 August 1905, p. 4.

the railroads communicate with him in writing their desire to be part of a terminal built on the land offered by the state.

The Major wrote to the governor that in his opinion the site was too small to accommodate the needs of the railroads going in and out of Atlanta and "would be just as inadequate ten years from now as the present depot facilities are today." The Major also stated that the financial terms being offered by the state were not appealing to the railroads. It was his recommendation that the railroads should decline the offer made by the state. Samuel Spencer, president of the Southern Railway, echoed the objections of the Major. The representatives of the other two railroads were willing to accept the site offered by the state, but the Major remained firm in his belief that the site was inadequate.[52]

Without the unanimous approval of the railroads, the state legislature could not proceed, opening the door for private enterprise. The Major wasted no time in getting involved in the construction of what would be one of the most beautiful public buildings in Atlanta's architectural history, Terminal Station. In January 1903 the Southern Railway and Central of Georgia Railway formed the Atlanta Terminal Company and requested a charter from the state to build a railroad terminal in Atlanta. The Major visited a potential site in the city with his friend Captain James W. English, with whom he had served in the Civil War. English had recently purchased a large tract of land in downtown Atlanta, and on a cool day in February, officials from the railroads made a site inspection and approved the English property for the new terminal. English was named president of the Atlanta Terminal Company and oversaw the construction of Terminal Station.[53] Architect P. Thornton Marye, who designed the Fox Theater, among many other commercial and residential buildings in Atlanta, was commissioned to design the station.[54] Marye's work resulted in a structure of "towered and arcaded Renaissance revival language that calls to mind the Beaux-Arts

---

[52]"Central Road Will Accept Depot Plan but under Protest," *Constitution*, 8 February 1902, p. 1.

[53]"Depot Company Will Organize," *Constitution*, 23 January 1903, p. 9.

[54]"Spencer and Party Greet Citizens, State and City Officers," *Constitution*, 16 October 1903, p. 1.

tradition of the late Victorian era," which belied the innovative reinforced-concrete infrastructure beneath.[55]

On May 14, 1905, Terminal Station, the magnificent railroad gateway to Atlanta for passengers and freight, opened to the public amid much fanfare. English arranged for the Sixteenth U.S. Infantry Band to attend. With visible pride in his accomplishment, and with his "Panama Hat in hand," English threw open the doors of the terminal and led the band into the building, receiving a grand ovation. From the building's telegraph station English sent the first telegram to Samuel Spencer and the second to the Major. Both telegrams declared, "The Atlanta Terminal is now open to the public. The people of this section and those who enter Atlanta's gates owe you and the Central of Georgia and the Atlanta and West Point Railroads an everlasting debt of gratitude."[56] The strength and foresight of the Major's vision served the city well. The terminal hosted travelers and received goods from Georgia and the Southeast for over sixty years, until 1971, when it was torn down to make way for the Richard B. Russell Federal Building.[57]

While making needed improvements to the Central, the Major was also mindful of the upgrades necessary for the Ocean Steamship Company to remain competitive. The steamships in the line did not have the modern advances that were available, such as double bottoms for safety, and only two ships had triple-expansion engines for improved efficiency. In addition, many of the competing lines were upgrading their passenger quarters to make them more luxurious, a market in which the Ocean Steamship Company wanted to remain competitive. The Major took on the task of modernizing the line by making significant overhauls to existing ships and adding new vessels to the fleet.[58]

The Major's first newly commissioned ship, the *City of Memphis*, was launched in February 1902. It had a double-bottom steel hull and a triple-expansion engine. The ship was able to carry fourteen thousand tons of

---

[55] *New Georgia Encyclopedia*, s.v. "P. Thornton Marye (1872–1935)," by Robert M. Craig, last modified 4 June 2013, http://www.georgiaencyclopedia.org/articles/arts-culture/p-thornton-marye-1872–1935.

[56] "Palatial Doors of Depot Swing Open Today," *Constitution*, 14 May, 1905, p. 41; Franklin M. Garrett, Atlanta and Environs, vol. 2, *A Chronicle of Its People and Events, 1880s–1930s* (Athens: University of Georgia Press, 1969) 477.

[57] *New Georgia Encyclopedia*, s.v. "P. Thornton Marye."

[58] Mueller, *Savannah Line*, 119.

cotton, doubling the capacity of the previous ships in the fleet, and had a cold compartment for perishables. This new vessel allowed the Major to compete favorably with the four other shipping companies in the port of Savannah.[59] While the Major was supervising upgrades to the fleet and the launch of the *City of Memphis*, he was also overseeing construction of the power plant and cotton mill in Columbus and upgrading the Central of Georgia Railway, a testament to his executive management skills, energy, and breadth of focus.

Soon after the christening of the *City of Memphis*, the board of the Central of Georgia Railway asked for Egan's resignation as president of the Ocean Steamship Company, ostensibly to allow him to concentrate more fully on his job as president of the Central and to separate the operation of the two companies "as much as it is practicable to do so."[60] With Egan's resignation, the Major became president of the Ocean Steamship Company. But a spirit of dissatisfaction was evident in Egan's letter of resignation, in which he stated, "I regret very much the course that matters have taken."[61] A possible rift between the two men was made known to the public in April 1903 with this headline in the *Atlanta Constitution*: "Hanson Said to Back Effort to Oust Egan."[62] The Major denied any such friction in an interview in New York, in which he stated, "I cannot imagine how such an idea started. We are in thorough accord."[63] Adding to the speculation, an unnamed friend of the two men was said to have witnessed the Major and Egan in Savannah "spending the entire day together and appearing to be the best of friends."[64]

In his efforts to make improvements to the enterprises he controlled, the Major needed strong financial investors who could provide access to capital. Courting investors and cultivating new board members was part of a chairman's responsibilities. To that end, the Major entertained wealthy New York investor James A. Blair of Blair & Co. in his private railroad car in Atlanta in late April 1903. The Major's car was luxuriously appointed and

---

[59]Ibid.

[60]"Egan Resigns Presidency," *Constitution*, 4 June 1902, p. 5.

[61]John Egan to Samuel Spencer, SRHA, LMS 2003.009 Box 121 Folder 5068, Southern Museum of Civil War and Locomotive History Archives, Kennesaw, GA.

[62]*Constitution*, 7 April 1903, p. 8.

[63]"Hanson Denies Friction Talk," *Constitution*, 8 April 1903, p. 5.

[64]Ibid.

served as a traveling office, providing all the elegance and privacy the Major needed when meeting with potential investors. Blair & Co. was an investment banking firm that had other railroad investments in its portfolio, and Blair was a New York millionaire interested in making investments in the South, and specifically in the Central of Georgia Railway. The Major was solicitous of Northern capital for his businesses and was also interested in building a more diverse board for the Central.[65]

In the fall, after witnessing the America's Cup yacht race aboard the *City of Savannah*, the Major received good news.[66] His meeting with Blair had borne fruit. After the October board meeting of the Central of Georgia, the Major announced that Blair would be joining the board of directors. The position would most likely come with an infusion of capital as well. The board also announced that all differences between the Major and Egan had been resolved.[67] Nonetheless, Egan tendered his resignation to the Major in November, seven months after the press had first reported a rift between the two men.[68] With Egan's departure, the board elected the Major president of the Central of Georgia Railway.[69] The board also voted to abolish the position of chairman, which had been created expressly for the Major more than three years earlier.[70]

By 1903 the Major was in complete financial and operational control of the Central of Georgia Railway and the Ocean Steamship Company. Within two years of his ascension to the presidency, the Major commissioned three more ships for the Savannah Line: the *City of Macon*, the *City of Columbus*, and the *City of Atlanta*, following the tradition of naming the ships after Southern cities.[71] Each ship was christened by an ingénue from that city accompanied by city dignitaries, with each young lady receiving a

---

[65]"Railway Notes," *Constitution*, 25 April 1903, p. 2.

[66]"Excursion Fleet at Race," *New York Times*, 23 August 1903, n.p.

[67]"Two New Faces on Directorate," *Constitution*, 13 October 1903, p. 3.

[68]"John M. Egan Out," *Constitution*.

[69]"Major J. F. Hanson, President Central," *Augusta (GA) Chronicle* (hereafter cited as *Chronicle*), 8 December 1903, p. 9.

[70]"Election of Hanson and Kline Unanimous," *Columbus (GA) Enquirer*, 9 December 1903, p. 7.

[71]"City of Macon Launched," *Constitution*, 15 March 1903, p. 31; "The City of Macon Launched," *New York Times* 15 March 1903, n.p.; "'City of Atlanta' Launched at Chester," *Telegraph*, 1 May 1904; "Christening of the City of Columbus," *Columbus (GA) Ledger*, 3 February 1904; Mueller, *Savannah Line*, 126.

diamond and gold watch engraved with a lifetime pass for the steamship line. For the christening of the *City of Atlanta*, in a departure from the custom of presenting a diamond-encrusted gold watch, Jenny English, daughter of the Major's good friend James English, received a Tiffany locket inlaid with diamonds attached to a diamond pendant and engraved with a lifetime pass.[72]

With the launch of the *City of Atlanta* in 1904, the Savannah Line was now being served by four large steel double-hulled beauties with capacities for cold storage and cargo that far surpassed those of the fleet's older ships.[73] Business in the port of Savannah was vigorous in both passenger and freight service. The port ranked third in the nation in cotton shipping and first in the shipment of naval matériel.[74] To further capitalize on the port's vitality, the Major would launch the *City of Savannah* in 1907 and two more vessels, the *City of St. Louis* and the *City of Montgomery*, in 1910.[75] This would bring the number of ships commissioned by the Major to seven in eight years, expanding the ability of Georgia's products and passengers to reach the East Coast and beyond.

Under the Major's leadership, the Ocean Steamship Company had become one of the most modern fleets on the Atlantic, with passenger service that was second to none. So successful had the Ocean Steamship Company become that in 1907 the Major would receive an offer to purchase the company from Charles Morse of New York, who was in the process of building his own shipping conglomerate. Morse's proposal was quite tempting, being larger than the combined value of the steamships, the port properties, and other assets, but the Major, after consulting with the board, declined.[76]

Fuel was critical to the Major's enterprises, in terms of his having both a constant, dependable supply and the ability to purchase it at the lowest prices that he could negotiate. The single largest operating expense for the Major in his transportation companies was fuel, not unlike transportation companies of today. He was already powering his railroad engines with

---

[72]"Miss Jennie English Who Christened Ship Presented with Diamond Locket," *Constitution*, 1 May 1904, p. 4.

[73]"New Ships Mark Era of Growth," *Telegraph*, 26 May 1909, p. 4.

[74]Mueller, *Savannah Line*, 119.

[75]Prince, *Central of Georgia Railway*, 36.

[76]Mueller, *Savannah Line*, 131, 141.

Alabama coal and had been powering his mills with it as early as 1887, when he joined an investment consortium to build a more expedient rail line between the coalmines around Birmingham and the city of Macon.[77]

The Ocean Steamship Company, however, fueled its ships with Pennsylvania coal stored at the company's bunkers in New York. At the turn of the century, while developing hydroelectricity to power his mill in Columbus and other industries in the region, the Major began to investigate the feasibility of using Alabama coal for his steamships. The efficiency of Alabama coal as compared to Pennsylvania coal would determine its cost effectiveness, including the logistics of transporting the coal to its point of consumption. As a test, in August 1901 the Major powered the northbound vessels out of Savannah with Southern coal. If this experiment was successful, the Major announced, he would close the ship's bunkers in New York and establish a coaling station at the wharves in Savannah.[78]

Alabama coal did indeed prove to be a more cost-effective substitute, and the Major transitioned to using nothing but Alabama coal for virtually all of his businesses. The Central of Georgia Railway additionally benefitted from this arrangement as the transporter of the coal.[79] Because his fuel consumption and transportation costs were high, the Major had the foresight to purchase the Gulf Coke and Coal Company, headquartered in Mobile, Alabama, for $1.25 million on behalf of the Central of Georgia Railway, in association with the Pratt Coal and Iron Company of Birmingham, in July 1906.[80] The acquisition included a 17,000-acre vein of coal, thus securing for the Central of Georgia Railway, the Ocean Steamship Company, and the Bibb Manufacturing Company their own source of coal. Not unlike his move into hydroelectric power, the Major's ownership of a coal mine is an example of vertical integration that gave him access to a reliable power supply at reasonable rates.[81] It would take another nine years from the day the first steamship had sailed with Alabama coal in its belly,

---

[77]"On to Birmingham," *Macon (GA) Weekly Telegraph*, 29 March 1887, p. 5.

[78]"Ships to Coal at Savannah," *Constitution*, 28 August 1901, p. 2.

[79]*Fourteenth Annual Report of the Central of Georgia Railway*, 31 July 1909, p. 7, Central of Georgia Annual Reports, 1362AP-30, Box 3, Georgia Historical Society, Savannah.

[80]"Maj. Hanson Buys Vast Coal Mines," *Columbus (GA) Ledger*, 6 July 1906, p. 1.

[81]"Major Hanson Buys Vast Mines," *Telegraph*, 6 July 1906, p. 1.

but in June 1910, the Major's dream of a coaling station for the Ocean Steamship Company in the port of Savannah came to fruition.[82]

In the Major's diverse efforts to enhance the industrial prosperity of Georgia he found himself facing a rising tide of sentiment against the very entities he represented. The strength and power of America's large corporations had fueled the economic growth of the nation during the late nineteenth century, but in some cases it had also fostered predatory pricing and reduced competition. Discontent with big business had contributed to the rise of the progressive or reform era in politics in the late nineteenth century, and in the early twentieth century it led to increased political and government intervention in business. The largest corporations in Georgia were its railroads, and the early years of the reform movement in the state were characterized by virulent anti-railroad rhetoric, with Georgia Populist Thomas Edward Watson being one of the loudest voices.

Watson was a practicing lawyer from Thomson and a master of rhetorical oration, which he used to great effect in defining the plight of farmers, with whom he sympathized.[83] As one of the wealthiest lawyers in the state, Watson owned more than three thousand acres in McDuffie County, land that was worked extensively by tenant farmers.[84] He disliked the movement toward industrialization in the South, and although his occupation as a lawyer precluded him from joining the Farmers' Alliance in Georgia, it did not prevent him from becoming the state's leading advocate for the Populist cause. He was elected to Congress as a Populist in 1891, and he ran against Democrat Charles Crisp of Georgia for Speaker of the House, upsetting many in the Democratic Party with his third-party leanings. His oratorical strength and passion for the Populist cause won him the party's nomination as vice president of the United States in 1896, and he was nominated as its presidential candidate in 1904.[85] In sympathy with the farmers, and particularly with the difficulty they faced in managing the high

---

[82]*Fourteenth Annual Report*, Georgia Historical Society, p. 7.

[83]Ferald J. Bryan, *Henry Grady or Tom Watson? The Rhetorical Struggle for the New South, 1880–1890* (Macon: Mercer University Press, 1994) 63–69.

[84]Robert C. McMath, Jr., *American Populism: A Social History, 1877–1898* (New York: Hill & Wang, 1993) 128–29, 157–58.

[85]*Biographical Directory of the United States Congress*, s.v. "Watson, Thomas Edward," accessed 23 February 2015, http://bioguide.congress.gov/scripts/biodisplay. pl?index=w000205.

cost of shipping their products, Watson became convinced that public oversight of the railroads was a necessity, describing railway executives as "railroad kings who shamelessly violate the penal statutes."[86]

Political sentiment in Georgia reflected the growing national antipathy toward American conglomerates, which resulted in Congress passing the Sherman Antitrust Act of 1890 to discourage corporations from forming trusts and monopolies. The law was rarely applied until the early twentieth century when presidents Roosevelt and Taft became more aggressive in prosecuting corporations.[87] In February 1902, much to the disappointment of the Major, President Roosevelt announced that he would prosecute J. P. Morgan for violating the Sherman Act with his Northern Securities Company, a consolidation of several large corporate interests.[88] The Major sympathized with Morgan; after all, without Morgan's capital investment in the Central of Georgia Railway, the company might not have survived. The Major saw Morgan's investment in the Central as an investment in Georgia and its development. As one who had not only lived through the wave of industrialization fervor in the South but carried its mantle, the Major was concerned for what he saw as a dangerous backlash against the corporations that had advanced the economy of his state and nation and provided jobs to millions who would otherwise have been unemployed.

An invitation to speak at a banquet hosted by the Atlanta Chamber of Commerce in spring 1903 gave the Major a venue to address the rising public hostility toward corporations. He spoke in the dining room of the Kimball House, along with a number of the state's business and political leaders, among them Samuel Spencer, Governor Joseph Terrell, G. Gunby Jordan, and Evan Howell, now the mayor of Atlanta.[89] In his talk the Major examined his accomplishments and how they had affected the fabric of his state. He candidly admitted that during the course of his lifetime "it has fallen to my lot to advocate policies that were not in favor with the people of this state." He explained that he had not had sinister motives, stating, "I have never done anything in my life that I did not think was for the best

---

[86]McMath, *American Populism*, 128–29; Thomas E. Watson, *The Life and Speeches of Thomas E. Watson* (Nashville: printed by author, 1908) 64.

[87]George Bittlingmayer, "Antitrust and Business Activity: The First Quarter Century," *Business History Review* 70 (Autumn 1996): 363–64.

[88]Strouse, *Morgan*, 440.

[89]"Eloquent Talks at Big Banquet," *Constitution*, 18 February 1903, p. 1.

interests of Georgia." In speaking about policies antithetical to the population, the Major expressed his apprehension. He described the economic progress of Georgia since the Civil War as having been "accomplished by a departure from her old methods, by breaking away from the traditions that have bound her," referencing the transition from agrarian roots to industrialization and the rise of the modern corporation. It was the Major's contention that the time had again come for Georgia to look to the new wave of American industrialism, which was the conglomerate form of corporations—or "the joining together of corporations," as he described it— as a pathway for success. He asserted that businesses joined forces "not because they make more money, but because of the protection of capital.... the world today is towards the combinations of corporations. The principal reason is that it perpetuates the invested capital." He implored his audience, "Why are you opposing the very forces that are advancing the world?"[90]

The Major was growing weary of government intrusion in corporate affairs. He had begun his career as an industrialist in a laissez-faire atmosphere in which business was conducted with little or no government regulation. During his lifetime he saw the implementation of a state railroad commission, the Interstate Commerce Act, and the Sherman Antitrust Act, and he would soon see the railroads of Georgia under the additional control of a newly formed public-utility commission. As government increasingly placed its hands around the throat of big business, investment capital dried up and the value of railroad companies declined. The Major told his audience that the Ocean Steamship Company needed to further upgrade its fleet to meet growing demand and that he didn't know where that money would come from "if the oppression that is now being directed toward the railroads is extended to steamship lines."[91]

In this anti-corporate climate the state legislature introduced the Houston Bill, in 1903, which would prohibit factories from employing children under the age of twelve. Four years earlier the Major had spoken out against similar legislation, which eventually failed.[92] In a reversal of his support of a child labor bill in 1887, when he went on record stating that outlawing child labor would be "wise and humane," the Major now saw the

---

[90]Ibid.

[91]"Hanson Said War Waged by Roosevelt Destroyed One-Fifth of the Values," *Telegraph*, 13 October 1907, p. 1.

[92]"Child Labor Bill," *Telegraph*, 10 November 1899, p. 2.

Houston Bill as an attack on the autonomy of the corporation rather than an instrument for the betterment of the children of Georgia. The Major argued against the bill on behalf of the Georgia Industrial Association, stating that as written it "would transfer parental responsibility to the mill and parental authority in the government of children to the state."[93] Although great economic strides had been made since the Civil War, the Major argued that economic circumstances for a certain segment of Georgia's population had not improved in the last twenty years. He explained that families, particularly those headed by single mothers, often needed their children's wages to survive, stating that "the cause of child labor was poverty and that the remedies proposed are impractical and inadequate." The Major made it clear that mill owners were neither encouraging nor in favor of child labor, but he also thought that the legislature should not play a role in regulating their operations.[94] The Major had clearly abandoned the moral high ground on which he had stood in the 1880s as an advocate for a child labor law in Georgia, but he viewed this bill as an opening salvo that would eventually lead to the regulation of the textile industry. His experience with such a heavily regulated industry as the railroads had given the Major a perspective he hadn't had in 1887.

Populist Party leader Tom Watson testified in favor of the Houston Bill.[95] In rebutting the Major's testimony, Watson sarcastically denounced him as being interested only in protecting his capital investments and made repeated derogatory references to him as a Republican. The attack's personal nature spurred the *Macon Telegraph* to print what it considered the other side of the issue. While stating that it was not the newspaper's "purpose or desire to defend Maj. Hanson [as he] is able to take care of himself," the *Telegraph* published what could only be described as a defense of the Major's character. The paper said that it understood Watson's support for the child labor bill but could not understand why he assaulted the manufacturers of Georgia with inflated statements, accusing them of "impoverishing the farm…and…blighting the prosperity of the farmer."[96] The *Telegraph* invited Watson to come to Macon and "go among the poor and he will find that Major Hanson has done his full share towards alleviating their conditions by

---

[93]"Cotton Mills and Child Labor, *Telegraph*, 30 June 1903, p. 3.
[94]Ibid.; "Child Labor Bill Strongly Urged," *Telegraph*, 7 July 1903, p. 6.
[95]"Child Labor Bill Strongly Urged," *Telegraph*.
[96]Ibid.

giving them employment. It would be interesting to compare Mr. Watson's weekly contributions to this cause with that of Maj. Hanson's." The paper also took exception to the fact that the Major was being criticized for being a Republican, a charge that the *Telegraph* described as "Mr. Watson's long suit, but we believe we tell the truth of history when we say that Mr. Watson has given the Democratic party more trouble in Georgia than Maj. Hanson," in a fine barb aimed at his Populist Party leadership. The paper concluded by stating that the Major is "an honored citizen of this city, and The Telegraph feels that this much by his home paper is due him."[97] When the Houston Bill came to a vote in July 1903, it was defeated with no motion to reconsider.[98]

On the national front, President Roosevelt won a landslide victory in his first presidential bid in 1904, giving him the political capital he needed to further his trust-busting ambitions, much to the Major's dismay. But even with strong political differences, the Major accorded full honor and respect to the president as part of the welcoming committee when Roosevelt visited Georgia on a tour of the Southern states in fall 1905. It was a quick eleven-hour visit, which began in Roswell, just north of Atlanta, at Bulloch Hall (the home of the president's mother, Mittie Bulloch) and included a short stop in Macon, the hometown of the man who was still wearing the mantle of Georgia Republican leadership. Although it was ten o'clock at night when the president's train arrived in Macon for the second visit to Macon of a seated president in the Major's lifetime, more than three thousand people waited in the station to greet him. Roosevelt spoke for about ten minutes and didn't fail to invoke the Confederacy and the names of Grant and Lee, but he placed a particular emphasis on the unity of the country today.[99]

Shortly after the president's visit, the Major found himself on the receiving end of government intervention by his own state in its pursuit of the ownership arrangements of the Central of Georgia Railway. Between 1897 and 1907 the courts and the Georgia Railroad Commission would

---

[97]"Mr. Watson and Maj. Hanson," *Telegraph*, 8 July 1903, p. 4.
[98]"House Refuses to Reconsider," *Telegraph*, 10 July 1903, p. 3.
[99]"Spoke at Depot to Macon Crowd," *Constitution*, 21 October 1905, p. 5.

question the Central's ownership no fewer than four times.[100] The same question was asked each time: Who owned the Central?

The scrutiny began in 1897 when Atlanta attorney and former Secretary of the Interior Hoke Smith represented the Southern Railway in the Superior Court of Macon in a suit filed by the Dunlap Hardware Company against the Southern Railway.[101] The company claimed that the Southern owned the Central in violation of the state constitution, which declared illegal and void any contract or agreement between corporations "which may have the effect or be intended to have the effect to defeat or lessen competition in their respective businesses or to encourage monopoly."[102] In commenting on the suit, Smith stated that he represented the Southern because he was convinced that it did not own the Central, emphasizing, "I could not be employed by the Southern Railway Company in any litigation which was in conflict with my views of the Constitution…or the interests of the public." The commission didn't share his conviction, however, and continued to pursue the Central and the Southern on this point well into the next decade.[103]

The Major found himself defending the ownership position of the Central before the state railroad commission in 1904. He presented stock certificates that showed the current ownership of the Central to be in the hands of three individuals: George Sherman, of New York; Adrian H. Joline, an attorney for the Southern and chairman of the Richmond Terminal Reorganization Committee; and Alexander Lawton, legal counsel for the Central and its first vice president.[104] None of the men were officers or directors of the Southern Railway, nor was the Southern ever in possession of Central of Georgia Railway stock, which remained in the hands of the Richmond Terminal Reorganization Committee.[105]

---

[100]Dewey W. Grantham, Jr., *Hoke Smith and the Politics of the New South* (Baton Rouge: Louisiana State University Press, 1967) 141; "Central Case up this Week," *Chronicle*, 3 December 1905, p. 13.

[101]Fairfax Harrison, *A History of the Legal Development of the Railroad System of the Southern Railway Company* (Washington, DC: Transportation Library, 1901) 559.

[102]GA Const. of 1877, art. IV, §2, para. 4.

[103]Grantham, *Hoke Smith*, 141.

[104]"Three Men Own Great Central of Georgia Railway System," *Chronicle*, 28 October 1904, p. 2.

[105]Harrison, *History of the Legal Development*, 559–62.

With the ownership question seemingly resolved, in 1905 the Major became concerned about a coming campaign for governor that could have a detrimental effect on the railroad industry. A three-column headline in the *Atlanta Journal* in May announced, "HOKE SMITH IS URGED TO RUN FOR GOVERNOR."[106] With Joseph Terrell having served two terms as governor, a new political contest was about to be waged, and Smith had thrown his hat into the ring. Despite his defense of the Southern in 1898, Smith had a reputation as an anti-railroad lawyer who had become wealthy in his pursuit of personal-damage cases, particularly against the railroads. In 1893 the *American Law Review* declared Hoke Smith "the damage lawyer of Georgia par excellence."[107] Woodrow Wilson described him as a lawyer who was definitely most successful in anti-corporation suits "representing anybody, and presently everybody, that had a grievance against any railroad especially."[108]

Smith wanted to give the state railroad commission greater control over the railroads, something to which the Major was adamantly opposed. Smith had been a strong advocate for Cleveland and had campaigned vigorously for him in his second bid for the presidency, for which Cleveland had tapped him to be secretary of the interior.[109] Running against Smith for the Democratic nomination for governor was the editor of the *Atlanta Constitution*, Clark Howell, son of Evan P. Howell, who had been the *Constitution*'s editor while the Major owned the *Macon Telegraph*. The Major's choice in the contest was Clark Howell, a protective-tariff advocate and pro-business politician who opposed disfranchisement.[110] Howell had served three terms in the Georgia House of Representatives and two terms in the state senate.

As the gubernatorial race was taking shape, in 1905 the Major and Spencer found themselves again testifying before the state railroad commission about the ownership of the Central of Georgia. Spencer attested that the Central was not owned by the Southern, but rather its stock was held by some members of the Richmond Terminal Reorganization Committee, Joline among them, and was emphatic that "the Southern has

---

[106]"Hoke Smith is urged to run for governor," *Atlanta Journal*, 21 May 1905, p. 1.

[107]"The New Secretary of the Interior," *American Law Review* 27 (March/April 1893): 264; Grantham, *Hoke Smith*, 18.

[108]Grantham, *Hoke Smith*, 18.

[109]Ibid.

[110]Ibid., 144.

absolutely no control of the policy of the Central of Georgia. There are no facts that show or are capable of the construction, that the Southern owns or controls in any way the policy of the Central of Georgia."[111] However, he admitted, when asked, that if the Richmond Terminal Reorganization Committee sold its stock in the Central the Southern would claim the money.[112]

When the Major was called to the stand, he was asked to explain his official connection to the Central of Georgia, to which he replied, "I am the president of the company, or as the *Atlanta Journal* calls me "the tin-horn president of that system," taking a poke at Smith, whose friends now managed the paper Smith had once owned. He went on further to say,

> I do not know of any rule, or ownership, or deal, or contract or lease, that would justify me in believing that the Central of Georgia is owned, leased, or other wise controlled by the Southern Railway, which would in any way destroy or defeat competition. On the contrary, I will say, that the Southern is one of our strongest competitors in the matter of securing business. Competition is more sharply drawn between the Central of Georgia and the Southern than between any other railroad or system of railroads in the state.[113]

The complicated nature of the financial ownership structure of each railway company prompted the *Cordele News* to write, "Major Hanson has been put upon the rack, the investigation has been pulled off, and yet the great conundrum remains—who owns the Central?"[114]

The gubernatorial campaign began in earnest in 1906. Hoke Smith was running as an anti-railroad, anti-corporation candidate, eventually adding disfranchisement to his platform in order to garner support from Tom Watson, an exponent of disfranchisement.[115] Smith's disfranchisement activism would have been enough to dissuade the Major from voting for him—a position he had vocally opposed since his 1891 Memorial Day address at Andersonville—much less Smith's antagonism toward the railroads. Anti-railroad sentiment was so virulent that politicians were competing with one

---

[111]"Southern Does Not Own the Fraction of a Share of Central," *Telegraph*, 9 December 1905, p. 1.

[112]"Georgia Central Control," *New York Times*, 9 December 1905, n.p.

[113]"Southern Does Not Own the Fraction," *Telegraph*.

[114]Quoted in "Cordele News," *Chronicle*, 24 December 1905, p. 15.

[115]Grantham, *Hoke Smith*, 146.

another to see who could most effectively tear down the railroad interests. In an interview with the *Washington Post* in early 1906, the Major observed that "every candidate for Governor in Georgia was trying to outdo the other in the virulence of his attacks on the railway corporations. Death to the Railroads is the slogan of the candidates."[116]

Because of his high profile as the leader of the Central of Georgia Railway, the Major was caught in the crosshairs of Hoke Smith's political guns. Smith stumped the state denouncing the railroads, the corporations, and the *Atlanta Constitution*, which had endorsed his opponent Clark Howell. In October 1905, while speaking in Bainbridge, Smith spoke harshly of some Democrats, proclaiming that "those who composed the state ring and professed to be democrats in reality belonged more to Major J. F. Hanson and the Republican Party and were dominated by Hanson and his railroad interests."[117] The Major, who had heartily fought the Atlanta Ring for most of the 1880s, was now being accused of heading a ring of railroad men. While the Major made no public statements about Smith during the gubernatorial campaign, Smith seemed to think that his campaign would benefit by casting aspersions on the Major.

In a rally in Decatur, Smith commented that the Major held a "strange influence over the Macon Telegraph."[118] The Major had no reaction to this comment, but the *Macon Telegraph* certainly did, accusing Smith of trying to discredit the newspaper in Democratic circles because it was not supporting Smith's candidacy. The paper was now a low-tariff advocate and staunchly Democratic, and had been for years following the Major's ownership, including during most of the 1890s when his brother Henry was the manager. The *Telegraph* contended that Smith was hoping that if the paper was aligned with someone who was a "despised railroad president and a Republican"—as Smith had referred to the Major—it would reflect poorly on the paper and perhaps negate the *Telegraph*'s harsh opinions of Smith's campaign.[119] Smith's depiction of the Major as a "despised railroad president and a Republican" demonstrates what a polarizing figure the Major had

---

[116]Quoted in "Major Hanson on the Georgia Campaign," *Columbus (GA) Ledger*, 15 March 1906, p. 5.

[117]"Hoke Smith Lines Up with Watson," *Constitution*, 28 October 1905, p. 5.

[118]"That Strange Influence," *Telegraph*, 5 May 1906, p. 4.

[119]Ibid.

become in his efforts to give the state and its citizens an economically viable railroad.

Smith's campaign was successful. He became the Democratic nominee and was elected governor in fall 1906. During his first term in office he accomplished two of his campaign promises. First, he passed a disfranchisement law that included requirements such as property ownership, veteran status (or status as the descendant of a veteran), and literacy criteria so stringent that it was nearly impossible for blacks to qualify to vote, not to mention many poor whites.[120] Second, he increased the power of the state railroad commission, through the efforts of Charles Murphey Candler in the house and E. K. Overstreet in the senate, who passed the Candler-Overstreet Act, commonly referred to as the Candler Act. The bill changed the railroad commission from a three- to a five-member panel and gave the body authority over streetcars, docks, wharves, cotton compress corporations, terminal companies, railway terminals, terminal stations, telephone and telegraphic companies, and persons owning, leasing, or operating the same. It was also given the authority to hire a rate expert, a provision that Smith particularly wanted.[121] Thus the railroad commission was transformed into a public-utility commission with broad powers.[122] The Major felt that the government oversight stipulated in the act was a further encroachment on business because of the commission's authority to ascertain the value of properties and the capitalization of all corporations, which meant that the railroads had to provide detailed financial records and statements to the commission. The act also gave the commission the authority to set rates, rules, and other regulations for each corporation under its jurisdiction.

Smith failed to get a number of other anti-corporation bills passed during his term, such as one that would increase corporate taxes. However, he did lend his support to a bill to investigate the ownership of the Central of Georgia Railroad.[123] This would appear to be a complete reversal of his stand in 1897, when he represented the Southern Railway in this very same matter, convinced that the Southern did not own the Central. Although the

---

[120]Robert Preston Brooks, *History of Georgia* (Boston: Atkinson, Mentzer & Co., 1913) 380.

[121]Railroad Commission of Georgia, *Thirty-Sixth Annual Report of the Railroad Commission of Georgia, 1908* (Atlanta: Foote & Davies, 1908) 64.

[122]Ibid.

[123]Grantham, *Hoke Smith*, 166.

bill was tabled during the session, the handwriting was on the wall for the Major and the Central of Georgia.

II

THE WAR ON CORPORATIONS

Let us remember that when capital won't work, labor can't work, and when labor is idle or working at low wages, or on reduced time, the country cannot prosper.

—J. F. Hanson

THE MAJOR HAD spent a lifetime driving Georgia's transformation from an agrarian society ravaged by the Civil War to a state flourishing atop a broad industrial foundation. By developing a textile empire that employed thousands, founding a technological school that trained Georgians for professional careers in manufacturing, building a hydroelectric facility that served as a catalyst for industrial growth, and expanding a railroad conglomerate and steamship line that gave businesses better access to the marketplace, the Major had unquestionably contributed to Georgia's economic advancement. Building on this foundation, he was determined to continue to expand and upgrade the industries he led to keep pace with the growing needs of a thriving economy. But by the turn of the century, the Major found himself defending the very institutions he felt were responsible for the prosperity the state had achieved. Once industry had been salvation's cry for Georgia; now the corporations formed to achieve industrial progress were under attack by politicians and grassroots movements. The Major accused the posturing from the White House of having a detrimental effect on business, in what he described as "the war waged on corporations...led by President Roosevelt, with all the demagogues in the country at his heels."[1] He spent his twilight years supporting the corporation and what he saw as the economic heart of the country, its capital. Going on the offensive at every speaking opportunity afforded him, the Major battled the anti-corporation, anti-railroad, and anti-capital sentiments emanating from the White House, Georgia's governor's mansion, and his own state legislature.

---

[1]"War Waged by Roosevelt," *Macon (GA) Telegraph* (hereafter cited as *Telegraph*).

Georgia railroads had played a significant role in the growth of the state's economy, particularly in the success of its agricultural and manu-facturing industries. In 1906 alone, more than 1.5 million fruit trees were planted and 194 new industries—worth over six million dollars and em-ploying 7,108 people—sprang to life along the Central of Georgia Railway.[2] In the hope of further accelerating commercial growth, the Major expanded his rolling stock by purchasing one thousand new freight cars, and in 1906 he was in negotiations to buy thirty new engines.[3] By 1907, also under the Major's leadership, the Central's reach hit its peak of approximately 1,974 miles of track.[4]

Macon, as the heart of the Central of Georgia, served as the railroad's maintenance hub. In order to support this new volume of rail cars and engines, the existing facilities needed to be expanded. They had also suffered from years of neglect due to the Richmond & West Point Terminal Com-pany's lack of investment. The report J. P. Morgan had commissioned during the company's reorganization described the maintenance shops and rail yards as "crude and uneconomical."[5] To that end, in late spring 1906 the Major purchased property in Macon for the Central of Georgia Railway on which he planned to construct a new million-dollar machine shop and roundhouse.[6]

The year 1906 ended on a tragic note for the Major with the death of his friend, business associate, and president of the Southern Railway, Samuel Spencer.[7] Spencer's death didn't eliminate the specter of another

---

[2] *Eleventh Annual Report of the Central of Georgia Railway Company*, p. 7, Central of Georgia Annual Reports, 1362AP-30, Georgia Historical Society, Savannah.

[3] "Central of Georgia Gives Contract for 1,000 Cars," *Telegraph*, 6 March 1906, p. 1.

[4] Richard E. Prince, *Central of Georgia Railway and Connecting Lines* (Salt Lake City: Stanway-Wheelwright, 1976) 43.

[5] Stuart Daggett, *Railroad Reorganization* (Boston/New York: Houghton Mifflin, 1908) 167.

[6] "Business Men Happy over Central Shops," *Telegraph*, 14 June 1906, p. 3; "Central of GA to Build Shops," *Columbus (GA) Ledger*, 14 June 1906, p. 5.

[7] Burke Davis, *The Southern Railway: Road of the Innovators* (Chapel Hill: University of North Carolina Press, 1985) 42–43. Spencer's personal rail car was slammed full force by another train while he and several friends were sleeping after a quail-hunting excursion to North Carolina. In tribute to him, the Southern employees collected money to commission Daniel Chester French (the sculptor of the seated Lincoln statue in the Lincoln Memorial in Washington, D.C.) to create a large bronze statue of Spencer,

investigation into the Central's ownership, however, with Governor Hoke Smith and other legislators still motivated to force the matter to a definitive conclusion. Fortuitously for the Major and the Central, larger forces were at work in a scheme to purchase the railway from its current stockholders. During spring 1907 the Major traveled to New York to negotiate the sale, which he hoped would put an end to any speculation about the relationship between the Central and the Southern. It took him approximately seven weeks to complete the transaction, but by the end of June the sale of the Central of Georgia Railway was finalized. Oakleigh Thorne of New York, president of the Trust Company of America, and Marsden J. Perry of the Union Trust Company of Providence, Rhode Island, purchased the stock, with a portion of the proceeds being paid to the Southern Railway. When asked about the sale, the Major told the press that this would bring the ownership of the Central of Georgia Railway in line with the "spirit as well as the letter of the laws of the state" and that he could at last bring the railroad out of the shadows of possible illegality.[8] In a final attempt to clarify the matter, he emphasized that the Central of Georgia Railway and the Southern Railway had operated independently from each other just as they operated independently from all the other railroads in Georgia and that the Central's "relationship to the Southern had never cost the people of Georgia one dime."[9] In using the word "relationship," the Major was referring to the "wretchedly tangled mass of securities," not an ownership position.[10] The Major remained president under the new ownership. As such, he assured the public that the current improvements to the railroad shops in Macon would be continued, and he expressed the hope that more money would be invested in improving the Central to "keep abreast with its opportunity as well as its duty to the public."[11]

---

which was placed at Terminal Station in Atlanta, where he cast his eyes on the traveling public for more than sixty years. After the terminal was demolished, the statue was moved to Brookwood Station and is now located in the plaza of the Norfolk Southern Corporation building on Peachtree Street in Atlanta.

[8]"Central Railroad Sold to Messrs. Thorne and Perry," *(Macon, GA) Twice-A-Week Telegraph*, 28 June 1907, p. 3.

[9]Ibid.

[10]Ulrich B. Phillips, "Railway Transportation in the South," in *The South in the Building of the Nation*, vol. 6, *Southern Economic History, 1865–1909*, ed. Thomas E. Watson (Louisiana: Pelican, 1909) 312–13.

[11]"Central Railroad Sold," *Twice-A-Week Telegraph*.

Although his ownership headaches appeared to be behind him, the Major still faced challenges in the management of the Central. In 1907 in its zeal to regulate railroad operations, the Georgia legislature was considering ninety-one bills that targeted the railroads.[12] With penalties attached to nearly every one, it seemed that the legislators had an unending appetite for punitive measures to an entity that was a key contributor to the growth and prosperity of its state. The Major had strenuously objected to the recently passed Candler Act, which had established a public-utility commission with broad government oversight of the railroads, and he was equally opposed to the pending bills, which included more rate reductions.[13] The Major appeared before a joint meeting of the house and senate judiciary and railroad committees to explain that the actions of the railroad commission and the state legislature were making it difficult for the Central to attract the capital investment needed to fund critical repairs and improvements to keep the road functioning and also to meet the standards established by the commission. The Major testified that he needed five million dollars to make the necessary improvements in the current fiscal year and that he lacked sufficient reserves because

> the increase in the cost of supplies of every character has been almost or quite as great as the increase in pay rolls while there has been no rate increase to correspond with the increased cost of their labor and material. On the contrary, the tendency has been to lower rates, and it is requiring half of the time of all the officials of the company in making preparations to oppose before the railroad commissions and the legislatures and courts, reductions in our passenger and freight rates.[14]

The Major's objections received support from Joseph B. Cummings of Augusta, head of the Georgia Railroad, who thought the ninety-one bills were "less of reform, than of revenge" and "less of progress than of punishment." Cummings also objected to the "extreme powers given the commission in the imposing of penalties." He noted that "the law provides for no hearing before or appeal after," showing that the Major was not alone in his concerns about excessive government interference without the

---

[12]"Ninety-One Bills Aimed at Railways," *Augusta (GA) Chronicle* (hereafter cited as *Chronicle*), 21 July 1907, p. 29.

[13]"A Plea for Protection," *Atlanta Constitution* (hereafter cited as *Constitution*), 21 July 1907, p. 10.

[14]Ibid.

possibility of appeal. Representatives from the Seaboard Air Line Railway and the Nashville, Chattanooga, and St. Louis Railway joined the Major and Cummings in their complaints before the committees.[15]

The *Griffin Daily News* attempted to support the Major in his defense of the railroads. The paper asked its "thinking people, if there are any of that class left in Georgia," to consider the Major's argument that increases in his cost of supplies, payroll, and maintenance were being countered by the state with reductions in freight and passenger rates. The *Telegraph* quoted the Major as stating that after crucial upgrades to the line the earnings of the railroad in 1906 were less than those in 1866, despite "carrying three or four times the tonnage and passengers to make even that showing."[16]

The Major's financial troubles began to mount when in August 1907 the second and third income bondholders of the Central of Georgia Railway brought suit against the new owners, Perry and Thorne, claiming that the bondholders had not been fairly treated in the payment of interest on their holdings. Income bonds are entitled to interest payments based on earnings, and the Central of Georgia bondholders were entitled to 5 percent non-accumulating interest per year if earnings warranted.[17] In 1907 the Central paid 5 percent interest on their first income bonds, 3.729 percent interest on their second income bonds, and no interest on the third income bonds.[18]

In addition to the bondholder suit, the Major faced a property tax assessment for the Central of Georgia that he thought was excessive. In September he appeared before a tax arbitration board to dispute the recent assessment of the railroad's property at $29 million. Thinking that political demagoguery had played a role in the valuation, he warned the tax arbitration board that "so long as politics, and not reason, holds the sway, railroads will suffer—and some of them may be wrecked, too."[19] The Major, in contesting the assessment of the Central's property, was doing everything

---

[15]"Ninety-One Bills," *Chronicle.*

[16]"No Increase for Railroads," *Telegraph*, 25 July 1907, p. 4, as reported in the Griffin (GA) *Daily News.*

[17]W. Lawrence Chamberlain and George W. Edwards, *The Principles of Bond Investment* (New York: Henry Holt and Company, 1911; Washington, DC: Beard Books, 1999) 103. Citations refer to the Beard Books edition.

[18]Floyd W. Mundy, ed., *The Earning Power of Railroads, 1911* (New York: Jas. H. Oliphant, 1911) 348.

[19]"President Hanson of Georgia Central Deplores Conditions in State," *New York Times*, 5 September 1907, n.p.

he could to hold on to the railroad's capital. Contrary to the prevailing opinion of the day, which held that the railroad executives were robber barons who gouged the public, the Central of Georgia Railway was struggling to remain profitable under a large bond debt, in addition to the decreasing rates and increasing costs.

The Major would need an infusion of capital in order to continue to successfully operate the railroad, but he felt that government interference in the managing of the railroads made railroads unattractive to investors. Historians and economists have analyzed the effect of the federal government's antitrust activity at the turn of the century to determine if it was responsible for the decline in business investments that occurred at the time. George Bittlingmayer, University of Kansas economics professor, for instance, contends that "turn-of-the-century antitrust policy was in fact unstable, and since it concerned the fate of the modern corporation, arguably the most important innovation in the history of business, fluctuating antitrust may very well have affected the business cycle."[20]

With a decline in earnings, a lawsuit pending, and a reduction in passenger and freight rates, the Major decided to halt construction of the new railroad repair shops and roundhouse in Macon, along with all other scheduled improvements except work that was absolutely necessary to the functioning of the road. In a statement to the press the Major stated,

> Railroads cannot borrow money under the present conditions, and with rate reductions being made[,] in justice to the Central it will be necessary to stop all the work of improvement now going on in order to have enough money to keep going. The new machine shops in Macon and the new roundhouse are included in the work that will be stopped. Contracts have already been made for the new car shops and these will be continued, and finished, but the machine shops and roundhouse will have to wait. We are simply unable to pay for the work, and the other improvements that we had under way and therefore will have to stop them.[21]

The Major's prediction that the railroad commission's oversight and the governor's war on the railroads would have a detrimental effect on the railroads and, therefore, the economy, was coming to fruition.

---

[20]George Bittlingmayer, "Antitrust and Business Activity: The First Quarter Century," *Business History Review* 70 (Autumn 1996): 364–65.

[21]"Work on Million and Half Dollar Central Shops Ordered Stopped," *Telegraph*, 4 September 1907, p. 6.

Government oversight of the railroads was not confined to Georgia. By the turn of the century more than thirty states had railroad commissions with various degrees of power and oversight, including Alabama, whose railroad commission was created in 1881.[22] Alabama also had a governor, Braxton Bragg Comer (brother of the Major's former partner Hugh Moss Comer), who had waged his own war on the railroads in his recent gubernatorial campaign. Following his lead, in 1907 the Alabama legislature introduced several railroad bills, which included rate reductions that the railroads felt were unjust. The Central of Georgia Railway ran several of its lines through Alabama. It and several other railroads, such as the Louisville and Nashville, appealed to the legislature for a hearing; they pled their case before the Alabama House Committee on Commerce and Common Carriers in November 1907.[23] When the Major spoke, he was "ruggedly frank" in his opinion that the rate reductions would cause serious financial harm to some of the railroads and could lead to bankruptcies, which would in turn cause a loss of rail service for travelers and businesses, an idea he had expressed at a previous meeting with the committee. He used his "sharp wit and ready repartee" in making his arguments, which "kept his audience in a roar of laughter."[24] He was very serious, however, about what the proposed legislation would do to the earnings of the Central, stating, "We would like to live in harmony with the people that we serve, but owing to the increased prices of everything and lack of money we cannot stand a cut in rates." He attributed the lack of money "to the political agitation which has destroyed the credit of railroads and all other big industries and until confidence is restored, there'll be a period of depression and bankruptcy."[25]

This loss of investor confidence was disheartening to the Major, who exclaimed, "For three decades, we knocked at the door of capital, but were turned down, but in the last ten years we have obtained an equal footing with the Central, Eastern and Western section of this country" only to have

[22]Frederick Converse Clark, *State Railroad Commissions and How They May Be Made Effective* (Baltimore: Guggenheimer, Weil & Co., 1891) 40; Allen J. Going, "The Establishment of the Alabama Railroad Commission," *Journal of Southern History* 12/3 (1946): 366.

[23]"Railroad Men Plead with Lawmakers for Fairness," *Montgomery (AL) Advertiser*, 23 January 1907, p. 1.

[24]"Committees Jump to Lash of Comer and Report Bills," *Montgomery (AL) Advertiser*, 10 November 1907, p. 1.

[25]Ibid.

seen it erode through the actions of politicians.[26] Further, he lamented the fact that he had voted for Roosevelt and contributed to his campaign fund, saying, "I wouldn't vote for him for a dog catcher"—a retort that made headlines in the *New York Times*.[27] With that comment, Alabama Senator George McWhorter challenged the Major: "You made a mistake on Roosevelt, might you not make a mistake with this thing [railroad rates]. Your words are not consistent." To which the Major replied, "Did you hear what Bob Toombs said to Ben Hill when Hill criticized him for being inconsistent? He said that there was not but one animal on earth that was consistent and that was a jackass," causing the chamber to erupt in laughter and applause. The Major concluded his testimony by asking the legislators to "do what you think is for your best interest and the best interests of your people."[28] The committee, although entertained by the Major, unanimously approved the pending bills.

Having no impact on the Alabama legislature, nor on the legislature and railroad commission in his own state, the Major took his appeal directly to the people of the United States by hosting a large contingency of Northern press officials at a Savannah Chamber of Commerce event. The press corps traveled to Savannah as guests of the Major on the *City of Savannah*'s maiden voyage from New York. In his address, the Major "caused a sensation by a denunciation of the governments, state and national, that have become arrayed against the railroad interests of the country."[29] He expressed the opinion that it was the war waged by Roosevelt and the rhetoric spewed by certain politicians to increase their political standing that had "diminished the value of railroad property all over the country by one-fifth of its previous value." In calling out politicians for their posturing, the Major was referring to people like Governor Hoke Smith and, more particularly, to Tom Watson, who had made inflammatory accusations against the railroads in his continued assault on corporations and urbanization. One of the most outlandish statements Watson had made against railroads appeared in *Tom Watson's Magazine*, a publication of his own, in which he told his readership that "we lost fewer lives to the invading

---

[26]Ibid.

[27]"Hanson on Roosevelt," *New York Times*, 10 November 1907, n.p.

[28]"Committees Jump to Lash," *Montgomery (AL) Advertiser*.

[29]"The Hon. Hoke Smith 'Is Not Strong Enough,'" *Chronicle*, 12 October 1907, p. 1.

host of Sherman than we have lost to the railroads under Sam Spencer."[30] While assaulting Spencer and the Southern, Watson also accused "the Republican President of the Central Railway"—one of the monikers by which Watson referred to the Major—of "trying to dominate the public policies and politics of Georgia."[31]

The Major also explained to his press audience that the stoppage order for the new maintenance facilities being built in Macon had been made "due to the lack of money…the shortage of which is due to the weakened credit of the company, which has been induced by the oppressive tactics of the Legislature." Claiming that he was ashamed to mention the name of his state when he was in New York because of the "senseless action the State's legislative body had recently taken," he appealed to his audience for "a more kindly feeling toward the systems he represents."[32]

The Major had become quite adept at using the press to disseminate his views, hoping to change the legislature's current course of action by appealing to the court of public opinion. His strategy produced some results. The *Macon Telegraph* quoted extensively from an article in the *Washington Star*, published immediately after the Major's Savannah address, that analyzed the annual reports of numerous railroad presidents and found them "unanimous in saying that the evil effects of unreasonable laws are not only injuring the property of railroads, but will surely produce a decided relaxation of the prosperity of the country." The *Star* reported that Edward P. Ripley of the Atchison, Topeka and Santa Fe Railway "insists that the hostility of the public is unreasonable, and has impaired the credit of railroads." In regard to the need for increased capital, George W. Stevens, president of the Chesapeake and Ohio Railway, felt that "investors are alarmed at the action of Legislatures and of State Railway Commissions in reducing rates and imposing burdensome restrictions." The *Telegraph* supported the Major's claims in his address at Savannah, stating, "It will be observed that this epitome by the *Washington Star* tracks closely the views of President Hanson."[33]

Not long after the Major's speech in Savannah, the Georgia Railroad Commission requested that the Major and the new president of the

---

[30]"Watson and the Telegraph," *Telegraph*, 5 July 1906, p. 4.

[31]"The Say of Other Editors," *Tom Watson's Magazine* 3 (January 1906): 301.

[32]"War Waged by Roosevelt," *Telegraph*.

[33]"As Railroad Presidents See It," *Telegraph*, 17 October 1907, p. 4.

Southern, William W. Finley, appear before them, once again concerning the ownership of the Central. Some of the proceeds from the Central's sale in June had been paid to the Southern Railway, which is what prompted this latest inquiry. The commission asked for a complete list of stockholders dating back to 1895, although previous hearings had already produced those documents. The inquiry was cut short, though, after the Major had a private meeting with the commission on November 8, 1907, which put an end to further investigations of the railroad's ownership.[34]

Over the previous several years the Major had focused a great deal of his energy on the Central and the Ocean Steamship Company. On January 7, 1908, during a board meeting of Bibb Manufacturing, a recess was called during which the Major and Hubert Duckworth, a long-time member of the Bibb Manufacturing board of directors, met in a private conference at the Major's railroad office. The board, acknowledging that the Major's time was being taken up by the management of the transportation enterprises he led, didn't feel that the Bibb was receiving its fair share. When the two men emerged from their conference, they announced that the Major would be retiring from Bibb Manufacturing, having agreed to the following terms: the board would buy the Major's stock holdings of 2,000 shares at $120 per share and would also buy his daughters' holdings, of 208 shares each, at the same price. Thus ended the Major's thirty-two-year association with the company in a meeting that was "affected by a feeling of sentiment which is proper to record as most unusual in dealing with business affairs."[35]

After the Major retired, shareholders elected Mills B. Lane to the board and elevated Walter T. Hanson, the Major's son, to the presidency. Walter had returned to the Bibb in 1906 as a vice president after a six-year absence, although the rest of his family continued to live in Point Loma, California.[36] His return must have comforted the Major in his retirement from Bibb Manufacturing, allowing the father to pass the mantle of leadership to his son, a dream fulfilled.

In March 1908 the *New York Times* and papers throughout Georgia announced that Edward H. Harriman had purchased the Central of Georgia

---

[34]"Southern and Central R. R.," *Chronicle*, 17 November 1907, p. 2.

[35]*History of Bibb Manufacturing Company, 1876–1929* ([Macon]: n.p., 1937) 38. There is a copy at Middle Georgia Archives, Washington Memorial Library, Macon, GA.

[36]Ibid., 34.

Railway. Harriman was a railroad magnate whose name was as familiar to the people of the day as was J. P. Morgan's.[37] In less than ten years Harriman had amassed a railroad dynasty, and his purchase of the Central was in fact part of a larger initiative.[38] The press revealed that Harriman had actually purchased the Central in June 1907 but had been forced to put the acquisition into a voting trust, which consisted of Perry and Thorne.[39] At the time, Harriman had been in negotiations for control of the Illinois Central Railroad, to which he intended to transfer his Central of Georgia Railway stock. In the Major's private conference with the railroad commission the previous November, he had requested, on Harriman's behalf, that the commission keep Harriman's ownership of the Central confidential until after the transaction involving the Illinois Central was complete, which the railroad commission agreed to do.[40] With his purchase of the Illinois Central secure, Harriman owned a controlling interest in several large systems, including the Union Pacific and the Southern Pacific. With the addition of the Central of Georgia to his already extensive holdings, Harriman now had a direct link to the port of Savannah and the first ocean-to-ocean system of railways in the country, part of his vision for a global "rail-water transportation system."[41]

Although the Central seemed to have received a new lease on life, the Major continued to advocate for an environment more sympathetic to business. He used his speech at the April 1908 opening of the new Hotel Patton in Chattanooga, Tennessee, the city's first skyscraper, to do just that.[42] Titled "The Present Crisis," his speech was an indictment of President Roosevelt, William Jennings Bryan, and Grover Cleveland, laying at their feet all of the country's financial troubles since the Panic of 1893,

---

[37]Maury Klein, *The Life and Legend of E. H. Harriman* (Chapel Hill: University of North Carolina Press, 2000) xiii.

[38]Ibid., xiii, xiv.

[39]Ibid., 427.

[40]"Southern and Central R. R.," *Chronicle*.

[41]"Harriman System Now Ocean to Ocean," *New York Times*, 9 March 1908, n.p.; Klein, *The Life and Legend of E. H. Harriman*, xiv.

[42]"Hanson Takes Fly at Roosevelt, Bryan and Mr. Cleveland," *Telegraph*, 5 April 1908, p. 1; John Shearer, "Hotel Patton Completed One Hundred Years Ago," *Chattanoogan.com*, 8 June 2008, http://www.chattanoogan.com/2008/6/8/129404/Hotel-Patten-Completed-One-Hundred.aspx.

when Cleveland and a Democratic Congress had been in control.[43] The nation had suffered another financial panic in 1907, which caused a near collapse of America's banking system and quickly spread to Wall Street, only to be averted by the orchestrated actions of J. P. Morgan and others.[44] The Major blamed Roosevelt for the 1907 panic, charging him with "turgid and bellicose deliverances against capital" resulting in the "loss of confidence in the basis of our prosperity…whether invested in the railroads and other corporations or in the hands of private citizens."[45]

Bryan didn't escape the Major's wrath either. The Major accused him of joining with Roosevelt against corporations and against what Bryan had termed "predatory wealth." He predicted that the country's unstable business climate would not be resolved "until the country is rescued from the influence of Roosevelt and Bryan." In a no-holds-barred declaration, the Major stated that "if Mr. Roosevelt and Mr. Cleveland both live until the close of Mr. Roosevelt's term, and if the latter retires, they will both enjoy the distinction of having each been elected to their last terms as President when the country was more prosperous, and of having left it with universal depression in every branch of business. They can also reflect that each destroyed his party." The Major left the audience with these words: "Let us remember that when capital won't work, labor can't work, and when labor is idle or working at low wages, or on reduced time, the country cannot prosper."[46] The Major actively blamed Washington for the lack of investor confidence, a theory that "had a wide following at the turn of the century," according to Bittlingmayer.[47]

With new ownership of the Central of Georgia came new personal and professional opportunities for the Major. In August, following his speaking engagement in Chattanooga, the Major moved the Central of Georgia headquarters to Atlanta into a "suite of rooms" in the Candler Building.[48] The Major and Cora had legally separated in June. Cora had received the

---

[43]"Hanson Takes Fly," *Telegraph*.

[44]Jean Strouse, *Morgan: American Financier* (New York: Random House, 1999) ch. 28; Harold Underwood Faulkner, *American Economic History*, 5th ed. (New York: Harper & Brothers, 1924) 507–509.

[45]"Hanson Takes Fly," *Telegraph*.

[46]Ibid.

[47]Bittlingmayer, "Antitrust and Business Activity," 363.

[48]"To Move Headquarters," *(Columbia, SC) State*, 23 July 1908, p. 1.

house in the separation, rented it, and then moved permanently to Point Loma, California, to be near her son's family as well as her daughter Frances and her husband, who had also moved there, and a growing number of grandchildren. Thus the Major found himself starting a new life on his own in a city that knew him well through many close business associations and a lifetime of friendships. He told the press that he regretted leaving Macon, having only a few years before moved the railroad's headquarters from Savannah to Macon for its more central location. However, the Illinois Central's ownership of the Central of Georgia had increased freight service between Chicago and Savannah, as had been hoped for in the sale. Atlanta, a much more active railroad center, was a more strategic location for the headquarters.[49]

When the bondholders' suit made it to court in fall 1908, the Major found himself defending his decision to pay limited dividends to his bondholders, claiming that profits had not been sufficient to allow all interest payments to be made without depleting cash reserves. The Central was using the money from its sale of consolidated bonds to finance capital expenditures. Bonds were a preferred way to finance railroad expansions and improvements because the alternative, the sale of stock, would dilute the holdings of existing shareholders. The Major testified that in the short term instead of using the money to make interest payments it was wiser to fund maintenance that was critical to the proper functioning of the road. He defended this strategy by explaining its long-term benefit: "I believe the policy we have pursued is a safe one and one which will get the income bonds to par quicker than any other that might be pursued."[50] Writing on the economic history of the South, historian Ulrich Phillips sympathized with the Major's plight, stating that "the Southern Railway and the Central of Georgia, along with several other overcapitalized corporations, have been sadly hampered in their betterments." Ulrich uses the term "overcapitalization" to describe the debts imposed on the railroad through its sales and restructuring; in contrast, other Southern railways, such as the Louisville and Nashville, had been making infrastructure improvements since 1895 without taking on heavy debt.[51]

---

[49]"Pres. J. F. Hanson Is Located in Atlanta," *Telegraph*, 4 August 1908, p. 7.
[50]"Maj. Hanson Talks Central Affairs," *Telegraph*, 22 October 1908, p. 3.
[51]Phillips, "Railway Transportation in the South," 313.

In their suit, the bondholders were critical of the high maintenance charges and other expenses incurred by the Central. In particular, they questioned the construction of the Miller-Ellen extension road to the coal mines of Alabama. The Major explained that this line had been built to facilitate access to the coal mines, the source of the Central's fuel, and one of its largest operating costs. The judge scrutinized the railroad's annual report and questioned the Major about an expense for a road survey between Albany, Georgia, and Quincy, Florida. This drew a rather humorous response from the Major, but one that showed how he protected his enterprise from competition. The Major explained that he had ordered the survey to prevent the Georgia, Florida and Alabama Railroad from encroaching on Central of Georgia territory: "I told the owner of the property if he stuck a spade in the ground north of a certain point that we would build to Quincy. He didn't build any further north and we abandoned the idea of building south."[52] The Major understood that the loss of revenue from a competing railroad line would far exceed the expense of a road survey.

Populist Tom Watson—as part of Watson's bloated rhetoric against the "Republican Hanson" and his railroad[53]—and others had often accused the Major of being interested only in his investors. However, the Central of Georgia's financial records paint a picture of a man who was trying to balance the needs of his railroad with the interests of his investors, whose capital kept the railroad going. Since the Major had taken the financial reins of the Central in 1900, the railroad had made full interest payments to the first bondholders from 1901 to 1907, along with the second and third bondholders in 1905 and 1906. It had made smaller interest payments to the second bondholders in 1904 and 1907 and, with the exception of 1905 and 1906, paid no interest to third income bondholders. In 1907 the Major was fighting to keep the capital he had in order to reinvest it in the business by reducing the payment to the second income bondholders and withholding it from the third. With his investors taking a backseat to a well-maintained railroad, the Major predicted that they would see stronger returns in the long run. The Superior Court of Georgia did not concur, however, ruling

---

[52]"Why G. F. & A. Didn't Build into Columbus," *Columbus (GA) Enquirer*, 23 October 1908, p. 4.

[53]"Mr. Egan Was Popular Here," *Chronicle*, 24 November 1903, p. 3; "Child Labor Bill Strongly Urged," *Telegraph*.

that the full 5 percent interest was due to the second and third income bondholders from the earnings of the 1907 fiscal year. The Central appealed the decision, but the Georgia Supreme Court upheld the Superior Court's decision.[54]

Almost two years after Harriman purchased the Central, he made his first inspection of the operations. In January 1909 he traveled to Georgia; he spent several days inspecting the facilities in Savannah and then accompanied the Major to Atlanta, where the Atlanta Chamber of Commerce played host.[55] On the state of the line, Harriman declared, "The railroad certainly needs uplifting." He was also determined "to show the people of the south what a real railroad looks like." In Harriman's assessment, the Central's entire roadbed needed to be rebuilt to address its "lateral curves" and "grades and dips."[56] Harriman biographer Maury Klein contends that Harriman was clearly "aware that strong anti-railroad sentiment in Georgia discouraged investment in new lines or modernization." As a result, he sent his own message to the state about government inference in the railroads by promising to invest ten million dollars in the Central of Georgia Railway if the state would curtail its war on the railroads.[57] Several days later, Hoke Smith fired back a response denying that the railroads had "been damaged financially as the result of state legislation affecting corporations," a claim that was supported by neither the Major's nor Harriman's experience.[58] By 1908 the Major had "exhausted the capital reserves of the company" in order to keep the road functioning.[59]

Harriman's assessment of the Central paid big dividends for the Major and for the Central of Georgia Railway. In the spring following Harriman's visit, the Major traveled to New York to meet with Harriman. On his return he announced that an additional one million dollars would be spent on the machine shops in Macon in addition to the three quarters of a million already invested. Additionally, the Major announced that he had purchased five thousand tons of steel rails for the Central and spoke optimistically to

---

[54]Mundy, *Earning Power of Railroads*, 348.

[55]"Harriman Here on Short Visit," *Constitution*, 26 January 1909, p. 1.

[56]"Harriman Plans for the Central," *Constitution*, 26 January 1909, p. 1.

[57]Klein, *The Life and Legend of E. H. Harriman*, 427; "$10,000,000 for the Central from Harriman," *Constitution*, 27 January 1909, p. 1.

[58]"Statement by Governor," *Savannah (GA) Tribune*, 20 February 1909, p. 8.

[59]Mundy, *Earning Power of Railroads*, 350.

the press about the coming improvements and prosperity for the Central of Georgia Railway under Harriman's ownership.[60]

The advances to the railroad were overshadowed that year by family tragedy. In May 1909, the Major's son, Walter, and Walter's wife, Estelle, were traveling in New York on Bibb Manufacturing business when Walter suffered a stroke. He died on May 23, 1909, at the age of forty-three. Bibb Manufacturing lost its president, and the Major lost his only son. This staggering personal loss was followed six months later by the death of Harriman, ending the Major's eighteen-month relationship with one of America's most successful railroad men. The Major immediately ordered the offices of the Central Railroad and Ocean Steamship Company to be draped in black for thirty days and the flags of the Ocean Steamship Lines to be placed at half-mast to honor the financier. Although the Major had long been in the company of U.S. presidents, railroad magnates, and successful industrialists, he had still found much inspiration in Harriman. The *Augusta Chronicle* quoted the Major as stating, "Personally I was very much attached to him as I found him always pleasant and the most satisfactory man to transact business with, with whom I have ever come in contact. His death is a national calamity, for as great has been his work, it was unfinished."[61]

Shortly after Harriman's death, James T. Harahan was elected president of the Illinois Central, becoming the Major's new boss. Because the Illinois Central owned the Central of Georgia Railway, Harahan came to Georgia to inspect the Railway, specifically the port property, amid rumors that the Major would be resigning as president of the Central. While in Savannah, Harahan attended the stockholders' meeting, during which the Major was reelected president of the railway just before his sixty-ninth birthday. The Major met the rumors of his resignation head-on by stating to the press, "Someone, I don't know who, seems to feel called upon to start a report every now and then that I have resigned or am about to quit the Central." Harahan displayed complete confidence in the Major: when asked questions about the future of the railroad, he replied, "Major Hanson is president of the Central, ask him."[62]

---

[60]"Central of Georgia Will Spend Million Dollars More on Shops," *Telegraph*, 20 June 1909, p. 1.

[61]"Major J. F. Hanson on E. H. Harriman," *Chronicle*, 11 September 1909, p. 2.

[62]"Maj. J. F. Hanson Re-elected President of Central," *Telegraph*, 12 October 1909, p. 3.

After many tumultuous years of leading the Central of Georgia, in February 1910 the Major undertook his final speaking engagement as the guest of honor at the annual banquet of the Macon Chamber of Commerce, held at the Hotel Lanier. The guest list included many of the Major's associates in Georgia and a large contingency of prominent businessmen from New York, John D. Rockefeller included, although he was not among those in attendance.[63] Accompanying the Major at the speakers' table were John T. Moore, mayor of Macon; Emory Winship, president of the Macon Chamber of Commerce; G. Gunby Jordan from Columbus; and Dr. Andrew M. Soule, dean of the University of Georgia College of Agriculture. The Major was introduced by the mayor, who praised him for his lifelong contributions to the city, stating that "to Major J. F. Hanson the city of Macon owes a debt of gratitude difficult to repay."[64] The Major spoke in a tone that was both sentimental and melancholy, as if he knew this was his last chance to express himself so personally. No longer a citizen of Macon, he missed passing among his friends on the streets, and he thanked the audience "for the opportunity of meeting my old friends and neighbors and fellow townsmen of Macon." He claimed "a deep and lasting interest in this city and its people, for here I passed the major portion of my active business life, and here I met the vicissitudes of fortune that come to men who from small beginnings strive to make their way in the world." He poignantly referred to his time in Macon as "the happiest years of my life."[65]

He couldn't leave the subject of Macon without mentioning the *Macon Telegraph*, the paper he had led for seven years, often in a head-to-head battle with Henry Grady and Atlanta Ring politics. He told the gathering that although he now lived in Atlanta, he continued to follow the civic affairs of Macon, and he complimented the *Telegraph* on its improvements, which he felt were reflective of the overall progress in the city's growth and development. And although he differed with the current editor on some points, he praised the newspaper as being a conservative leader in the state and its editor as loyal to both the people of the community and the South, which benefitted Georgia.[66]

---

[63]"Men of Prominence Invited to Banquet," *Telegraph*, 1 February 1910, p. 3.

[64]"Maj. J. F. Hanson Urges an Increased Trade with Latin America," *Telegraph*, 11 February 1910, pp. 1–2.

[65]Ibid.

[66]Ibid.

He also took pride in the recently completed Central of Georgia machine shops in Macon, which exemplified the Major's core belief in the value of industry as an engine for economic prosperity for all people. He enthusiastically referenced the ability of the new facilities to enhance Macon's economy "by providing a large force of skilled mechanics who will need homes, and the essentials of life that go to make up the trade of a city."[67] He didn't move far from his business principles in a segue from the economic interests of Macon to the enterprises of government, declaring, "I believe that government in its simplest form of statement is business upon a large scale, and that the same intelligence, enterprise and energy, essential to the success of a private corporation should characterize the policies of government."[68]

By introducing government into the conversation, the Major had reached the central theme of his speech: increasing trade with Latin America. He had championed trade with the region as early as 1888 in his speech before the Cotton Exposition in Augusta and later when he served as a member of the first Pan American Congress. All these years later he was still carrying the torch on this issue. He pointed out that inequities in the trade balance with Latin America and the lack of a U.S. merchant marine had not been adequately addressed in the twenty years since the conference, despite Roosevelt having described the absence of a merchant marine as "discreditable to us as a nation" in his first address as president.[69] President Taft also supported the idea, speaking about the need for subsidies to establish a merchant marine in his inaugural address, on March 4, 1909, and again at the Alaska-Yukon-Pacific Exposition in Seattle, which the Major attended, in summer 1909.[70] The United States was still underrepresented in shipping, not only in Latin America, but worldwide. The Major told his audience that "during the last year 3,700 merchant ships passed through the Suez Canal and not one of them carried the United States flag."[71]

---

[67]Ibid.

[68]"Maj. Hanson Urges an Increased Trade," *Telegraph*.

[69]"First Message of President Roosevelt Conservative and Marked by Dignity," *Constitution*, 4 December 1901, p. 4.

[70]*International Marine Engineering* 14 (January–December 1909): 486-C; "Our Merchant Marine," *Marine Review* 40 (1910): 497.

[71]"Maj. Hanson Urges an Increased Trade," *Telegraph*.

The Major closed by asking the chamber of commerce to continue to discuss the matter of foreign trade at its annual meetings and to make it a priority at its monthly meetings. He encouraged the audience to ascertain all the facts "so that an intelligent public opinion may be exercised upon our representatives in congress, in favor of such measures as necessary to protect all the interests of the country."[72] The National Board of Trade, a national association of chambers of commerce and boards of trade, had just held its annual meeting in Washington, in January, and had already passed a resolution to encourage President Taft to push Congress to enact legislation that would help private enterprise compete with other maritime powers, although it would be six years before the United States would pass federal legislation to establish a national merchant marine.[73]

The banquet's organizers chose G. Gunby Jordan, the Major's business associate and friend, to speak in tribute to the Major. Jordan eloquently praised the Major, predicting that his legacy "would stand as a monument to sound judgment, rare foresight, and energy par excellence, with successful monuments of industry as living, pulsing, throbbing evidence of his success throughout the state."[74] Jordan applauded the difference the Major had made to the counties and cities in the state by providing jobs to the thousands of operatives who worked in his mills and his railroad and steamship operations. Jordan also praised the Major's "intuitive knowledge of men, experienced business methods and ever-present resolve to aid his people and his state, while acting always in the best interest of the owners of the property." Regarding the Major's proficiencies, Jordan distinguished him

---

[72]Ibid.

[73]*Proceedings of the Fortieth Annual Meeting of the National Board of Trade Held in Washington, January 1910* (Philadelphia: John R. McFetridge & Sons, 1910) 215. The first Merchant Marine Act was the Shipping Act passed in 1916 in support of an American merchant marine, which established a U.S. shipping board. An amended version was passed in the form of the Merchant Marine Act of 1920, commonly called the Jones Act, which provided for the maintenance of an American Merchant Marine; it was amended in 1936. The U.S. Merchant Marine Academy opened at Kings Point, New York, in 1943 ("USMMA History," U.S. Merchant Marine Academy website, last modified 23 January 2013, http://www.usmma.edu/about/usmma-history; Clarence G. Morse, "A Study of American Merchant Marine Legislation,"_*Law and Contemporary Problems* 25 (Winter 1960): 57–81.

[74]"Splendid Tribute Paid Maj. Hanson by Gunby Jordan," *Telegraph*, 11 February 1910, p. 6.

as "direct and forcible as a writer, of splendid address, and convincing as a speaker, it is accorded to few men to have filled so many plates as completely." His most personal and poignant remarks described the Major as being in the "October of his Life," where the "feverish passion of early manhood has been consecrated into noble purpose; when experience has imparted its discipline to character; when arduous work has at least partly finished and the tempting grapes are ripe and one has earned the right to pluck and enjoy them."[75] On this last point, however, Jordan may have been too optimistic.

In mid-July the Major was returning from a trip to New York when he became ill and nearly died aboard the train. He underwent gall bladder surgery in August in Atlanta and remained in the hospital nearly a month, after which he was taken to his Atlanta residence to complete his recovery. By early October the papers were reporting that his friends and business associates were showering congratulations on the Major for his complete recovery. The Macon Chamber of Commerce, for example, sent him a telegram that read, "The Macon Chamber of Commerce in meeting assembled, congratulates you on your restoration to health."[76] In fact, so many well wishes had come his way that the Major issued a public statement of thanks through the press: "During my illness, from which I have about recovered, I received many expressions of sympathy from friends in all parts of the country. From necessity I must adopt this method of assuring them of my great appreciation of their kindness, to most sincerely thank them."[77] To complete his recovery the Major took a three-week rail trip to New York and other points in the east for a little rest. His recovery seems all the more remarkable given that many had given up hope, what with newspaper offices "preparing obituary notices, and extensive accounts of his career [that] were already put into type."[78]

The Major was rested and refreshed from his excursion by the time of his seventieth birthday, on November 25, 1910. He spent the day in his office in the Candler Building receiving congratulations from friends, who remarked that they found him in better health than he had been in for quite

---

[75]Ibid.

[76]"Sent a Telegram to President J. F. Hanson," *Telegraph*, 2 October 1910, p. 12.

[77]"Major Hanson Thanks Many Kind Friends," *Telegraph*, 5 October 1910, p. 9.

[78]"Maj. J. F. Hanson Leaves Hospital," *Columbus (GA) Enquirer*, 12 October 1910, p. 2.

some time.[79] He was feeling so well that he traveled to Savannah on Central of Georgia Railroad business on December 3 and traveled again on December 8 to Birmingham, Alabama, to attend the funeral of his friend and business partner, coal magnate Henry F. DeBardeleben.[80] He returned home in time to be with his brother Newt, who had come to visit him for the holidays. The two were in the Major's home together on the evening of December 14 when the Major complained of not feeling well. Newt called the Major's physician, Dr. Goldsmith, who made a house call and stayed until quite late in the evening. When the doctor returned early the next morning, the Major greeted him with a cheerful "Good morning, Doctor" and then rolled over on his side and passed away. Besides the doctor, the Major's brother was the only one present when he "crossed over," as his death was referred to by the *Macon Telegraph*.[81]

The Major's funeral was scheduled for the next afternoon. His daughter Annie made immediate arrangements to travel from Baltimore by train with her sons, arriving just in time to accompany her father's body from Atlanta to Macon. Joining her on this special train was Newt, the only other family member in attendance, along with dignitaries from Atlanta, including Mayor Robert Maddox and the Major's Civil War comrade-in-arms Capt. James W. English. The train departed Atlanta at 11:30 a.m., and with it the Major took his last ride on the Central of Georgia Railway, in his own private car, number 100.[82]

---

[79]"Maj. Hanson Seventy Years Old on Friday," *Telegraph*, 27 November 1910, p. 5.

[80]"Major Hanson Pays Visit to Savannah," *Chronicle*, 3 December 1910, p. 1; "Maj. J. F. Hanson Dies Suddenly," *Montgomery (AL) Advertiser*, 16 December 1910, p. 1.

[81]"J. F. Hanson, One of the Greatest Builders of the South, Crosses Over," *Telegraph*, 16 December 1910, p. 1.

[82]"Funeral Services in Macon This Afternoon," *Constitution*, 16 December 1910, p. 1. The Major's private rail car rendered extensive service to him during his lifetime, transporting the state's most important businessmen, such as Hugh Moss Comer, Mills B. Lane, G. Gunby Jordan, and John D. Little, and several governors, including McDaniel and Terrell. Visiting dignitaries to the state, such as Samuel Spencer, president of the Southern Railway, also traveled in the Major's car. In 1946 the car was sold to author Lucius Beebe and his partner, Charles Clegg, who used the car as their traveling residence for many years, renaming it "The Gold Coast." In 1954 they donated the car to the Pacific Coast Chapter of the Railway and Locomotive Historical Society, where it was used in many railroad displays and even appeared in the Walt Disney movie *Pollyanna*. The Pacific Coast Chapter presented the car to the state of California in 1969 to be part of the future California State Railroad Museum. In 1970 the Sacramento

When the train pulled into the Macon station, a long funeral procession awaited. The Major's car was met by eight pallbearers, "toil-stained men of the shops chosen from the oldest mechanics regardless of their rank or station" because "it was to these men that the president of the road had the tenderest leaning."[83] The men carefully lifted the casket from the train, took it to the hearse, and then joined their fellow workers in the long processional to the graveyard. Although the active pallbearers were chosen from the men in the railway shops, the Major's honorary pallbearers, twenty in number, included a who's who of turn-of-the-century Maconites, such as William. J. Massee, Emory Winship, Harry Stillwell Edwards, Robert. J. Taylor, Roland Ellis, and Charles R. Pendleton, the owner of the *Telegraph* at that time.[84]

A slow stream of people flowed through Macon's streets in a somber tribute to the man whose life had prospered in this Middle Georgia town. Leading the cortege in their carriages on the warm winter day were the chief officers of the Central of Georgia Railway, including William. A. Winburn, vice president of the Central; Col. Alexander R. Lawton, another vice president; and twelve other business associates and friends. Members of the board of directors from both Atlanta and Savannah followed behind the officers with Mills B. Lane, a Bibb board member, heading the delegation of Savannah dignitaries who attended the funeral. According to the *Macon Telegraph*, more than four hundred white and two hundred black workers from the railway shops walked four abreast behind the carriages filled with dignitaries.

Trust, along with the Southern Pacific Railroad and Pacific Coast Chapter, hosted then-governor Ronald Reagan and his wife, Nancy, at a memorable evening event in the Major's private car. After the event, Governor Reagan signed the first funding legislation in support of the California State Railroad Museum. Because of its presidential provenance, the elegantly restored car is a centerpiece in the California State Railroad Museum in Sacramento and looks exactly as it appeared at the event with the Reagans, with all of its original interior embellishments from the Major's day completely intact (California State Railroad Museum, Information Sheet No. 2. "Georgia Northern Private Car No. 100 "The Gold Coast.")

[83]"Major John F. Hanson Is Taken by Death," *Savannah (GA) Morning News*, 16 December 1910, p. 1.

[84]"This Afternoon at Riverside Remains Will Be Laid Away," *Telegraph*, 16 December 1910, p. 1.

As the Major was not affiliated with any church in Macon, an ecumenical service took place graveside at Riverside Cemetery.[85] The processional arrived quietly, and then the singing of "Abide with Me" by the First Baptist Church choir broke the silence. Reverend J. E. Wray, pastor of the Mulberry Street Methodist Church, began the service with these words of praise: "A great and good man has passed away. This fair city of ours may well bare and bow her head, for Major Hanson was one of her best friends. The vast shops of the Central of Georgia are not his only monument. His monuments are all over Macon and all over the south."[86] Thus began a eulogy that described a man who was dedicated to his city, his state, and his country. Wray went on to say, "Not only was he a builder of industries, he was one of the strongest advocates of popular education in the state. In looking over his files of the *Macon Telegraph* during the years that he owned and edited the paper, the burden of his editorials was always the plea for an ever widening education and enlightenment." Wray concluded by paying tribute to the Major's "causes of public spirit and to his helping hand that was always held out to every worthy object." Reverend R. E. Douglas of the First Presbyterian Church pronounced the benediction, and the choir concluded with "Lead Kindly Light."[87]

Savannah mourned the loss of the Major as much as Macon did. All the shops of the Central of Georgia Railway in the seaport town were ordered draped in black, as were its offices and passenger terminal. All flags on the Ocean Steamship Company's fleet were lowered to half-mast in memory of the man who was their president. The Citizens and Southern Bank office at Liberty and Montgomery streets was also draped in black bunting out of respect to the bank's relationship with the Major and the businesses he directed.[88]

---

[85]The Major was a founder of Riverside Cemetery; he and other Macon businessmen applied for a charter in April 1887. The Major served on the original board of directors that chose the renowned landscape architect Calvert Vaux and his firm, Vaux & Co., to design the meandering pathways that would carry the Major to his final resting place ("Application for Charter," *Telegraph*, 6 April, 1887, p. 5; "Riverside Cemetery," *Telegraph*, 18 May 1887, p. 7).

[86]"Major J. F. Hanson[,] the South's Empire Builder[,] Is At Rest," *Telegraph*, 17 December 1910, p. 1.

[87]Ibid.

[88]"Major John F. Hanson Is Taken by Death," *Savannah (GA) Morning News.*

In Macon the shops at Bibb Manufacturing were closed at noon on the day of the funeral. In an age when labor laws forced sixty-hour workweeks on its employees and child labor was a standard practice, this gesture showed a strong measure of respect for the man who was one of the founders of this textile giant. In another display of admiration, at three o'clock in the afternoon the mighty engines of the Central of Georgia Railway stopped running for five minutes on every line in the system, and all machinery in the shops ceased operation. In solidarity, every streetcar in Macon paused for five minutes. On December 16, 1910, in mute tribute to a great Georgia industrialist, the wheels of industry stood still.[89]

---

[89]"Major J. F. Hanson[,] the South's Empire Builder[,] Is At Rest," *Telegraph.*

EPILOGUE

In my judgment they slew him.

—Harry Stillwell Edwards

AS THE MAJOR was leading the Central of Georgia out of a state of neglect and advocating for the virtue of the corporation, a scandal on the home front erupted in the headlines from coast to coast. What had been a rumor on the streets of Macon for two years became fodder for gossip when Cora Hanson filed for divorce from the Major in 1909, immediately after their son's death.[1] In her suit, Cora claimed that the Major had been verbally abusive to her and that he was once infatuated with her friend and former Atlanta resident Daisy Emerson Horner, then thirty-two years old and heiress to the Bromo Seltzer fortune.[2] The Major filed his legal response to the divorce, which appeared in full in both the *Macon Telegraph* and the *Atlanta Constitution*.[3] Newspapers across the country from Bellingham, Washington, to New York and Baltimore immediately picked up the story, publishing details of the accusations and refutations, including denials from a reportedly shocked Daisy Horner, now Mrs. James McVickar of New York.[4] As far away as Ogden, Utah, people read about the scandalous divorce over their morning coffee.[5]

The seeds that germinated into divorce were planted some years prior. In the 1890s the Major's son, Walter, joined an international spiritual movement sweeping the nation called Theosophy, which within a few short years had drawn most of the Major's family into its fold. Walter founded a

---

[1]"Macon Expected the Divorce Suit," *Atlanta Georgian & News*, 18 August 1909, p. 1; "Mrs. J. F. Hanson Files for Divorce," *Macon (GA) Telegraph* (hereafter cited as *Telegraph*), 19 August 1909, p. 5.

[2]"Maj. J. F. Hanson Is Sued for Divorce," *Atlanta Georgian & News*, 18 August 1909, p. 1.

[3]"Suit for Divorce," *Telegraph*, 15 September 1909, p. 7; "Suit for Divorce," *Atlanta Constitution* (hereafter cited as *Constitution*), 15 September 1909, p. 9, 10.

[4]"Theosophy Wrecks Home," *Bellingham (WA) Herald*, 16 September 1909, p. 7; "Theosophy Divided Hansons," *New York Times*, 20 August 1909, n.p.

[5]"Theosophy Is Blamed for Marital Troubles," *Ogden (UT) Standard*, 15 September 1909, p. 8.

chapter of Theosophists in Macon and later moved with his family to the Theosophical colony at Point Loma, California, a commune founded by Katherine Tingley. Tingley was the charismatic leader of the American branch of Theosophy, which she christened the Universal Brotherhood and Theosophical Society. With a particular emphasis on the occult and reincarnation, its focus was on "the study of comparative religions, philosophies, and sciences," as well as "unexplained laws of nature and the powers latent in man."[6] The Major's daughter Frances and her husband, Ross White, and their children also became Theosophists and followed Walter to the colony. Walter, like his father, had strong powers of persuasion and convinced others in Macon to move to Point Loma, such as his cousin Ethel Green Small, who was persuaded by Walter to send her infant son to the colony. As part of their spiritual training, children were separated from their parents at birth and placed in dormitory-style dwellings and educated at the Raja Yoga Academy, a school founded by Tingley located at the colony. Walter's proselytizing for the Theosophical movement included pressing his sister Annie, the only one of the Major's children who wasn't a Theosophist, to send her two sons to be educated with their cousins at the school, but the Major thwarted his efforts, causing a breach between father and son.[7] Despite the continued pleadings of his family, including his wife, the Major refused to embrace Theosophy or to contribute money to the movement. He considered it a cult, often telling his family that "every brotherhood scheme within his knowledge had ingloriously failed" and if this was the life they chose to lead they could not depend on him for any financial support.[8] The Major had already watched Walter divest himself of his only asset—his stock in Bibb Manufacturing—to support the colony at Point Loma.[9] Concerned that Frances intended to do the same, the Major denied her request, made several years before he died, to be given her inheritance early.[10] The Major finally accepted his family's conversion, but his refusal to support the colony

---

[6]Emmett A. Greenwalt, *The Point Loma Community in California, 1897–1942* (Berkeley/Los Angeles: University of California Press, 1955) 3, 6–7.

[7]"Suit for Divorce," *Constitution*, p. 10.

[8]Ibid., 9.

[9]Ibid.; Walter Hanson Dunn, interview by author, 1998.

[10]"Suit for Divorce," *Telegraph*; "Suit for Divorce," *Constitution*, p. 9.

financially or have anything to do with Theosophy caused a rift in the household that, over time, tore the family apart.[11]

The Major and Cora, who had become a Theosophist in 1900, legally separated in 1908, after which Cora permanently moved to Point Loma to be with her family.[12] As part of the separation agreement, the Major had given her their home in Macon, which she immediately rented, and a generous monthly allowance. The next year, Cora's divorce suit asked for no more money from the Major than what the couple had already agreed to in the separation, indicating to the Major that her only motive for the divorce was retaliation for his "refusing to bend to the yoke of Theosophy."[13]

Fifteen months after the initial filings, the suit had been carried no further, and at the time of the Major's death the couple was still legally separated. When the Major's will was filed in the probate court on December 21, 1910, a week after he died, his net worth was splashed across the headlines. The total value of his estate was approximately $500,000 ($12.5 million in 2015 dollars).[14] Cora received $50,000 in securities to be held in trust to satisfy the financial arrangements of the separation agreement, including their home in Macon. Despite the Major's distrust of Theosophy, he had provided for all of his children and grandchildren— although his will did favor his daughter Annie and her children, none of whom were Theosophists, with $110,000 in cash from the estate. The remainder was divided equally among Frances, Annie, Walter's children, and Frances's children. Annie was immediately entitled to the corpus of her bequest, while Frances could receive only the income from her share, with the corpus passing to her children upon her death. The Major's grandchildren living in the Theosophical commune would similarly receive the income from their share of the corpus, but in order to receive their full inheritance before the age of thirty-five, they had to renounce Theosophy; otherwise they would receive their full inheritance at age thirty-five with no restrictions.[15] The Major had structured his will so as to prevent his money

---

[11]"Suit for Divorce," *Constitution*, p. 9.

[12]Membership certificate in possession of the author.

[13]"Suit for Divorce," *Telegraph*.

[14]"Choose: Faith or Fortune? J. F. Hanson's Will Leaves a Fortune to Grandchildren," *Atlanta Georgian & News*, 20 December 1910, p. 1.

[15]J. F. Hanson, will dated 17 August 1910, Book E (1909–1916), Fulton County (GA) Record of Wills, Fulton County Probate Court, Atlanta.

from falling into the hands of the Theosophical Society, to the extent possible, while still providing an income to all of his inheritors.

Less than two months after the will was filed Cora, Frances, and the Major's daughter-in-law Estelle (Walter's wife) launched a bitter fight to have it overturned, landing the family on the front pages once more.[16] The women accused Annie of exercising undue influence over the Major in his drafting of the will. The Major's alleged infatuation with Daisy Horner was also revived.[17] The jury took no time in returning a verdict two days later in favor of the will as it was written.[18] However, the superior court judgment did not end the fight. Cora, Frances, and Estelle took their fight to the Georgia Supreme Court. The case was not heard until February 27, 1913. Because no one was disinherited and no further evidence of any substantive nature was provided, the Supreme Court upheld the Major's will as he wrote it.[19] But damage was already done. The Major's contentious will and personal life had remained alive in the news for more than two years after his death, gossip that in some circles eclipsed the substance of his career.[20] Alluding to the divorce scandal in his tribute to the Major shortly after his death, Harry Stillwell Edwards, the Major's lifetime friend and former associate editor at the *Macon Telegraph*, wrote, "The sorrows that came to him late in life are not for this column." He added, "In my judgment they slew him."[21]

While the Major's family seemed more concerned about his money than his good name, his friends and business associates started a fund shortly after his death with which to erect a monument to his memory in Macon. Several thousand dollars had been collected when his good friend Gunby Jordan was struck with the idea that an endowment for Georgia Tech would be a more fitting tribute, because "the money we put into this will go toward making self-reliant boys, upbuilding the state and carrying into loving

---

[16]"Mrs. Hanson Files Suit to Break the Will of Her Husband," *Augusta (GA) Chronicle*, 7 February 1911, p. 1.

[17]"Name Mrs. Garrett in Hanson Will Suit," *New York Times*, 24 October 1911, n.p.

[18]"Fight on Hanson Will Thrown Out [of] Court," *Columbus (GA) Ledger*, 26 October 1911, p. 3.

[19]"Major Hanson's Will Stands as He Made It," *Telegraph*, 28 February 1913, p. 1.

[20]Ibid.

[21]Harry Stillwell Edwards, "John F. Hanson—The Man," *Telegraph*, 18 December 1910, p. 6.

memory the name of a man who was one of the first to suggest a School of Technology, and who always believed that the South needed enlightenment on this line." Jordan wrote immediately to Charles R. Pendleton, chairman of the monument fund, explaining the idea and assuring him that "being intimate with Major Hanson I had concluded that this would please him best, if he knew we were trying to appropriately honor his memory." All members of the monument fund committee concurred, and the J. F. Hanson Endowment Fund at Georgia Tech was established, though it is no longer in existence today.[22]

As appropriate as the gesture was, it left no tangible evidence of the Major's significance on the landscape of Georgia's history. Instead, his legacy speaks in the crowded halls on the campus of Georgia Tech, in the wind that howls through the abandoned mill buildings across the state, in the water that flows over the North Highlands Dam, and in the roar of the engines that continue to run the rails of Georgia, none of which can speak for him, yet in their way speak volumes about his foresight and energy. Reflecting on the Major's life after his death, Edwards had this to say: "His life had been a fierce conflict. Through school days, farm days, and the bloody days of '61–'65 it was an unending battle. In the days of Reconstruction it was still a battle, with no rest. He rose from the ranks through sheer force of ability, and character, not to rest, but to govern, to build up, to provide for. The lofty soul was never shaken; the splendid body sustained the fierce demands of war, privation and relentless labor.... it was only his great loving heart that gave way."[23]

---

[22]"Scholarship; Not Monument," *Columbus (GA) Daily Enquirer*, 23 July 1911, p. 3.
[23]Edwards, "John F. Hanson," 6.

BIBLIOGRAPHY

1. Books, Articles, and Scholarly Works

Anderson, William D. *A Bench Mark: Bibb Manufacturing Company, Macon, Georgia, USA*. New York: Newcomen Society in North America, 1950.

Andrews, J. Cutler. *The South Reports the Civil War*. Princeton: Princeton University Press, 1970.

Andrews, Mildred Gwin. *The Men and the Mills: A History of the Southern Textile Industry*. Macon: Mercer University Press, 1987.

Avery, Isaac W. *History of the State of Georgia from 1850–1881*. New York: Brown & Derby, 1881.

Ayers, Edward L. *The Promise of the New South: Life after Reconstruction*. Oxford: Oxford University Press, 2007.

Bacote, Clarence A. "Negro Office Holders in Georgia under President McKinley." *Journal of Negro History* 44/3 (1959): 217–39.

Baker, Raymond F. *Andersonville: The Story of a Civil War Prison Camp*. Washington, DC: National Park Service, 1972.

Barr, Christopher. "The High Watermark of Slavery: Andersonville as a Monument to Emancipation." Paper presented at the biennial meeting of the Society of Civil War Historians, Baltimore, June 2014.

Bernhardt, Joshua. *The Tariff Commission: Its History, Activities, and Organization*. New York: D. Appleton, 1922.

Bittlingmayer, George. "Antitrust and Business Activity: The First Quarter Century." *Business History Review* 70 (Autumn 1996): 363–401.

Blaine, James Gillespie. *Foreign Policy of the Garfield Administration: Peace Congress of the Two Americas*. Cambridge, MA: Harvard University, 1882.

Blight, David. *Race and Reunion: The Civil War in American Memory*. Cambridge, MA: The Belknap Press of Harvard University Press, 2001.

Britt, Bill. *History and Directory of Ebenezer United Methodist Church*. Forsyth, GA: n.d.

Brittain, James E., and Robert C. McMath, Jr. "Engineers and the New South Creed: The Formation and Early Development of Georgia Tech." *Technology and Culture* 18/2 (April 1977): 175–201.

Brittain, Marion L. *The Story of Georgia Tech*. Chapel Hill: University of North Carolina Press, 1948.

Brooks, Robert Preston. *History of Georgia*. Boston: Atkinson, Mentzer & Co., 1913.

Brown, [?]. *A History of Barnesville*. n.d. Old Jail Museum and Archives, Barnesville, GA.

Browne, Waldo R. *Altgeld of Illinois: A Record of His Life and Labor*. New York: B. W. Huebsch, 1924.

Bryan, Ferald J. *Henry Grady or Tom Watson? The Rhetorical Struggle for the New South, 1880–1890*. Macon: Mercer University Press, 1994.

Butler, John C. *Historical Record of Macon and Central Georgia*. Macon: Middle Georgia Historical Society, 1969. Originally published 1879 by J. W. Burke.

Carlton, David L. "Carlton on Gaston." Review of *The New South Creed*, by Paul M. Gaston. H-South, H-Net Reviews. Article published January 2003. https://networks.h-net.org/node/512/reviews/685/carlton-gaston-new-south-creed-study-southern-mythmaking.

"Central of Georgia and Bibb Manufacturing: An 88-Year Partnership in Progress." *Ties Magazine* 18/5 (August 1964): 6.

Chamberlain, W. Lawrence, and George W. Edwards. *The Principles of Bond Investment*. Washington, DC: Beard Books, 1999. Originally published 1911 by Henry Holt.

Chandler, Alfred D., Jr. "Patterns of American Railroad Finance, 1830–1850." *Business History Review* 28 (September 1954): 248–63.

Clark, Frederick Converse. *State Railroad Commissions and How They May Be Made Effective*. Baltimore: Guggenheimer, Weil & Co., 1891.

Coleman, Kenneth. *A History of Georgia*. Athens: University of Georgia Press, 1977.

Conant, Charles A. *The Plans for Currency Reform*. New York: Bankers, 1906.

Crain, Barbara. *Biography and History*. New York: Palgrave Macmillan, 2010.

Crews, Pamela. *A Biography on Hugh M. Comer*. Savannah: Georgia Historical Society Archives, 1991.

Crimmins, Timothy J., and Anne H. Farrisee. *Democracy Restored: A History of the Georgia State Capitol*. Athens: University of Georgia Press, 2007.

Croly, Herbert David. *Marcus Alonzo Hanna: His Life and Work*. New York: Macmillan, 1923.

Daggett, Stuart. *Railroad Reorganization*. New York: Houghton Mifflin, 1908.

Davis, Burke. *The Southern Railway: Road of the Innovators*. Chapel Hill: University of North Carolina Press, 1895.

Davis, Harold E. *Henry Grady's New South: Atlanta, a Brave and Beautiful City*. Tuscaloosa: University of Alabama Press, 1990.

Eckert, Ralph Lowell. *John Brown Gordon: Soldier, Southerner, American*. Baton Rouge: Louisiana State University Press, 1989.

Faulkner, Harold Underwood. *American Economic History*. 5th ed. New York: Harper & Brothers, 1924.

Felton, Rebecca Latimer. *My Memoirs of Georgia Politics*. Atlanta: Index, 1911.

Fogel, Robert William. *Railroads and American Economic Growth: Essays in Econometric History*. Baltimore: Johns Hopkins Press, 1964.

Friedman, Milton. "The Crime of 1873." *Journal of Political Economy* 98/6 (December 1990): 1159–94.

Fry, Joseph A. *Dixie Looks Abroad: The South and U.S. Foreign Relations, 1789–1973*. Baton Rouge: Louisiana State University Press, 2002.

Garrett, Franklin M. *Atlanta and Environs: A Chronicle of Its People and Events, 1880s–1930s*. Athens: University of Georgia Press, 1988.

Gaston, Paul M. *The New South Creed: A Study in Southern Mythmaking*. New York: Alfred A. Knopf, 1970.

Georgia Genealogical Society. *The Third and Fourth or 1820 and 1821 Land Lotteries of Georgia*. Easley, SC: Georgia Genealogical Reprints/Southern Historical Press, 1973.

Gerster, Patrick, and Nicholas Cords, eds. *Myth and Southern History*. Vol. 2, *The New South*. 2nd ed. Urbana: University of Illinois Press, 1989.

Ginn, Leonora. *Days to Remember: Commemorating the 150th Anniversary of the Founding of the Town of Barnesville, Georgia*. Barnesville, GA: Lamar County Historical Society, 1983.

Grantham, Dewey W., Jr. *Hoke Smith and the Politics of the New South*. Baton Rouge: Louisiana State University Press, 1958.

Greenwalt, Emmett A. *California Utopia: Point Loma, 1897–1942*. San Diego: Point Loma, 1978.

———. *The Point Loma Community in California, 1897–1942*. Berkeley/Los Angeles: University of California Press, 1955.

Going, Allen J. "The Establishment of the Alabama Railroad Commission." *Journal of Southern History* 12/3 (1946): 366–85.

Haines, Henry Stevens. *Restrictive Railway Legislation*. New York: Macmillan, 1905.

Hall, James Davidson. "On an Old-Field School." Composition for the Dialectic Society, 23 April 1828. Documenting the American South website, University of North Carolina Library. Last modified 16 November 2006. http://docsouth.unc.edu/true/procs/hi_name.html?das_id=mss02-14&name_id=pn0000655.

Hanson, J. F. *A Memorial Address*. Macon: News Publishing, 1891.

Harden, William. *A History of Savannah and South Georgia*. Vol. 2. Chicago: Lewis, 1913.

Harris, Joel Chandler, ed. *Life of Henry W. Grady, including His Writings and Speeches: A Memorial Volume*. New York: Cassell, 1890.

Harris, N. E. *Address on Technical Education*. Macon: J. W. Burke, 1884.

Harris, Nathaniel E. *Autobiography: The Story of an Old Man's Life with Reminiscences of Seventy-Five Years*. Macon: J. W. Burke, 1925.

Harrison, Fairfax. *A History of the Development of the Railroad System of the Southern Railway Company*. Washington, DC: Transportation Library, 1901.

Harrold, Charles C. *The Story of Riverside Cemetery, 1887–1948*. Salt Lake City: Genealogical Society of Utah, 1959.

Harte, Geoffrey Bret, ed. *The Letters of Bret Harte*. New York: Houghton Mifflin, 1926.

Hearden, Patrick J. *Independence and Empire: The New South's Cotton Mill Campaign, 1865–1901*. DeKalb: Northern Illinois University Press, 1982.

Hild, Matthew. *Greenbackers, Knights of Labor, and Populists: Farm-Labor Insurgency in the Late-Nineteenth-Century South*. Athens: University of Georgia Press, 2007.

———. "A Pro-Labor Industrialist in the New South? J. F. Hanson and the Knights of Labor." Paper presented at the Tennessee Conference of Historians, University of Tennessee, Knoxville, 1998.

Hirshson, Stanley P. *Farewell to the Bloody Shirt: Northern Republicans and the Southern Negro, 1877–1893.* Bloomington: Indiana University Press, 1962.

Hubbard, R. Glenn, ed. *Financial Markets and Financial Crises.* Chicago: University of Chicago Press, 1991.

Iobst, Richard W. *Civil War Macon: The History of a Confederate City.* Macon: Mercer University Press, 1999.

Kinney, Abbott. *The Tariff: Protection vs. Free Trade.* n.p., [1883?]. Copy from University of California Libraries.

Klein, Maury. *The Life and Legend of E. H. Harriman.* Chapel Hill: University of North Carolina Press, 2000.

Knight, Lucian Lamar. *A Standard History of Georgia and Georgians.* Vol. 3. Chicago: Lewis, 1917.

Kousser, J. Morgan. *The Shaping of Southern Politics: Suffrage Restriction and the Establishment of the One-Party South, 1880–1910.* New Haven: Yale University Press, 1974.

Lambdin, Augusta, and Tallu Brinson Jones (Mrs. Edward A.) Fish, eds. *The History of Lamar County, 1825–1932.* Sponsored by United Daughters of the Confederacy, Willie Hunt Smith chapter. Alpharetta, GA: W. H. Wolfe Associates, 1932.

Lane, Mills. *Savannah Line: 70 Years of the Ocean Steamship Company.* Savannah: Beehive, 1999.

Lane, Mills B., ed. *The New South: Writings and Speeches of Henry Grady.* Savannah: Beehive, 1971.

Link, Arthur S. "The Progressive Movement in the South, 1870–1914." In *Myth and Southern History*, vol. 2, *The New South*, edited by Patrick Gerster and Nicholas Cords, 172–95. Urbana: University of Illinois Press, 1989.

Lynch, John W. *The Dorman-Mashbourne Letters, with Brief Accounts of the Tenth and Fifty-Third Georgia Regiments, C. S. A.* Senoia, GA: Down South, 1995.

Martin, Cathie Jo. "Sectional Parties, Divided Business." *Studies in American Political Development* 20/2 (Fall 2006): 160–84.

Massee, Jordan. *Accepted Fables: An Autobiography.* Compiled and edited by Richard Jay Hutto. Macon: Henchard, 2005.

McCarthy, James Patrick, Jr. "Commerce and College: State Higher Education and Economic Development in North Carolina and Georgia, 1850–1890." PhD dissertation, University of Georgia, 2002.

McMath, Robert C., Jr. *American Populism: A Social History, 1877–1898.* New York: Hill & Wang, 1993.

——— et al. *Engineering the New South: Georgia Tech, 1885–1985.* Athens: University of Georgia Press, 1985.

Meyer, Balthasar Henry. *Railway Legislation in the United States.* New York: Macmillan, 1903.

Mitchell, Broadus. *The Rise of Cotton Mills in the South.* Columbia: University of South Carolina Press, 2001. Originally published 1921 by Johns Hopkins Press.

———. *William Gregg, Factory Master of the Old South.* Chapel Hill: University of North Carolina Press, 1928.

Monroe County Historical Society. *Family Histories of Monroe County, Georgia.* Fernandina Beach, FL: Wolfe, 2000.

———. *Monroe County, Georgia: A History.* Fernandina Beach, FL: Wolfe, 1979.

Moore, Anne Chieko. *Benjamin Harrison: Centennial President.* First Men, America's Presidents, edited by Barbara Bennett Peterson. New York: Nova Science, 2008.

Morse, Clarence G. "A Study of American Merchant Marine Legislation." *Law and Contemporary Problems* 25 (Winter 1960): 57–81.

Mueller, Edward A. *The Savannah Line: The Ocean Steamship Company of Savannah.* New York: Purple Mountain; Providence, RI: Steamship Historical Society of America, 2001.

Mundy, Floyd W., ed. *The Earning Power of Railroads, 1911.* New York: Jas. H. Oliphant, 1911.

Nesmith, Achsah. "A Long, Arduous March toward Standardization." *Smithsonian Magazine* 15/12 (March 1985): 176.

Nixon, Raymond B. *Henry W. Grady, Spokesman of the New South.* New York: Alfred A. Knopf, 1943.

Nottingham, Carolyn Walker, and Evelyn Hannah. *History of Upson County, Georgia.* Macon: J. W. Burke, 1930.

Olcott, Charles S. *The Life of William McKinley.* 2 vols. Boston: Houghton Mifflin, 1916.

Perman, Michael. *Struggle for Mastery: Disfranchisement in the South, 1888–1908.* Chapel Hill: University of North Carolina Press, 2001.

Phillips, Ulrich B. "Railway Transportation in the South." In *The South in the Building of the Nation,* vol. 6, *Southern Economic History, 1865–1909,* edited by Thomas E. Watson, 305–16. Louisiana: Pelican, 1909.

Porch, Faith Walton, comp. *Heritage of Gordon Military College in the Heart of the Deep South.* Barnesville, GA: n.p. [1965?].

Prince, Richard E. *Central of Georgia Railway and Connecting Lines.* Salt Lake City: Stanway-Wheelwright, 1976.

Rauchway, Eric. *Murdering McKinley: The Making of Theodore Roosevelt's America.* New York: Hill & Wang, 2003.

Rezneck, Samuel. "Distress, Relief, and Discontent in the United States during the Depression of 1873–78," *Journal of Political Economy* 58/6 (December 1950): 494–512.

Rothbard, Murray N. *A History of Money and Banking in the United States: The Colonial Era to World War II.* Auburn, AL: Ludwig Von Mises Institute, 2002.

———. "The Indianapolis Monetary Convention." *Mises Daily.* Mises Institute website. Article published 27 September 2011. http://mises.org/daily/5609/.

———. "Origins of the Federal Reserve." *Quarterly Journal of Austrian Economics* 2/3 (Fall 1999): 3–51.

Rouse, Parke, Jr. *The Great Wagon Road: From Philadelphia to the South.* Richmond, VA: The Dietz Press, 1995.

Shadgett, Olive Hall. *The Republican Party in Georgia from Reconstruction through 1900.* Athens: University of Georgia Press, 1964.

Shaw, Lucille Ivey. *The History of Porterdale, from the Newton Country* [sic] *History Reference*. Accessed 29 June 2006. http://home.earthlink.net/~porterdale/porterdale/history/porterdale-history.htm.

Sheinin, David. "Flaccid Anti-Americanism: Argentine Relations with the United States at the Turn of the Century." Paper presented at the Annual Meeting of the Latin American Studies Association, Guadalajara, Mexico, April 1997.

———. *The Organization of American States*. New Brunswick, NJ: Transaction, 1995.

Snyder, Carl. *American Railways as Investments*. New York: Moody, 1907.

Stewart, William C. *Gone To Georgia: Jackson and Gwinnett Counties and Their Neighbors in the Western Migration*. Washington, DC: National Genealogical Society, 1965.

Strouse, Jean. *Morgan: American Financier*. New York: Random House, 1999.

Taylor, F. M. "The Final Report of the Indianapolis Monetary Commission." *Journal of Political Economy* 6 (June 1898): 293–322.

Taylor, R. J., Jr. *An Index to Georgia Tax Digests: 1789–1817*. 5 vols. Atlanta: R. J. Taylor Foundation, n.d.

Taylor, Robert J. "Currency Reform." *Century* 55, New Series, vol. 33 (November 1897–April 1898): 627.

Tindall, George Brown. *The Disruption of the Solid South*. New York: W. W. Norton, 1972.

Wallace, Robert B., Jr. *Dress Her in White and Gold: A Biography of Georgia Tech*. Atlanta: Georgia Tech Foundation, 1963.

Warren, Mary Bondurant, ed. *Georgia Marriages 1811 through 1820*. Danielsville, GA: Heritage Papers, 1988.

Watson, Thomas E. *The Life and Speeches of Thomas E. Watson*. Nashville: printed by author, 1908.

Whites, LeeAnn. "The De Graffenried Controversy: Class, Race, and Gender in the New South." *Journal of Southern History* 54/3 (August 1988): 449–78.

Wiebe, Richard H. *Businessmen and Reform: A Study of the Progressive Movement*. Cambridge, MA: Harvard University Press, 1962.

Wiggins, William H., Jr. *O Freedom! Afro-American Emancipation Celebrations*. Knoxville: University of Tennessee Press, 1987.

Williams, Ron. *On Railroad Street: The Story of Carrie Hanson Breedlove and Her Family*. Valley, AL: printed by author, 1998.

Woodward, C. Vann. *Origins of the New South, 1877–1913*. Baton Rouge: Louisiana State University Press, 1951.

Wynne, Lewis Nicholas. *The Continuity of Cotton: Planter Politics in Georgia, 1865–1892*. Macon: Mercer University Press, 1986.

Young, Ida, Julius Gholson, and Clara Nell Hargrove. *The History of Macon, Georgia*. Macon: Lyon, Marshall & Brooks, 1950.

2. Periodicals

American Economist (American Protective Tariff League publication, New York)
Americus (GA) Times-Recorder
Athens Banner-Watchman
Atlanta Constitution
Atlanta Georgian and News
Atlanta Journal
Atlanta Post-Appeal
Atlanta Weekly Constitution
Augusta (GA) Chronicle
Barnesville (GA) Gazette
Bellingham (WA) Herald
Boston Daily Advertiser
Century (magazine, New York)
Charleston (SC) News and Courier
Charlotte (NC) Observer
Chicago Inter-Ocean
Chicago Railway Age
Cincinnati Enquirer
Cleveland Leader
Columbus (GA) Daily Enquirer
Columbus (GA) Ledger
Evening Star (Washington, DC)
Georgia Weekly Telegraph, Journal and Messenger (Macon)
Griffin (GA) Daily News
Macon Telegraph
Macon Weekly Telegraph
The Madisonian (Madison, GA)
Manufacturers' Record (Baltimore)
Marietta (GA) Journal
Milledgeville (GA) Union and Recorder
Montgomery (AL) Advertiser
New York Herald-Tribune
New York Times
New York Tribune
New York World
Ogden (UT) Standard
Oregonian (Portland)
Philadelphia Inquirer
Philadelphia Patriot
Philadelphia Press
Richmond (VA) Dispatch
Rome (GA) Courier
San Diego Union

Savannah Morning News
Savannah Tribune
Southern Christian Advocate (Macon and Augusta GA)
Sparta (GA) Ishmaelite
State (Columbia SC)
Sunny South (Atlanta)
Tariff League Bulletin (American Protective Tariff League publication, New York)
Tom Watson's Magazine (New York)
Twice-A-Week Telegraph (Macon, GA)
The Whistle (Georgia Tech faculty newspaper)
Wilmington (NC) Star
Worcester (MA) Daily Spy

3. Reference Works

Dictionary of Georgia Biography. Edited by Kenneth Coleman and Charles Stephen Gurr. Athens: University of Georgia Press, 1983.
Encyclopedia of Georgia Biography. Vol. 1. Edited by Lucian Lamar Knight. Atlanta: A. H. Cawston, 1931).
Encyclopedia of Tariffs and Trade in U.S. History. Vol. 3. Edited by Cynthia Clark Northrup and Elaine C. Prange Turney. Westport, CT: Greenwood, 2003.
GeorgiaInfo: An Online Georgia Almanac. Digital Library of Georgia, 2008–. http://georgiainfo.galileo.usg.edu.
The National Cyclopaedia of American Biography. 71 vols. New York: James T. White, 1891–.
New Georgia Encyclopedia. Georgia Humanities Council and University of Georgia Press, 2004–. http://www.georgiaencyclopedia.org.

4. Private Papers and Manuscript Collections

Baldwin, George Johnson, Papers. No. 850. Southern Historical Collection, Wilson Library, University of North Carolina, Chapel Hill.
Bibb Manufacturing Company. The Bibb Company Collection. Middle Georgia Archives, Washington Memorial Library, Macon.
Central of Georgia Railway Company Collection. MS 1362. Georgia Historical Society, Savannah.
Comer, Hugh Moss, Family Papers. MS 2235. Georgia Historical Society, Savannah.
Drew, Stephen E. *Georgia Northern Private Car No. 100 Gold Coast.* California State Railroad Museum Library, Sacramento, CA.
Felton, Rebecca Latimer, Papers. MS 81. Hargrett Rare Book and Manuscript Library, University of Georgia, Athens.
History of Bibb Manufacturing Company, 1876–1929. Macon: n.p., 1937. Middle Georgia Archives, Washington Memorial Library, Macon.
J. P. Morgan & Co. syndicate books, Morgan Library and Museum, New York.

Jordan, G. Gunby, Papers. MC 12. Columbus State University Archives, Columbus, GA.

McDaniel, Henry D., Family and Business Papers. Box DOC-6066, Accession 1966–400M. Georgia Archives, Morrow.

McKinley, William, Papers. MSS 32268. Manuscript Division, Library of Congress, Washington, DC.

Ocean Steamship Company of Savannah Records. MS 1362OE. Georgia Historical Society, Savannah.

Records of US Participation in International Conferences, Commissions, and Expositions. National Archives, Washington, DC.

Spencer, Samuel, Papers. LMS 2003.009. Southern Railway Historical Association Collection of Southern Railway Presidents Files. Southern Museum of Civil War and Locomotive History, Kennesaw, GA.

"The Story of Cotton." Bibb Manufacturing Company Booklets. SMC 82. Columbus State University Archives, Columbus, GA.

6. Legal and Public Documents

Committee on Communication on the Gulf of Mexico and the Caribbean Sea. RG 43, A1 11, box 1. National Archives and Records Administration.

Compiled Service Records of Confederate Generals and Staff Officers, and Nonregimental Enlisted Men. Microfilm 331, Records from the Military and Military Agencies: Civil War. National Archives at Atlanta.

Congressional Record, 48th Congress, 1st session, vol. 15. Debate on floor regarding letter from J. F. Hanson read to Congress. Washington, DC: Government Printing Office, 1884. Law Library of Congress, Washington, DC.

County Marriage Records, 1828–1978. Georgia Archives, Morrow.

Fulton County (GA) Record of Wills. Book E (1909–1916). Fulton County Probate Court, Atlanta.

Hanson, J. F. "Speech of J. F. Hanson of the *Macon Telegraph*, before the House Committee on Railroads, Delivered in the Senate Chamber at Atlanta." 10 December 1886. Hargrett Rare Book and Manuscript Library, University of Georgia, Athens.

Historical American Engineering Records (HAER). Historic Preservation Division, Georgia Department of Natural Resources, Atlanta.

International American Conference. *Reports and Recommendations, together with the Messages of the President and the Letters of the Secretary of State Transmitting the Same to Congress.* Washington, DC: Government Printing Office, 1890. LCCN 01023417.

Macon City Directories, 1860–80. Genealogy and History Collection. Washington Memorial Library, Macon, GA.

Monetary Commission of the Indianapolis Convention. *Report of the Monetary Commission to the Executive Committee of the Indianapolis Monetary Convention.* [Indianapolis]: Secretary of the Monetary Commission, 1897. LCCN 05004619.

Monroe County (GA) Marriage Book. Book A (1824–1845). Monroe County Ordinary Court. Georgia Archives, Morrow.

Monroe County (GA) Wills Book. Book C. Monroe County Library, Forsyth.

Morgan County (GA) Deed Books. Books A–G (1808–1820). Genealogy and History Collection. Washington Memorial Library, Macon.

Munn v. Illinois, 94 U.S. Supreme Court 113 (1876).

National Park Service. Civil War Soldiers and Sailors System (CWSS). Database. Accessed 23 January 2014. http://www.nps.gov/civilwar/soldiers-and-sailors-database.htm.

———. "Lowell Machine Shop." *Lowell National Historical Park Handbook 140*. *Accessed 23 January 2014*. *http://www.nps.gov/lowe/photosmultimedia/machine_shop.htm*.

National Register of Historic Places. National Park Service, US Department of the Interior. http://www.nps.gov/nr/.

Pan American Union. *Fifth International Conference of American States: Special Handbook for the Use of the Delegates*. Washington, DC: Government Printing Office, 1922. LCCN 22027325.

Poythress, David B. *Georgia Surveyor General Department*. Atlanta: Georgia Surveyor General Department, n.d. Georgia Archives and Records Building, Morrow.

Proceedings of the Fortieth Annual Meeting of the National Board of Trade Held in Washington, January 1910. Philadelphia: John R. McFetridge & Sons, 1910.

Railroad Commission of Georgia. *Semi-Annual Report of the Railroad Commission of the State of Georgia, Submitted to the Governor*. Atlanta: Constitution Publishing, 1881.

———. *Thirty-Sixth Annual Report of the Railroad Commission of Georgia*. Atlanta: Foote & Davies, 1909.

Russell, William A. "The Tariff: Revenue for the Government, and Protection for All." Speech, H.R., 48th Cong., 16 April 1884. Washington, DC: 1884.

Southern Manufacturers' Association. Extract from official proceedings, 30 November 1888. Miscellaneous Documents of the Senate of the United States for the Second Session of the Fiftieth Congress. Library of Congress, Washington, DC.

Transactions of the Georgia State Agricultural Society, from August 1876 to February 1878. Atlanta: James P. Harrison, 1878.

US Bureau of the Census. *1910 Federal Population Census*. National Archives microfilm roll 172. Bibb County, GA.

US Census Office. *Fifth Census of the United States, 1830*. National Archives microfilm M19. Roll 19. Monroe County, GA.

———. *Sixth Census of the United States, 1840*. National Archives microfilm M704. Roll 47. Monroe County, GA.

———. *1850 Federal Population Census*. Slave Schedule. National Archives microfilm M432. Roll 88. Bibb County, GA; M432. Roll 78. Monroe County, GA; M432. Roll 80. Pike County, GA.